To Address You as My Friend

To Address You as My Friend

African Americans' Letters to
Abraham Lincoln

EDITED BY
Jonathan W. White

FOREWORD BY
Edna Greene Medford

The University of North Carolina Press CHAPEL HILL

This book was published with the assistance of the John Hope Franklin Fund of the University of North Carolina Press.

Set in Merope Basic by Westchester Publishing Services
Manufactured in the United States of America

The University of North Carolina Press has been a member of the
Green Press Initiative since 2003.

Library of Congress Cataloging-in-Publication Data
Names: White, Jonathan W., 1979– editor.
Title: To address you as my friend : African Americans' letters to Abraham Lincoln / edited
    by Jonathan W. White ; foreword by Edna Greene Medford.
Description: Chapel Hill : University of North Carolina Press, [2021] | Includes bibliographical
    references and index.
Identifiers: LCCN 2021027328 | ISBN 9781469665078 (cloth) | ISBN 9781469665092 (ebook)
Subjects: LCSH: Lincoln, Abraham, 1809–1865—Correspondence. | African Americans—
    Correspondence. | African Americans—Social conditions—19th century. |
    United States—History—Civil War, 1861–1865—African Americans. |
    BISAC: SOCIAL SCIENCE / Ethnic Studies / American / African American &
    Black Studies | HISTORY / United States / Civil War Period (1850–1877)
Classification: LCC E457.2 .T625 2021 | DDC 305.896/07309034—dc23
LC record available at https://lccn.loc.gov/2021027328

Cover illustration: Heard and Moseley, "Watch meeting, Dec. 31, 1862—Waiting for
the hour," carte de visite, 1863. Gladstone Collection of African American Photographs,
Library of Congress Prints and Photographs Division (LC-DIG-ppmsca-10980).

For my teachers at the
University of Maryland

Contents

Foreword by Edna Greene Medford xi

Prologue: One of Lincoln's Oldest Friends xv

Note on Method xxi

Introduction 1

PART I | *Chief Executive*

  1   Petitioning for Pardon 9

  2   Debating Colonization 33

PART II | *Commander in Chief*

  3   Recruiting for the Ranks 59

  4   Protesting Unequal Pay for Black Soldiers 89

  5   Requesting Discharge from the Service 116

  6   Navigating Military Justice 136

PART III | *Chief Citizen*

  7   Appealing for Equal Treatment 165

  8   Soliciting Aid for Christian Ministries 181

  9   Seeking Economic Rights and Opportunities 201

 10   Mementos 227

Epilogue: "I Have Lost a Friend" 235

Acknowledgments 239
Notes 241
Bibliography 259
Index of Correspondents 271
Subject Index 275

Illustrations

William Florville xvi

J. Willis Menard 51

J. Sella Martin 63

Dr. Alexander T. Augusta 65

William Slade 70

Paschal B. Randolph 72

"The War in the South—Paying Off Negro Soldiers
at Hilton Head, S.C." 91

Sgt. John Freeman Shorter 101

Thomas Pepper 112

Twenty-Sixth U.S. Colored Infantry at Camp William Penn 113

Col. Louis Wagner 114

Sgt. Charles R. Douglass in uniform 126

"Avoiding the Draft—Agents of Northern States Engaging
Negro Substitutes at Norfolk" 128

E. Arnold Bertonneau 172

Abraham H. Galloway 178

Rev. Leonard A. Grimes 183

John H. Kelly and Jane E. W. Kelly 185

Rev. Jeremiah Asher 186

Rev. Richard H. Cain 191

Group at L'Ouverture Hospital, Alexandria, Va. 195

Chaplain Benjamin Franklin Randolph 200

Laura M. Towne's School, St. Helena Island, South Carolina 211

Foreword

EDNA GREENE MEDFORD

Historians have long grappled with the challenge of capturing the voices of mid-nineteenth-century African Americans. A people who largely existed at the margins of society, it was thought, did not leave a record that is easily accessible or particularly robust. Indeed, illiteracy, intimidation, and relegation to a second-class status did prevent many, even the free born, from fully and effectively communicating the many trials they had endured, the victories they had enjoyed, and their expectations for the future. A fortunate few men and women, gifted with oratorical abilities and a skilled pen, used these talents to seize the opportunities available to them to speak for those who, through circumstance, remained voiceless. For so long, we have tended to interpret the lived experiences of black people through the writings and orations of these privileged few.

Jonathan White, author of the highly acclaimed *Emancipation, the Union Army, and the Reelection of Abraham Lincoln* (among several other works), seeks in this volume to expose us to the more diverse voices emanating from the African American community. The edited collection of letters to President Lincoln, many of them never published until now, illuminates the fears and the desires of Civil War–era African Americans as they dealt with the problems of the day and the uncertain future that awaited them. Their boldness in writing to the president, a common enough practice among white Americans at that time, says much about African Americans' faith in his ability and willingness to address their concerns. Their belief that they enjoyed a special relationship with the president—many saw him as their protector and friend—encouraged them in their determination to enjoy the same rights and privileges shared by the rest of the nation's residents.

As Professor White notes, Americans viewed the presidency much differently a century and a half ago. In the era of the Civil War, the citizen's relationship with the chief executive was more personal, with the expectation that the president would not simply assume responsibility for the collective needs of the country but intervene to solve the problems of the individual as well. Hence, it was assumed that the occupant of the White House would be accessible, even empathetic, as petitioners of all kinds approached him without reservation. A select group of well-positioned African Americans tested the president's racial tolerance by seeking an audience with him among the many white men (mostly) lobbying for office or special favors. The ordinary folk, white and black, more often resorted to personal letter-writing or to dictating their requests to those with a stronger hold on literacy. The disposition of their cases rested, it appears, less on racial considerations than on whether the president was ever made aware of their concerns. Initial lower-level reviews or routing errors often prevented these letters and petitions from reaching his desk. When they did, his responses bore out his reputation for compassion and fairness. He commuted prison sentences or pardoned convicted offenders, returned sick soldiers to their families, and questioned the ill treatment shown to black men and women. But the letters also reveal a tough-minded chief executive and commander in chief, who consistently weighed societal interests against the requests of the individual. Mercy, although prominently displayed, was never a certainty.

Professor White has gathered a collection of letters and petitions that thoroughly conveys the complexity of issues affecting the African American community and the urgency with which community members sought to have their concerns addressed. A formerly enslaved husband appeals for the release of his pregnant wife, who has received a prison sentence of sixteen months for allegedly stealing forty dollars from her employer. A prominent member of the community pens a blistering indictment of the president in an open letter in response to his colonization scheme. A mother petitions for the release of her wounded soldier son, her only means of support. A wife, made destitute by the infrequent pay of her soldier husband, pleads for assistance in the support of her children. These letters represent a level of frustration that extended beyond that of the average white American, who, through privilege and legal rights, had other avenues in which to redress their grievances.

For all the difficulties African Americans faced, their letters were not always pleas for financial assistance or complaints of ill treatment. Through their correspondence with the president, black men sought appointments as recruiters or offered themselves for military service. They expressed gratitude for his having issued the Emancipation Proclamation or shared their private thoughts through poetry and the recounting of their dreams. They connected with the president in ways that reveal a familiarity heretofore unknown between these marginalized Americans and this embodiment of the American government.

Drawn from a broad range of record groups, the letters are sometimes humorous, frequently tragic, and always poignant. They were penned in a variety of styles, exhibiting the imprecise hand of the unlettered, the structured manner of legal advocates, and the florid prose of the highly educated. Professor White's expert contextualization positions each request in the struggle of the larger African American community and demonstrates that black people were worthy and persistent self-advocates. This volume reveals that the African American voice, at least during the Civil War, may have been muffled at times but never muted.

Prologue
One of Lincoln's Oldest Friends

One evening in the fall of 1831, a young black man named William de Fleurville—he later anglicized his name to Florville—approached the sleepy village of New Salem, Illinois, on his way to Springfield. According to an Illinois county history from the 1880s, Florville met a young Abraham Lincoln that night—himself a recent arrival to the village. The twenty-two-year-old Lincoln was "wearing a red flannel shirt and carrying an axe on his shoulder, just returning from a day's labor in the woods." The two men walked to a nearby store, conversing the whole way. Lincoln then took Florville to the Rutledge Tavern, where he was boarding, so that the weary traveler could rest that night. The next morning, Florville continued on his way to Springfield.

Florville had been born in Haiti about 1806. In the 1820s he immigrated to Baltimore, where his godmother placed him in St. Mary's Convent. After her death a short time later, the Orphan's Court apprenticed him to a barber. But Florville did not much care for Baltimore, so he traveled to New Orleans and then St. Louis. Eventually he decided to head to Springfield, where a former employer of his from Baltimore, Dr. Elias H. Merriman, lived. It was on this journey that Florville met Lincoln at New Salem.

In Springfield, Florville married a Kentuckian named Phoebe Rountree in 1831. With Dr. Merriman's assistance, he opened up a barbershop the following year. Florville became a prominent citizen of Springfield, eventually owning a significant amount of real estate near the capitol building. Always seeking new business, he regularly placed witty advertisements in the local newspapers. In one 1833 advertisement, he wrote, "William Fleurville, the barber king of the village, announced that he had erected a new barber pole, against which the storms of factions, the hurricanes of the prairies, a common size earthquake or a runaway team will dash in vain."

Affectionately known as "Billy the Barber," Florville and Lincoln developed a close friendship over the years. Lincoln spent many hours in conversation at Billy's barbershop and also advised him in legal matters and investments, even paying the property taxes on several of Florville's properties. Lincoln also represented Florville in at least three legal cases. Years later, the *Illinois State Journal* wrote, "Only two men in Springfield

William Florville. Courtesy of the Abraham Lincoln Presidential Library and Museum, Springfield, Illinois.

William Florville
(Billy the Barber)

understood Lincoln, his law partner, William H. Herndon, and his barber, William de Fleurville."[1]

In the middle of the Civil War—on December 27, 1863—Florville sent Lincoln a long, heartfelt letter. Lincoln had apparently sent Florville "good wishis" through Illinois governor Richard Yates as well as their old friend Dr. Anson G. Henry, whom Lincoln had appointed surveyor general of Washington Territory. Florville celebrated emancipation and offered Lincoln his hope that he would be reelected in 1864. He also apprised Lincoln of how things were back in Springfield—such as that the Lincolns' dog, Fido, was doing fine with the Rolls family. In addition, Florville showed strong support for Lincoln's actions as commander in chief. But most poignantly, Florville sent his regrets that Lincoln had been ill with varioloid, a mild form of smallpox, in late 1863, as well as his condolences for the loss of Lincoln's son Willie.

The death of Willie Lincoln on February 20, 1862, had been a great tragedy in the lives of the Lincolns. Only eleven years old, Willie had succumbed to typhoid fever after having been sick for some time. Mary Lincoln's black seamstress, Elizabeth Keckly, later noted that she was immediately called into the room after Willie died. "I never saw a man so bowed with grief," Keckly wrote of the president. "He came to the bed, lifted the cover from the face of his child, gazed at it long and earnestly, murmuring, 'My poor boy, he was too good for this earth. God has called him home. I know that he is much better off in heaven, but then we loved him so. It is hard, hard to have him die!'" Keckly continued, "Great sobs choked his utterance. He buried his head in his hands, and his tall frame was convulsed with emotion." Standing at the foot of the bed, Keckly's eyes also welled up with tears.[2] One can imagine that Lincoln felt some encouragement and consolation upon receiving the following letter from his old friend, Billy.[3]

Springfield Ills Decr 27th 1863

President Lincoln—

Dear Sir—I, having for you, an irrisisteble feeling of gratitude for the kind regards Shown, and the manifest good wishis exhibited towards me, Since your residence in Washington City; as Communicated by Doctor [Anson G.] Henry Sometime ago, and lately by his Exelency Governor [Richard] Yates, have for the above reasons and our long acquaintance, thought it might not be improper for one so humble in life and occupation, to address the President of the United States—

yet, I do so, feeling that if it is received by you (and you have time for I know you are heavily Tax) it will be read with pleasure as a communication from Billy the Barber. this I express and feel. for the truly great man regards with corresponding favor the poor, and down troden of the nation, to those more favored in Color, position, and Franchise rights. And this you have Shown, and I and my people feel greatful to you for it. The Shackels have fallen, and Bondmen have become freeman to Some extent already under your Proclamation. And I hope ere long, it may be universal in all the Slave States. That your authority may Soon extend over them all, to all the oppressed, releiving them from their Bondage, and cruel masters; who make them work, and fight, against the Goverment. And when so released, they would be glad I have no doubt, to assist in putting down this infamous Rebellion—

May God grant you health, and Streangth, and wisdom, so to do, and so to act, as Shall redown to his Glory, and the Good, peace, prosperity, Freedom, and hapiness of this nation. So that War Shall be known no more, that the cause or pretext for war be removed. that Rebellion and Secession Shall have no plea to make, and nothing to ask for, that all the States may not have an equal right to demand. then, and not till then, will the Government be Steadfast and abiding. and for that reason, I hope and trust, that you may be chosen for a Second term to Administer the affairs of this Government. I think, after a four years experiance, you are posted in matters relating thereto. and better calculated to carry out your own designs, and the wishes of the people, than any other man in this nation. And the people here so think.

And if it Shall be the wish of the men, who Support the Goverment, anxious to put down the Rebellion, Sustaining the Army, loving Freedom and the union, and who Sustain your acts, and your Administration, that you Should again accept the office of Chief Magistrate of this nation, I hope you will not decline: but accept it, and put things and matters through, to their termination and when these troubles Shall end, the nation will rejoice, the Oppressed will Shout the name of their deliverer, and Generations to come, will rise up and call you blessed. (so mote [must?] it be)   I was Sorry to hear of your illness, and was glad when I learned that your health was improving. I hope by this time, you are able, or soon will be, to attend to your arduous buisness

I was Surprised at the announcement of the death of your Son Willy. I thought him a Smart boy for his age, So considerate, So Manly: his Knowledge and good Sence, far exceeding most boys more advanced in years. yet the time comes to all, all must die.

I Should like verry much, to See you, and your family, but the priviledge of enjoying an interview, may not soon, if ever come.

My family are all well. My son William is married and in buisness for himself. I am occupying the Same place in which I was at the time you left. Tell Taddy that his (and Willys) Dog is a live and Kicking doing well   he stays mostly at John E Rolls with his Boys Who are about the size now that Tad & Willy ware when they left for Washington

your Residence here is Kept in good order. Mr Tilton has no children to ruin things.[4] Mrs Tilton and Miss Tilton are verry Strong Union Ladies and do a great deal for the Soldiers who are suffering So Much for us & to sustain the Goverment

please accept my best wishis for yourself and family. and my daily desires for yourself that your Administration may be prosperous,

Wise, and productive of Good results to this Nation, and may the time Soon come, When the Rebellion Shall be put down; and Traitors, receive their just recompence of reward. and the People be at Peace, is the Sincere feelings of your obt Servant
  William Florville the Barber

Florville's long-standing relationship with Lincoln may have had some international implications. During his administration, Lincoln offered diplomatic recognition to both Haiti and Liberia. Many whites had opposed such a move, fearing that doing so would lead to black diplomats in the nation's capital. But Lincoln exhibited no such fears. When Lincoln learned that Haitian president Fabre Nicolas Geffrard was willing to appoint a white diplomat to go to Washington, Lincoln said, "Well—you can tell Mr. Geffrard that I shan't tear my shirt if he does send a negro here!" The Haitian government appointed a black army officer, Ernest Roumain, as its first minister to the United States. Several generations later, in 1942, African American folklorist and teacher John E. Washington observed (in what is almost certainly an overstatement), "Undoubtedly Fleurville's influence upon Lincoln during their long acquaintance had much to do with bringing this event to pass."

Following his assassination in April 1865, Lincoln's body was returned to Springfield, Illinois, for burial. Florville was invited to walk toward the head of the funeral procession, but he instead opted to mourn with the other black residents of Springfield at the back of the line. According to Florville's granddaughter, "He was never the same" after learning of Lincoln's death. "His high spirits went when his old friend was shot." Florville died three years later, in April 1868.[5]

Note on Method

The research for this book is based largely in two sources—the Papers of Abraham Lincoln (PAL) website, and the Library of Congress's digitized collection of Lincoln's papers. PAL is a long-standing project that seeks to locate, transcribe, and make available to the public every document sent to or from Abraham Lincoln. Thus far the project has published four volumes of papers from Lincoln's legal career. It has also placed online (without transcriptions) more than eighty-one thousand documents from the National Archives and Library of Congress. Using this database, I browsed through a number of record groups from the National Archives that I believed were likely to contain letters or petitions from African Americans. Some of these—like RG 94, which contains the records of the Office of the Adjutant General's Colored Troops Division—have been thoroughly mined by the Freedmen and Southern Society Project and other scholars. Others, however, have not. For instance, scholars of African American history have made little use of the presidential pardon records in RG 204—records that give extraordinary insights into the daily lives of African Americans in Washington, D.C. I read through thousands of pages of documents, turning up many of the letters in this book.

Browsing and searching through the Library of Congress's collection, I was able to locate a number of letters written by African Americans. After I had completed my searches of the PAL and Library of Congress collections, I consulted the volumes of the Freedmen and Southern Society Project, where I found a few additional letters that had not yet been scanned by PAL, as well as supplementary information for some of the documents I had already found and transcribed. Finally, some of the letters in this book turned up during the course of my own research at the National Archives for other projects. Letters that were located in the PAL database contain a citation to the record's original location at the National Archives followed by a citation in parentheses that contains PAL's identifying number for each particular document.

Most of the more than 120 letters in this book have never been published. Only fourteen appear in the volumes of the Freedmen and Southern Society Project. The diverse array of record groups at the National Archives that contain letters from black men and women (each record group represents a different federal department or agency) speaks to the wide array of problems people of color faced during the war, as well as the various levers of government that they attempted to pull in order to resolve their dilemmas. As such, this book makes a valuable contribution to our understanding of African American life.

This collection of African American correspondence to Lincoln is by no means exhaustive; more letters are certainly still buried in the National Archives and at other libraries and repositories around the country. But I hope that the book's size and scope will make it of interest to general readers, of use to scholars, and conducive to use in high school and college classrooms. The letters are arranged according to type/topic of correspondence. Part 1 contains letters that Lincoln would have handled in his capacity as chief executive—meaning those constitutional powers that he wielded in domestic affairs. Part 2 consists of letters related to his role as commander and chief of the army and navy. Part 3 contains correspondence Lincoln received as "chief citizen"—an informal role in which a president works to "represent all of the people of the United States."[1] Each chapter is divided into subsections that contain one or more letters from a particular correspondent or group of correspondents. The only exception to this organizational plan is chapter 2, which reproduces full transcriptions of letters as part of a narrative on colonization. Chapter 2 also includes several public letters that African Americans published in response to Lincoln's plan for colonization. Although it is unknown whether Lincoln read these particular public letters, there is evidence that he read public letters written by African Americans.[2]

The annotation varies in length throughout this book, with some documents receiving extensive annotation and others receiving very little. To a large extent, the amount of annotation depends on how much evidence was available for each particular correspondent, and also on how the annotation could either humanize the writers and illuminate their life circumstances, or provide useful context for the documents. In one instance, I include three lengthy reactions to an event mentioned in a letter, which I believe will lend themselves well to classroom discussion.

In transcribing the letters, I have kept them as close to the originals as possible. All obvious spelling errors have been retained except in a few instances where I inserted missing letters, words, or punctuation in brackets to provide clarity for the reader. Retaining spelling helps preserve the authors' voice and speech patterns, as the historian Stephen W. Berry has so eloquently pointed out.[3] Words or phrases that could not be deciphered are marked as illegible; words for which I have rendered a guess are followed by a bracketed question mark, or a bracketed word with a question mark. Underlined words have been rendered in italics, and superscripted letters have been retained. Words or letters that were crossed out have been retained with a ~~strike through them.~~

Capitalization and spelling are often difficult to decipher in letters composed by semiliterate writers. I made hundreds of judgment calls as I did my best to interpret which words should be capitalized and which should not. Moreover, many letters are completely devoid of punctuation. For the sake of clarity, I have indented all paragraphs with a single indentation. In the place of missing periods, I have followed the Freedmen and Southern Society Project's model of inserting five blank spaces to denote where I believe there should be a break between sentences. I have also silently omitted duplicate words and phrases in the few places they appeared.

I have made minor interventions in the salutations and headings of letters. Some letter writers used multiple lines for their salutations, date, and return address, in some cases spreading salutations over several lines across the top of the first page. These headings looked nice on a manuscript page but appeared awkward when transcribed. Accordingly, I moved all salutations onto a single line, starting on the left, and moved all dates and return address information to the right (I left these as one or two lines as they appear in the original letters). The closing and signatures of the letters vary widely in form, with some looking like a jumble of words. I have dealt with them on a case-by-case basis, attempting to capture some sense of how they appear in the manuscript while making them easy to read on the printed page. As a general rule, I indented each closing and signature and kept address information flush left. Petitions that contain more than thirteen signatures reproduce only the names of those who appear to have written the document, followed by bracketed information about the remaining signatories. In the headings and signatures of the letters I have inserted three spaces between words where a comma would have been appropriate.

It may be impossible to render *perfect* transcriptions of these letters, as some words, letters, marks, and characters are open to multiple interpretations.[4] (One of the particular difficulties with this project is that almost every letter is in a different hand, so I was not able to "learn" writers' idiosyncrasies over the course of reading multiple letters by them.) In some cases I have rendered words or letters differently than they appear in the Freedmen and Southern Society Project's volumes. I have proofread the transcriptions multiple times on my own, as well as with two of my research assistants.

Nevertheless, some errors may have slipped through. All errors in transcription are my own.

I decided to create this book with my students in mind. The stories collected here are those of ordinary individuals who struggled to survive and prosper during an immense social upheaval. Most of their voices have not been heard for more than a century and a half. I hope that their lived experiences will captivate students and general readers alike, helping Americans in the twenty-first century to reenter the tumultuous, uncertain, and compelling world of the Civil War. Intimately intertwined with these stories is that of Abraham Lincoln—a self-taught prairie lawyer who rose to become one of the world's greatest leaders and yet who never lost his down-to-earth approach to life, nor his interest in the lives of ordinary Americans.

Introduction

Americans went to the polls on Tuesday, November 6, 1860, to elect a new president. Largely forgotten today is that black men were voters in six states.[1] African Americans in the North also actively campaigned for Abraham Lincoln. "Colored" Wide Awake organizations sprung up in several northern cities to march in torchlight processions and help turn out the vote for the Railsplitter — even in states like Pennsylvania, where black men were disenfranchised.[2] A year after the election, several black men in Cleveland, Ohio, wrote to Secretary of War Simon Cameron, telling him "that we are colored men (legal voters); all voted for the present administration." In exchange for that support, they asked for "the poor privilege of fighting, and, if need be, dying, to support those in office who are our own choice."[3] Unfortunately, they would be denied the opportunity to support their country in that way for another year and a half.

Although most African Americans could not vote, free and enslaved black men and women still had strong opinions about the election. On November 5, 1860, Richard Hackley, a slave in Charlottesville, Virginia, wrote a curious letter about the impending contest to Baptist minister John A. Broadus. "I hope that Mr. Lincoln or no such man may ever take his seat in the presidential chair," Hackley began. His reasoning had to do with his fears about civil war. "I do most sincerely hope that the Union may be preserved," he continued. "I hear through the white gentlemen here that South Carolina will leave the Union in case he is elected. I do hope she won't leave, as that would cause much disturbance and perhaps fighting. Why can't the Union stand like it is now? Well do I recollect when I drove a wagon in the old wars, carrying things for the army; but I hope we shall have no more wars, but let peace be in all the land."[4]

Hackley's letter is undoubtedly an anomaly. Most evidence suggests that enslaved men and women exulted in Lincoln's election. In late 1860, for example, slaves in Alabama asked one northern visitor "if 'Linkum' was elected" and "how soon he would set us free." In South Carolina, slaves were whipped for singing "We'll fight for liberty / Till de Lord shall call us home; / We'll soon be free / Till de Lord shall call us home" when they heard about Lincoln's election. Similarly, a Missouri slave was knocked down three times and sent to a slave trader's yard for a month as punishment for hanging a newspaper-print picture of Lincoln on the wall of her room. In early 1861, one slave owner in Virginia found that he could no longer control a twenty-two-year-old gardener and house servant who held Lincoln "in great favor." To solve his problem, he turned the slave over to slave traders, instructing them to sell the young man in Alabama or Louisiana to "put him far out of the way of Lincoln." By March 4, 1861—the day of Lincoln's inauguration—a group of slaves in Florida refused to work for their enslavers, believing that the ascendance of a Republican administration had brought them freedom.[5]

In truth, enslaved men and women had been politically aware for years. Although denied formal education, they gleaned information about national politics from discussions in their masters' homes, from educated or skilled slaves with whom they worked, and from standing on the outskirts of political meetings and rallies. As the historian Douglas R. Egerton has shown, slaves learned a great deal about Republicans like Lincoln from the "overheated Democratic rhetoric" that emanated from newspapers and public speeches throughout the South. Booker T. Washington wrote famously in his memoir *Up from Slavery* of "the 'grape-vine' telegraph" that kept slaves abreast of what was going on in the country. "During the campaign when Lincoln was first a candidate for the Presidency, the slaves on our far-off plantation, miles from any railroad or large city or daily newspaper, knew what the issues involved were," he later recollected. "When war was begun between the North and the South, every slave on our plantation felt and knew that, though other issues were discussed, the primal one was that of slavery. Even the most ignorant members of my race on the remote plantations felt in their hearts, with a certainty that admitted of no doubt, that the freedom of the slaves would be the one great result of the war, if the Northern armies conquered."[6]

The Civil War opened up new opportunities for ordinary African Americans to participate in the political process and to make claims for equality.[7] For many, it was of utmost importance to prove their manhood on the battlefield. In a recruiting speech in March 1863, Frederick Douglass proclaimed that by fighting, black men could "rise in one bound from social degradation to the plane of common equality with all other varieties of men."[8] Sgt. Tillman Valentine of the Third U.S. Colored Infantry echoed this sentiment in a letter to his wife, telling her that "this war has caused me to think in terly [entirely] diferent from what i did" and that he hoped "to live like a man and . . . act as a man."[9] Corp. James Henry Gooding of the Fifty-Fourth Massachusetts Infantry similarly commented on the importance of being treated as a soldier. "To say even, we were *not* soldiers and to pay us $20 would be injustice," he wrote to the editor of the New Bedford *Mercury*, "for it would rob a whole race of their title to manhood."[10]

Black soldiers realized that their sacrifices for the nation entitled them to lay claim to the rights of citizenship. One Philadelphia barber exchanged his scissors and combs for a musket and bayonet so that he could fight for "the proper enjoyment of the rights of citizenship," while another black Pennsylvanian wrote from Virginia, "I cannot see why we should still be kept from exercising the full rights of citizenship" when we "are called upon to lay down our lives."[11] On numerous occasions, black soldiers protested against discrimination—particularly the lack of equal pay and unequal treatment by white officers.[12] As historians Ira Berlin, Joseph P. Reidy, and Leslie S. Rowland have written, "In learning how to deal with abstract law as well as personal authority, previously enslaved black soldiers took their first steps as free men. And in the process, they not only asserted their claim to citizenship, but also broke down the barriers that distinguished freemen and bondsmen."[13]

African American participation in politics during the Civil War included sending petitions and requests to members of Congress, cabinet officials, state houses, military officers, and the president. On a few notable occasions, black men personally delivered their petitions to Lincoln, handing them to him in his White House office. These actions represented a new form of integration for African Americans into the American body politic. By petitioning the president and other national leaders, black men and women were making bold claims to the rights of citizenship—that they, too, deserved the First Amendment "right *of the people* peaceably to assemble, and to petition the Government for a redress of grievances" (emphasis added). At the same time, Lincoln acknowledged and accepted these claims when he heard their petitions and did what he could to respond to them.

During his presidency, Lincoln had extensive involvement in the struggles of ordinary Americans. Whether he was meeting with private citizens in his office, reviewing their petitions, or answering their mail, he connected with his constituents in ways that few politicians have. "Stories of Lincoln's accessibility to even the humblest petitioner, his patience, and his humanity spread throughout the North," writes Lincoln biographer David Herbert Donald. "For the first time in American history, citizens began to feel that the occupant of the White House was *their* representative."[14] This view became true—at least to a limited extent—of African Americans as well. When people of color approached him, he gave them the same respect and attention that he gave to white callers. "To the lowly, to the humble, the timid colored man or woman, he bent in special kindliness," observed Union nurse Mary Livermore.[15]

WHILE SEVERAL COLLECTIONS of African American writings from the Civil War exist, none is quite like this one. Many of the best volumes—such as Edwin S. Redkey's *A Grand Army of Black Men: Letters from African-American Soldiers in the Union Army, 1861–1865* and Virginia M. Adams's *On the Altar of Freedom: A Black Soldier's Civil War Letters from the Front*—reproduce letters that soldiers sent to newspapers. These published letters—which tended to be written by army chaplains and noncommissioned officers—typically offered polished accounts of troops' movements as well as finely crafted statements of black soldiers' sentiments on important social and political issues. Their content has been invaluable to historians, yet they must be read with the understanding that they were written for public consumption, and they were likely edited for clarity before appearing in the newspapers.[16]

Private writings by ordinary African Americans are far less common, in large part because literacy rates among African Americans were low. It is estimated that only 5 to 10 percent of American slaves could read; fewer could probably write.[17] When Redkey published his landmark volume in the early 1990s, he noted that "private letters of black soldiers [have] vanished."[18] Indeed, very few substantial collections of personal correspondence between black soldiers and civilians are extant today. And yet scattered across several record groups at the National Archives, a significant number of original letters do survive. In the late nineteenth century, widows often submitted their deceased husband's wartime correspondence to Pension Office examiners to prove that they had been married so that they could receive a pension. Only through this process were many African Americans' letters preserved.[19] (In at least one instance, a veteran's children submitted their father's photograph to prove that he had served in the Union army, and the picture remains in his pension file to this day.)[20] The National Archives also preserves a great deal of correspondence that black men and women sent to federal officials, including the president of the United States. Many of these letters stem from the injustices experienced by black soldiers and their families. They offer intimate, uncensored, desperate, and often heart-wrenching portraits of African American soldiers' and civilians' wartime experiences. They also reveal a great deal about race relations in the mid-nineteenth century—especially the ways that African Americans interacted with white civilians, soldiers, missionaries, teachers, and government officials.

Many of the letters contained in this book were written at what one correspondent described as "the darkest hour of my life." The letters thus reveal the tenuousness of life in wartime, and the desperate need for financial support that many Americans—especially black Americans—experienced while the nation was in upheaval. For many, writing to Lincoln was "a last resort." At the same time, however, the letters demonstrate the determination of many African Americans to resist discrimination, injustice, and oppression. They protested demeaning punishments and unequal pay for black soldiers. In doing so, black communities—whether as soldiers in regiments or civilians at home—often mobilized collectively to make appeals to Lincoln. Corp. James Henry Gooding of the Fifty-Fourth Massachusetts, for example, told Lincoln that he wrote because of the "earnest Solicitation of my Comrades in Arms." Other groups of people organized to write petitions or collaborated to send multiple letters at the same time.

In writing to the president, enslaved and free African Americans were making an explicit claim to the rights of citizenship. One former bondsman who was serving in the Union army asked Lincoln to "remember me to all of my Brothers felow cittysons of the united States." In fact, the very act of writing became an act of political engagement. In their letters and petitions, black men rejected the status of "contraband" (or laborer) and insisted that they be treated as soldiers. They discussed political issues like colonization and demanded economic justice for wrongs that had been inflicted on them by their former owners. Several correspondents reminded Lincoln that African Americans were the most loyal people to the Union, while southern whites were traitors. With this in mind, they suggested that Lincoln could best save American democracy by securing the right to vote for black men. Many black soldiers and their families expressed full devotion to the Union cause despite the intense and unwarranted discrimination they faced. Taken together, the letters offer deep reflections on what "nation," "sacrifice," and "loyalty" meant to mid-nineteenth-century African Americans.

The correspondents in this book had a deep knowledge of American history. They wrote about the role that African Americans played in winning the American Revolution and in fighting to secure American independence during the War of 1812. They appealed to the nation's founding ideals to claim for themselves the rights that Thomas Jefferson wrote belonged to "all men." Their letters also reveal a rich biblical literacy and are seasoned with scriptural quotations. (Some, but not nearly all, of the biblical allusions are identified in the notes.)

Finally, the letters contained in this book give new and unique perspectives on how African Americans viewed Abraham Lincoln. One difficulty that historians have faced in assessing black views of Lincoln during the Civil War is that their analysis is frequently based on published documents, narratives written by whites, and postwar recollections.[21] The letters in this book give a valuable glimpse into how black Americans thought about Lincoln *during* the Civil War, and what they expected of him. Many saw him as a "friend" and savior, as one poor teenager about to be wrongfully imprisoned wrote: "Now being friendless—I implore your mercy." Others addressed him as a "Friend and protector," or as a "kine [kind] Dear and Honorable friend to we pore african race."

One gets the sense when reading these letters that some of the correspondents felt a personal connection to Lincoln—almost as though they knew him. Some likely believed that he could empathize with them, since he, too, had grown up in extreme poverty and hardship.[22] They therefore wrote to him in very personal ways. A black Union soldier, who was just learning how to read and write, sent Lincoln a poem with this postscript: "I. Sends this for you to look at . . . you must not laugh at it." Lincoln retained this missive in his personal collection of papers, likely indicating that he was personally moved by the sentiments it contained. To be sure, Lincoln likely read only a small number of the letters that appear in this book—his private secretaries screened the two hundred or three hundred letters he received each day, working under the rule "Refer as little to the President as possible." John Hay estimated that Lincoln "did not read one [letter] in fifty that he received."[23] Nevertheless, that these correspondents felt confident petitioning someone they considered *their* friend and *their* president, who had been concerned with *their* freedom and rights (for working to destroy slavery), speaks volumes about Lincoln's reputation among poor free black people and slaves, as well as about their own place in American society.

PART I | Chief Executive

CHAPTER ONE

Petitioning for Pardon

Some of the first African Americans to write to Lincoln during the Civil War were men and women somehow connected to a federal crime, including convicts and their relatives, and victims of crimes. Under the U.S. Constitution, the president has the "power to grant reprieves and pardons for offenses against the United States." In the nineteenth century, there were very few federal crimes; these included treason, murder on the high seas, mail robbery, and counterfeiting, the last of which happened to be the most commonly prosecuted federal crime before the Civil War. Because Congress legislated for the District of Columbia, convicts in Washington, D.C., could also appeal to the president for pardon just as a person from a state might appeal to the governor.[1]

From the moment Lincoln took office, convicts — both white and black — began petitioning him for pardon. These letters all went through the Office of the Attorney General, where a clerk reviewed each case and made a recommendation to the attorney general. If the attorney general believed that the convict was worthy of clemency, then he made a recommendation to the president. If he did not, then the president likely never saw the case. Lincoln often followed the advice of these subordinate officials.

Lincoln's inclination toward mercy became legendary during his lifetime and continued following his death. In an 1896 political stump speech, a Republican operative recounted overhearing several exchanges between Lincoln and White House visitors. In one, a Virginia slave owner came to the White House sometime in late 1863 or early 1864 with a petition. "Well, my good friend, what can I do for you?" the president asked him. The man presented the petition to the president, explaining that it was a request for the pardon of a black man, "formerly belonging to himself," who had been convicted of larceny in the District of Columbia. The petition stated that the convict "was a man of good character and had never been guilty of any offence before." Lincoln asked what he had stolen. "Thirty dollars in silver," replied the Virginian. "Why," remarked the president, "where did he find so much silver these days. Surely the temptation was great, and, as you say, he is a good kind of fellow and he is not likely to be soon tempted in the same way again, I guess we will have to let him out."[2]

A story like this almost seems too cute to be true—especially when considering that it was told in a political speech more than three decades after the event. And yet the pardon records at the National Archives bear much of it out. On October 30, 1863, a man named Lambert A. Whiteley wrote a petition to Lincoln asking for the pardon of a convict named Hamilton Anderson—"a young colored man" who, "upon his own confession," was found guilty of larceny in the federal court in Washington and sentenced to a year imprisonment in the Albany Penitentiary. Whiteley told the president that Anderson had already served four months in jail, that he had never before committed a crime, and that he had "an excellent character." If he was released, Whiteley believed Anderson would "become a useful member of society."

Lincoln wrote on the back of the petition: "Inclining to believe that this boy has been sufficiently punished in the four months['] imprisonment he has already endured, I have concluded to say 'Let a pardon be made out in this case.[']" Lincoln dated this endorsement October 31, 1863, presumably the day that Republican orator observed Whiteley at the White House. A few days later, on November 2, Lincoln granted the pardon.[3]

Only one small detail from the 1896 story does not align with the original records from 1863. While the 1896 account states that the convict stole thirty dollars in silver, the criminal case file at the National Archives states that Anderson had stolen fourteen dollars worth of silver coins and a pistol (valued at $7.50) from Whiteley.[4] Perhaps the Republican orator misremembered the amount—which would be understandable given the lapse of time—or perhaps he used poetic license to connect Lincoln's redemption of this convict to Jesus Christ and Judas Iscariot (who betrayed Christ for thirty pieces of silver). Regardless, the 1896 story now appears to be fairly reliable, and it is revealing on several levels. First, Lincoln's endorsement shows how the president used some of the pejorative language of his day, referring to the convict as a "boy." But more importantly, the case underscores the empathy Lincoln had for a convicted ex-slave, and his hope that this man could overcome his circumstances. For Lincoln, freeing this particular defendant was an act of justice.

Lincoln received more than a dozen petitions for pardon in cases involving African Americans. In some instances, he chose to show mercy, such as in an 1864 case in which a group of white Philadelphians wrote to Lincoln on behalf of a black inmate at Eastern State Penitentiary, describing the prisoner as "a person of good moral character and a peaceful and law abiding citizen."[5] In other cases, Lincoln chose not to act. When a servant of Lincoln's former political rival Stephen A. Douglas was convicted of stealing silver from Willard's Hotel in Washington, D.C., Lincoln opted not to pardon the man—despite the inclusion of a letter from the late senator's widow.[6] In these cases, African Americans did not write to Lincoln on their own behalf. In the stories that follow, they did.

A Desperate Wife Pleads for Her Husband's Release from Prison

On March 22, 1861, John Booth, a free black man in Georgetown, in the District of Columbia, stole twenty sticks of wood from Charles Myers & Son. Booth was found guilty in the Criminal Court of the District of Columbia and sentenced to pay a one-dollar fine and serve six months in the common jail. Several petitions arrived on Lincoln's desk, including one from Henry Addison, the mayor of Georgetown, who wrote on April 17 that he had known Booth "for many years" and that Booth was "a worthy and industrious colored man" who should be granted executive clemency. Another letter sent that same day came from the victims of the crime, Charles Myers & Son. Their letter noted that Booth had been in jail for a month and that since he was "exhibiting signs of penitence for his fault, we would be much pleased to see him pardoned."[7] Included among these papers was a petition from Booth's wife, written in the hand of attorney F. W. Jones, seeking pardon for her husband:

> To His Excellency Abraham Lincoln, President of the United States:
> The petition of Elizabeth Booth colored, the wife of John Booth colored, respectfully shews, that on the 22[d] day of March last past her husband John Booth was convicted in[8] the Criminal Court for the County of Washington of the District of Columbia of *larceny of 20 sticks of wood valued at 60 cents* from C. Myers & Son and was the same day sentenced to be imprisoned in the common jail for this county and District for the term of six months and to pay a fine of one dollar and costs, as by reference to a copy of the record thereof herewith filed more fully appears: Your petitioner further shews that she is dependent upon the daily labor of the said John Booth for her support and the support of her children and that she is put to great poverty and distress by reason of the deprivation of the monies derived from his daily labor—that the said John Booth is now contrite and sincere in his repentance for the act committed, the first with which he was ever

charged or suspected, and she prays that the clemency of your Excellency in his behalf will be exercised in his favor so far as to extend to him a pardon, and as in duty bound she will ever pray &c.

Elizabeth Booth
by her atty
F. W. Jones.

I would add from my own knowledge that the petitioner has five small children, the oldest about eleven years of age, — that the prisoner John Booth is a blacksmith, and the family are entirely dependent upon his services for support and are now in a destitute condition.

F. W. Jones
April 18. 1861.[9]

On May 3, the pardon clerk read through these papers but concluded, "There is nothing in this statement of facts to justify the extension of clemency to the prisoner at this early day after his conviction. His guilt is not disputed, and there is reason for believing that he stole more wood than he was convicted for stealing." Six weeks later, however, the pardon clerk changed his recommendation, writing on June 15, "Recommend pardon, prisoner having served three months and behaved well." Two days later, Lincoln pardoned Booth.[10]

Nine Sailors Convicted of Mutiny Seek Pardon

A dramatic scene unfolded aboard the American ship *Challenger* in April 1861. After having sailed about eight hundred miles from Liverpool toward New York, Captain Henry D. Windsor saw one of the black members of the crew, a man named Jones, smiling. Windsor thought the men were laughing at him and he ordered Jones to be locked in the cabin as a punishment. Jones protested that he was not misbehaving and had never done so before, but the captain was unmoved. This took place on April 9.

A short while later, on April 21, Captain Windsor ordered the boatswain to call the men on deck. Eight crewmen replied that they were sick and resting in the forecastle. Windsor exploded with rage. "I'll have them out, dead or alive; I will blow the forecastle up," he exclaimed. After another failed attempt to get the men, Windsor armed the ship's mates with pistols. Then, without provocation, he struck one of the crew, Thomas Woodberry, in the head two or three times with a horse pistol as Woodberry manned the ship's wheel. Blood flowed out of the black sailor's skull and onto his face. Windsor walked around the deck barking orders at the men, threatening them. He then hit another member of the crew, Anthony Jones, in the head with his horse pistol while Jones was merely "at this duty." Jones fell to the deck, but Windsor continued to strike him. Windsor and the officers then went into the forecastle, with the captain shouting, "Let me see the man that will raise a hand here, and I will blow his brains out, and every one of you s—s of b—s go out on deck."

The sick men put on their shoes and mustered onto the deck. Windsor said to them, "Let me see how many of you are sick; step out and go in the forecastle again." Six men stumbled back to the forecastle. Enraged, Windsor again struck Jones in the head with the horse pistol, then beat him six more times as he lay on the ground, begging for mercy. "For God's sake, Captain, spare my life," Jones pleaded. "No, I mean to kill you," replied Windsor. When Jones tried to run, one of the officers stabbed him in the back with a knife. "Murder!" cried Jones as he fell to the ground with the knife handle sticking out of him.

Windsor pulled out the knife and then went after another member of the crew, Isaac Hamilton. Seeing what had just happened, Hamilton ran. Windsor fired at him and missed. Hamilton then climbed up the rigging, at which point the captain ordered him down, saying he "would not hurt him." Foolishly, Hamilton obeyed. When Hamilton came down, Windsor struck at him with the horse pistol. Hamilton again tried to climb up the rigging, but this time Windsor and the officers punched him repeatedly and pulled him onto the deck.

Seeming to be in control of the situation, Windsor put his gun down and shouted, "Let me see the man among you that will come out and fight me [in] a fist fight; I can whip any d—n black s—n of a b—there is in the crowd." None of the men dared utter a sound. Windsor then told Anthony Jones to kneel down and say his prayers. Jones obeyed, at which point Windsor said, "Now, I mean to shoot you." "Pray, Captain, spare my life, for God's sake," begged Jones. Then Windsor called on all of the crewmen on deck to kneel down. "Captain, I have done nothing to you or any of your officers since I have been on board your ship," uttered Samuel Havens. The officers confirmed that Havens "had been respectful to all," and Windsor spared him any further threats. Windsor then turned to the men on their knees and said, "Pray to your God, and say that you have used me wrong—you have used me shamefully." The men replied, "We have done nothing wrong—we have only done as we were ordered." At that, the captain stormed off and "the row ceased."

Upon reaching New York, Windsor had fifteen of his black sailors arrested and charged with "endeavor[ing] to make a revolt or mutiny" on April 9. One newspaper said the defendants were "as black as the ace of spades." The trial took place on May 24, 1861, in the U.S. Circuit Court for the Southern District of New York. The presiding judge was U.S. Supreme Court justice Samuel Nelson, a Democrat from New York. Captain Windsor testified that the crew "had refused to obey his orders, and had attempted mutiny." He further claimed that he "behaved very mercifully" toward the crew when they misbehaved, merely making them "go down upon their knees, beg his pardon and say they were sorry." Despite evidence contradicting the captain's testimony, the court found all fifteen defendants guilty. Nelson sentenced Isaac Hamilton, Anthony Jones, and a third crewmember to three years in prison; three of the men received two years in prison; and the remaining nine were sentenced to one year in prison.[11] From prison, the nine, who were all between the ages of twenty-two and thirty, sent Lincoln a letter asking for pardon:

To, His Excellency Abraham Lincoln   President of the United States
The Petition of John Peterson, William Penn, Henry Hundy, James Russell, Alfred Suffon, George Pierce, Charles Tennant, John Davis, and James Evans, of the City of New York,
Respectfully shows:
That your Petitioners and six others were part of the crew of the American Ship Challenger, and were convicted on the 24th day of May A.D. 1861 in the U.S. Circuit Court at New York, of the crime of endeavor[ing] to make a revolt and your Petitioners were on the 28th day of said May sentenced to be imprisoned at Blackwells Island for the period of One Year, while the other six defendants were sentenced three of them to three years imprisonment and three of them to two years imprisonment.
And your Petitioners further show that although present at the mutinous acts of the other seamen your Petitioners took no active part in them.
And your Petitioners further show that they have already suffered severely for the offence aforesaid both before and after conviction. Wherefore they humbly pray that your Excellency would extend to them the executive clemency.
And your Petitioners will ever pray &c

James Russell		[illegible word]
his John X Petersen mark	—	New Haven Ct
his Wm X Penn mark	—	Frederick Md
his Henry X Hardy mark	—	Easton Md
his Alfred X Suffon mark	—	Del
his George X Peirce mark	—	Del
his Charles X Tennat mark	—	Del
his John X Davis mark	—	Concut
his James X Evans mark	—	Del

Unfortunately, this letter was misfiled. Rather than go to the Attorney General's Office, it was routed to the Department of the Navy—Lincoln's secretaries likely mistook the *Challenger* for a warship. Thus, the letter never got into the proper channels for consideration for a pardon.[12]

A Free Black Man Sells Whiskey to a Soldier

Soldiers getting drunk was a major problem during the Civil War. According to one scholar, "Alcohol was involved in 18 percent of the [roughly 75,000] incidents that came before general courts-martial; 3,133 men were charged with being drunk on duty in general courts-martial, and a conservative estimate is that thousands more were punished for this military crime at the regimental level."[13] Demon rum, in other words, was often at the root of the army's disciplinary issues.

In order to combat this problem, Congress enacted several laws that made it illegal "to sell, give, or administer to any soldier or volunteer in the service of the United States, or any person wearing the uniform of such soldier or volunteer, any spirituous liquor or intoxicating drink" in the national capital. The initial punishment for violating this law was a twenty-five-dollar fine or imprisonment for thirty days, but during the same session, Congress amended the fine to twenty dollars or thirty days in the Washington jail. Curiously, Lincoln signed the amendatory law before signing the first, which led to some confusion among judges in the District of Columbia.[14] The following petition, presumably written by a lawyer, involved a free black man who provided whiskey to a soldier in September 1861:

To the President of the United States

The petition of John Ames a free man of colour respectfully represents

That on the 26th of September—the day appointed for humiliation, prayer and fasting—your petitioner having come from the country (where he is usually employed) into the city of Washington, (where his family is) was in passing down Seventh Street accosted by a person wearing uniform and asked as a favour to buy him some whiskey. Your petitioner laid out 30 cents received from him, in whiskey to fill his canteen, and returned the canteen to him with its contents. For this your petitioner did not receive, and was not promised any reward. What he did was a mere act of civility and kindness, arising from motives which often actuate persons in your petitioners class towards those above them. And it was such conduct as your petitioner and others in his class have been accustomed to think was becoming in them—conduct indicating a willingness to oblige citizens or soldiers who are placed above them.

It never occurred to your petitioner that he was doing any thing improper; still less that he was violating any law. Yet for this and nothing more a justice of the peace has punished him by a fine of twenty five dollars, as will be seen by a statement of the justice which accompanies this petition. To terminate his imprisonment in jail—

where your petitioner was for the first time and hopes never to be again — a clergyman in whose employment he has been (the Rev^d Mr. Buck) kindly advanced the amount of the fine and according to the statement of the justice it has been paid over to the superintendent of the Metropolitan police. — Mr Buck is unable to lose the amount and your petitioner feels bound to indemnify him out of the future earnings of his labour, on which he depends for the support not only of himself but of his wife and two children. To be relieved from the necessity of making such an application of those earnings is the object of this petition.

Your petitioner is advised 1st that if he has unintentionally offended against the provisions of the act of Congress, it is in the power of the President — in whom is vested the Executive power and especially the power to grant reprieves and pardons for offences against the United States — to afford him relief; and that the circumstances of his case furnish just and proper ground for granting such relief. 2dly Your petitioner is advised that the circumstances do not show a case of liquor or drink either sold given or administered by your petitioner; the *sale* certainly was not by your petitioner but by the shopkeeper who received the price for it; the liquor was not *given* by any one to the soldier but was paid for by him; nor was it *administered* by your petitioner as doctor, nurse or otherwise, in the sense in which the term is commonly understood. And therefore your petitioner should not have been regarded as a person offending against the provisions of the act of Congress. 3dly he is advised that even if he had offended against those provisions, there was a want of jurisdiction in the justice to impose the fine and therefore the conviction was illegal. and 4[t]hly he is advised that even if it had been proper to impose a fine on him, the fine should not have been the sum of twenty five dollars mentioned in the act of Congress of last session p 291, 2 [pp. 291–92] but only the sum of twenty dollars mentioned in the amendatory act p 286.

Wherefore, your petitioner prays that under all the circumstances there may be repayment to him of the twenty five dollars, either in whole or in part, and such relief given as upon the whole case shall appear reasonable. —

John D. Clark, the justice of the peace who had fined Ames twenty-five dollars, appended a note to Ames's petition stating that he had made his decision "under the erroneous impression . . . that the act of Congress gave Jurisdiction to the Justices of the Peace" to determine the amount of the fine. Moreover, Clark stated that he believed Ames "was entirely Ignorant of the law and that he was the victim of a soldier who induced" him to "procure the liquor for him." Despite this explanation, it does not appear that Lincoln ever acted in this case.[15]

A Convicted Arsonist Asks for Pardon

On August 1, 1853, two homes in the District of Columbia burned to the ground, and two biracial teenage boys—Jack Shepherd (alias John Fisher) and John Francis West—were arrested for the crime. Both boys accused the other of the crime, and both were found guilty and sentenced to twelve years in prison (six years for each house).

While in prison, Shepherd gained a reputation for unimpeachable honesty. So trustworthy was he that for five years the warden would permit him to work outside the prison and make deliveries into the city. Writing on Shepherd's behalf in October 1861, the warden told Lincoln that several police officers had colluded with West in order to frame Shepherd and split a $1,000 reward. "He in Court swore that he saw Fisher set the house on fire, which testimony convicted Fisher, though during the trial the rottenness of those acts became so visible that the reward money was withheld from them, and they were both (Fisher and West) sentenced to the Penitentiary." Moreover, the warden continued, "West often frankly admits that *Fisher had nothing to do with it*, but, *Plainly says he done it himself* and that his object in swearing it on Fisher was to get the five hundred dollars reward."

Upon reading through this testimony in December 1861, the pardon clerk wrote, "The request strikes me as reasonable. Eight years is long enough to hold in confinement a poor unlettered boy of thirteen, for almost any offence he could commit." Lincoln agreed and pardoned Shepherd on December 30, 1861.[16]

For his part, West had been trying to get release from prison for several years. In 1857, he had petitioned Franklin Pierce for pardon, telling the Democratic president that a police officer had coerced him into saying that he had seen Shepherd set the fires. According to West, "The poor terror stricken boy perhaps muttered some incoherent phrases which was immediately construed by the avaricious man into a confession of guilt." But West's appeal was in vain; Pierce chose not to grant a pardon.[17]

Upon learning that Lincoln had pardoned Shepherd, West thought he would try again. In early 1862 he sent the following petition to the White House. The tone in this petition to Lincoln was far different from the more defensive petition to Pierce:

To His Excellancy President Lincoln,

The following is the Petition & Prayer, of your humble servant, (John Francis West) a Prisoner in the U.S. Penitentary District of Columbia, as herein after set fourth.

Your Petitioner would humbly set fourth, that at the time of his conviction which was for the crime of Arson, nearly nine Years ago. He was then very young & did not understand the true Principals of Morality, or his duty to his fellow man. And although convicted of the above dreadfull crime in two cases, yet he was in company with one John Fisher *whom* Your Excellancy Pardoned on the first day of January *last past,* in one case only.

And furthermore, that your Petitioner ought not to have been Prosecuted *atall,* from the following good & sufficient reasons, namely.

In the first place, your Petitioner being the main *witness,* the government ought not to have Prosecuted its own witness, more especially as indusements of acquittal were held out to your Petitioner, by the Prosecution, that they might obtain the evidance of your Petitioner.

Secondly as conviction was had only, by the Arresting Officers swearing to information imparted by your Petitioner—in the hope of an Acquital. Your Petitioner therefore Prays, Your Excellancy to release him from these Bonds, from the above good & sufficient Reasons.

Thirdly, your Petitioner having already served nearly nine years, or long enough to expiate any ordinary crime, your Petitioner would beg a release.

Fourthly, as the punishment of crime looks to the Moral Reformation of the crimnal; as well as the protection of the community, your Petitioner would say that he now understands the true Principals of Morality; & if released hopes to practice them, & live a sober & industerious life in the future.

Your Petitioner hopes to have your Excellancy's early consideration of the above, & Your Petitioner will ever Pray

Prisoner   John Francis West,
Atorney   D^r. W^m. Boyd
Thomas C. Down, Committing Magistrate
                                        Jno. H. Johnson JP [Justice of the Peace]
J. R. S. Van Vleet, [editor of the] Nat. Repub.
Geo. W. Garrett   ƚ James M. Eliason
Henry D. Gunnell   W. A. Crofferty
J. F. Page   John West [the prisoner's father]
Benja. F. Clark

Lincoln pardoned West on November 5, 1862.[18]

A Mother Begs for Her Wayward Teenage Daughter's Release from Prison

In January 1863, Elizabeth Byington of Washington, D.C., hired Mary L. Easton, a seventeen-year-old black girl, to work for her. Mrs. Byington was apparently disappointed with Easton's work, seeing her as "a very thoughtless, childish, careless servant." She threatened to fire Easton without pay "for some act of omission grosser than common," at which point Easton decided to take "the law into her own hands" by stealing some valuable items (including undergarments) from Byington and running off with them. Some people familiar with the case believed that Easton had been induced to do this by another, older servant.

Easton's mother, Lettecia Johnson, pleaded with Lincoln for a pardon for her daughter:

> Washington city
> Jenury the 13 1863
>
> To the Honabl Mr Lincoln   president of the u States
>   sir   i the mother of Mary Luesia Easton do this day aske of you pardon for her from the u s penatentia to witch she has Bin sentenc fore 18 monthes for taken som severil artickels of under cloathin from a Mrs Biengton and it Being the first offence i do hunbley Bege of you parden for her witch i hope you will grant in the name of the Lord and for som partickalar reason i am antious is that her health is quit indifferent   She is trubel with a desease of the thought [throat] and has Bin very sike in Jail But is now Beter   she has Bin in Jail for near Six weekes tharfo i aske of you pardon it Being the first affen[c]e and i hope it ma Be the Last   and i hope this ma prove a warning to her for

the time to com   She quit[e] young 17 years of age witch i hope as she grose older the lord ma inspier her hart to do Better that she ma Be a comfort in my oldest days &

to witch i now close askin of you anawnser [an answer] your Servent Mrs Lettecia Johnson

Easton's pardon file contains other letters in support of her release. Mrs. Byington wrote that she "would do all in my power to have Mary L. Easton repreived from prison." Another woman pledged to hire Mary if she was released. And other letters praised her mother, with one calling her "a person of veracity of moral worth, and very reliable."

For some unknown reason, the Attorney General's Office did not look into the case until February 9, 1864—more than a year after Johnson sent her initial petition. At that point, Easton had served two-thirds of her sentence. While the pardon clerk seemed inclined to pardon her, Attorney General Bates wrote on the file on February 20, "Her time is nearly out, & as there is nothing of controlling influence in her favor, Declined." Lincoln never saw the case.[19]

A Contraband Asks for His Pregnant Wife's Release from Prison

Robert Williams, a contraband, worked as a servant with the Fifteenth New York Independent Battery since April 1862. In August of that year, while the battery was stationed near Fredericksburg, Williams married a fugitive slave from Virginia named Elizabeth, who was about nineteen or twenty years old. Elizabeth stayed with the battery until December 12, 1862, working as a washerwoman, at which point she began boarding with an African American midwife in Washington, D.C., named Fanny Tyler.

When Tyler was absent from her home, she left Elizabeth "in charge of the house." On one such occasion a woman came by and offered Elizabeth a job. Elizabeth locked up Tyler's home and took forty dollars from it. Upon learning of this, Tyler notified the authorities. Elizabeth was arrested soon thereafter. Tyler testified against Elizabeth in court, and she was found guilty and sentenced to sixteen months imprisonment in Albany, New York.

Utterly distraught, Robert Williams met with several lawyers in Washington who refused to take the case. Finally, in early February 1863, an attorney named Henry Cooper agreed to represent the Williamses. Cooper traveled to Tyler's home and found that "she expressed *in substance* and in the most earnest manner her regret" for having testified against Elizabeth. He continued, "She assured me without knowing my object that she believed said Elizabeth Williams innocent and that she was told that she would be compelled to testify against her." He then had Tyler give a sworn statement to that effect:

Washington Feb'y 9th 1863

To His Excellency The President of the United States.

Sir.

At a recent session of the Criminal Court of the District of Columbia Elizabeth Williams a colored woman aged 20 years was convicted of grand larceny and sentenced to the Penitentiary for 16 months.

The circumstances of the case are simply these. About the 15th or 20t of December she came to Washington and applied to me for lodgings. She was an escaped fugitive from her owners in Virginia and was at the time of her arrival in delicate health. She secured lodgings at my house. I am by occupation a midwife, and frequently during my absence from home she was left in charge of the house with an injunction to take care of my property among which was a small sum of money say $40. — She was desirous of procuring a situation in some private family and once during my absence a lady called and hired her. She locked up the house and took the money with her and I have no doubt from subsequent developments with the most honest intentions for upon being called upon every cent of the money was delivered to me. Prior to this I have now no doubt I acted hastily in procuring her arrest after which I understood that it was incumbent upon me to appear in evidence against her and upon my evidence she was convicted and sentenced. I am sure now that she is innocent at heart. I would freely have lost the whole amount afterwards rather than that she should have been convicted, and ask of you as the only reparation and act of justice in my power to render to pardon her. She is young and was always faithful and amiable in her disposition. Though a poor offering in one so humble as myself I would ever feel deeply grateful and thankful for her pardon and her husband who is connected with army as a servant would I am sure bless you, always. May I not hope Mr President that this humble petition will meet with success, and that a matter so trivial to all save those immediately interested will not be thought impertinent by your Excellency.

I am Your Excellency's
Most obt and humble servant.

her
Fanny X Tyler
mark

Attest:
W. M. Duncan

In addition to Tyler's statement, Robert Williams submitted the following petition to President Lincoln, asking for pardon for his wife:

Washington Feb'y 10ᵗ 1863.

To his Excellency Hon Abraham Lincoln   President of the United States.

My name is Robert Williams. Since the 1st of April 1862 I have served as an officers servant in the Army. My wife Elizabeth Williams was formerly a servant (wash woman) also for the officers of the battery in which I am serving and on account of her health left some time in December 1862 and came to Washington. Some two weeks since I procured a pass to come to Washington to see her and found out on my arrival that she had been tried convicted and sentenced to the Penitentiary for 16 months for having (as alleged) stolen some forty (40) dollars from the person with whom she secured lodgings, and upon whose testimony alone, she was convicted. That person's statement accompanies this, and I do hope Mr President that amid the arduous duties which surround you, you will find time to give a small attention to this matter and do justice to one who though occupying the humblest position in life, has yet been wrongfully dealt with. Although a colored man I have presumed unaided to ask your assistance in this the darkest hour of my life, and ask you to restore her to me and the freedom which has been wrongfully wrested from her. We have both cheerfully performed the duties assigned to us always and even under the hardships of our former servitude in Virginia we gained the commendation of our owners. My wife is young and soon to become a mother, and my feelings in view of every thing connected with the case are almost more than I can bear. The only witness against her and upon whose testimony she was convicted acknowledges in the letter accompanying this that she is innocent. Mr President she is all that I looked to for happiness in life, and if restored to her liberty, our prayers though humble shall always ask blessings on your head and our future lives prove that your clemency was not undeserved. I am informed at the jail that my wife has been sent to Albany New York. Hoping that my petition be successful

I have the honor to be
Your most obt and humble servant
his
Robert X Williams
mark

Attest:
Henry C Cooper

Upon receiving Williams's petition and Tyler's statement, the pardon clerk was suspicious, suggesting that they may have "been made up for the occasion, or that improper influences [may have] been used upon the woman Tyler." Another lawyer in the Attorney General's Office marked the file on July 5, 1863, "Declined."[20]

A Young Black Boy Accidentally Shoots a Fellow Sailor on the High Seas

The U.S. Constitution gives jurisdiction to the federal courts in "all cases of admiralty and maritime jurisdiction." Thus, criminal cases that occurred on the high seas were tried in a federal district court. In the case that follows, Benjamin Brown—an African American youth who was serving as a cabin boy on the bark *George and Henry*—was convicted of killing another man aboard the vessel. When the ship returned to port in Baltimore in 1860, Brown was arraigned before U.S. district judge William F. Giles. He was found guilty of manslaughter and sentenced to three years in prison and ordered to pay a one-dollar fine plus court costs. He would not be released from prison until he paid the fine and costs.

After having served his prison sentence, Brown asked Lincoln to remit the financial penalties that had been assessed against him, as his inability to pay them meant that he would remain in prison for the rest of his life:

To His Excellency, Abraham Lincoln President of the United States,
Your Petitioner, Benjamin Brown, a Col boy, Respectfully represents to your Excellency, that at the April Term AD 1860 he was

indicted in the District Court of the Unted States, in and for the Maryland District, for the Killing of a Certain boy, by the name of Thomas Crozier, and was tried and Convicted of Manslaughter, and sentenced to Three years imprisonment, in the Jail for Baltimore City, and pay a fine of one dollar and Cost, a copy of which said Judgment, is herewith filed, your Petitioner, will here state the facts in the case, and they are those, at the time of the occurrence, your Petitioner, was a cabin boy on board of the Barque George & Henry on the West Coast of Africa, and one day whilst the Captain of the Barque was absent, your Petitioner was playing with a gun in the cabin of the said Barque, and whilst so playing with the said gun, the gun went off, and killed the said Thomas Crozier, at the trial of the case your Petitioner admmitted the killing, but pleaded that it was purely accidentally, your Petitioner states that he has suffered, and satisfied, the judgment, as far as it is in power, that the Term of his imprisonment, expires on the 23rd day of April AD 1863, and he further states that he is a poor Colloured boy, and, is unable to pay said fine & Cost, he therefore prays that your Excellency, will be pleased to Remit said fine and Cost, and as in duty bound he will ever pray &c.

Benjamin Brown

Brown's lawyer, C. Dodd McFarland, also submitted several letters on his client's behalf asking for the fine and court costs to be remitted so that Brown could be released from prison.

On April 21, 1863, the federal prosecutor in Baltimore, William Price, endorsed Brown's petition: "I respectfully recommend that the fine & costs within referred to be remitted as it is impossible that Brown by remaining in jail can ever pay them." The court costs were $666.50—an amount Brown never could have paid and that essentially gave him a life sentence. Judge Giles wrote a note concurring. Lincoln recognized the justice of these requests. On June 18, 1863, he granted Brown "a full and unconditional pardon."[21]

Black Convicts in New Jersey Ask for Release So That They Can Fight for the Union

The correspondents in this letter were convicted of horse stealing in New Jersey. Since this was a state-level crime, Lincoln had no authority to pardon them. Nevertheless, they wrote to the president asking for pardon so that they could fight for the Union cause and afterward emigrate to Liberia:

Middlesek Co
New brunswick
Sept 20 [1864]

To Your Honor sir — Mr Lincolon Presdent of the U — S

    If it pleases Your Honor sir I will address you a few line in writting   sir we have been in confinement for some three months and have got enough of confinement   sir we are willing to serve in the defence of our country sir three year with out any payment sir — sir we know we are colored and that the reason we got in the difficulties we are in sir but we see it no use sir   I suppose you want to know what we are in for   sir to your honor sir we are for takeing Horses   we took them and went to trenton to a great colored meeting intending to be home before morning but being invited to stay all night we over slept ourslefs [ourselves] an[d] they was there before we got off and had us arrested   sir we did not intend to steal the Horses   sir we had no such a Idea sir & but sir Ɨ we would most dearly love to see [our] own native country once before we die   but sir if we die in the service of this country sir we will die Just as Happy   sir we are Happy to know that you are still going to retain your Honor and sir if the colored people could vote sir you could stay till you [are] ready to leave sir   & sir to your Honor will you please to let me have an answer soon as this letter reach you if it pleases your Honor

[The following appears to be a poem titled "Johnny Rebs," which they enclosed in their letter.]

Johnny Rebs
Oh foolish owner wherefore did you ebb from so generous a nation to be a cruel reb. the appearance of your house call forth the exclamation that no higher value awaits you than relentless despoliation teacups pans and kettles all broken into bits while your sofas chairs and stands are use[d] in the rifles pits thus while you've lost your house your books your furniture and dishes Jeff Davis and his crew will have the loaves and the fishes Now take advice and come in the union again for you have had your bloody fun an[d] affectionate country will even greet a prodigal son then will a warlike nation with

patriotism full drive the frenck [French] from mexico and Handle old John Bull S S S S S

Sir we are willing and ready to join the defence of the union without any payment and serve for the trem [term] of three years or during the war and then emagrat after to Liberia If it please your Honor

From Your ever willing Servants Colored

William J C Bounds

Philip Conover

and Francis — M — Roe

~~and~~ New Brunswick Jail   Sept 20

[The men then appended another note written in pencil and in a different hand.]

We will address you afew more lines   sir if pleases your Honor we have sir ~~y use~~ been use very badly here   the turn key has use us very badly   he give us no bread at all some time and lets the white call us all the name they want because they go for Little Mac as they call him and they also let whites list [enlist] ~~and~~ and colored men they wount   we no we are colored but sir what the differents as long as we can carry ~~and use it~~ a gun and use it where some of them same white men are afraid to   so ~~peas~~ please sir to pardon us if it please Your Honor and let us Join the rest of our colored men in the field sir ~~my~~ may it please your Honor

Your Ever Willing Servant

William Bounds

Francis — M — Roe

Philip Conover

New Brunswick Jail   Sept[22]

A clerk in Washington misinterpreted the letter, mistakenly thinking that these men were already soldiers who wished to be restored to their regiment. The correspondence was forwarded to the assistant adjutant general, who wrote on the back of the letter on October 1, 1864, "These men are citizens; have been arrested for horse stealing—Have not now, and do not pretend that they ever had any connection with the service." It is unclear when they were ultimately released from prison.

In hindsight, Lincoln may have been lucky not to have these men in the Union army.[23] At least one of them appears to have been something of a career criminal. In 1861, Philip Conover had been arrested for dog stealing; in 1863, he was indicted with several others for "disorderly conduct and disturbing religious worship" at a church; in 1867, he escaped from prison following his second conviction for horse stealing (although he was quickly apprehended at Princeton); in 1881, he was arrested for assault; and in 1884, he was arrested for home robbery and attempted murder.[24]

A Victim of Sexual Assault Asks for Release from Prison

On November 3, 1863, an African American teenager named Elizabeth Shorter gave birth to a biracial daughter named Rosina. Lizzie apparently never told her friends or acquaintances who the father was, and when she had the baby baptized at St. Aloysius Church on December 2, she appears to have told the priest that the father was her "husband," William Davis.

During the war, Lizzie had been working as a servant in the home of William Francis Pruett (sometimes spelled Pruitt), a thirty-two-year-old shoemaker and streetcar conductor, in Washington, D.C. According to testimony she later gave in court, when Lizzie went to bed one night on the sofa in Pruett's store, he came in after dark and sat next to her. When she asked who was there, he replied, "It is me Liz, Frank. I want to get into bed with you, but don't want you to tell Lib; will you?" Lizzie said she was tired and told him to go away, but he "persevered and got in bed with her, and put his arms round [her] neck, and had illicit intercourse with her then and afterwards."

When Lizzie realized she "was in the family way" (meaning pregnant), she told Pruett. "He asked if it was his," and she confirmed that it was. (According to testimony in court, she had slept with only one other man earlier in her life.) Pruett initially told Lizzie that "if it was his he would sustain the child." However, after the baby was born, Pruett "told me he had no money to give [me], but he had a bedstead . . . he would give [me]." Lizzie asked incredulously "what use was a bedstead without a bed." Sometime around Christmas 1863, Pruett "urged [Lizzie] to go away from his house with the child." She replied that "if he would support the child she would go, if not, she would stay till the child was old enough to wean."

In May 1864, Lizzie learned that Pruett intended to kick her out of the house. On a Saturday when Mrs. Pruett was at the local market, Lizzie asked him "what he meant by wanting to send her out of the house." He denied having said such a thing and "shut the door" on her. Lizzie next decided to confront Pruett in front of his wife, who had also recently given birth. She asked him why he planned to "turn her away." Pruett replied that it was because Shorter was not an effective wet nurse for Mrs. Pruett's child "and the expense was too great."

The next morning, a Sunday, Shorter packed up her belongings, dressed her baby, and then knocked at the Pruetts' bedroom door. Frank stayed in bed while his wife answered the door. Lizzie went in and told him to "look at the baby and at her, and remember what he had done to her." He simply replied, "Well." She then reminded him that he had promised to take care of the child, and she threatened that if he did not provide support, she "would disgrace him on the morrow."

Pruett became angry and turned to his wife, saying, "Lib, do you believe that d—d black b—h?" "Yes, Frank, I do," she replied, "for the last three months you have acted as if you were afraid of Liz." At that he allegedly jumped out of bed and grabbed a revolver from his dresser. "God d—n you, I never intended to die a natural death, and I will blow your d—d brains out," he shouted. But Mrs. Pruett grabbed the pistol and scolded him, "Frank! a murder over my child!" Pruett then ran to Lizzie, "choked her and ran her up against the wall, and ordered her out of the house."

As Lizzie hurried away with her baby in her arms, Pruett "told her to get her trunk as soon as possible, or he would throw it out." When she returned later that day to retrieve her belongings, Mrs. Pruett gave her some money. The next morning, Monday, Lizzie went to a judge to file a complaint against Pruett, but the judge refused. She went to another judge who issued the warrant. But Pruett decided to act, too, and he had Lizzie arrested for grand larceny later that very same night. She spent the rest of the week in prison before being released on bail.

On June 16, 1864, a judge in D.C. heard the case against Pruett. According to a newspaper reporter, "The case excited great interest from the fact that it is among the first where negro testimony has been used upon such a charge," and a crowd of people packed into the judge's chambers to hear the case of this "good-looking colored girl."

Shorter laid out the foregoing testimony, although several white witnesses contradicted some of what she said. One witness who lived nearby testified that he had seen her "go in an alley with colored men several times; and also into a house of ill-fame nearly opposite, both of which are reputed to be used for improper purposes," although he added that he had "never seen [her] do anything improper in the alley; but have seen others."

The trial went on for several hours, and the lawyers chose not to give closing statements. The judge then immediately rendered a verdict, acquitting Pruett of all charges against him. According to a news report, Pruett "immediately had the girl arrested for perjury," and bail was set at $200. But since

Shorter was already charged with grand larceny, the judge dismissed the perjury charges a few days later.

Shortly before the June trial, the Pruetts' baby had died. Rosina also died at some point in early 1864, likely before Pruett's trial.

On October 22, 1864, Shorter was tried before a Washington jury and found guilty of larceny. On November 3—what would have been her daughter's first birthday—she was sentenced "to suffer imprisonment and labor" at the prison in Albany, New York, for one year.[25] The following day, she sent a letter to President Lincoln:

Washington Novr 4^t 1864.

To his Excellency the President of the United States
Sir:

On yesterday I was sentenced to serve at hard labor for the period of one year in the Albany Penitentiary. The fault was my own, for which I was convicted, but I most solemnly declare before my maker, that I am guilty of no crime. (charged in the indictment)

I was employed as a Servant in the family of one Francis Prewitt a resident of Washington D.C. and in an evil hour gave way to the importunities of Mr Prewitt, —I had carnal intercourse with him and the consequence was that I became pregnant and was afterwards delivered of a child—which lived but a few months, —*That child was begotten by Mr Prewitt.*

I was always trusted in the family of Mr Prewitt with the management of the house, and now being friendless—I implore your mercy.

I applied to Mr Prewitt after the birth of my baby on several occasions for the means to support it, but having tried ineffectually to obtain means for its subsistence I applied to a Justice of the Peace in the City of Washington D.C. for legal redress—Mr Prewitt as I am informed obtained a warrant for my arrest on a charge of Grand Larceny after learning that I had a warrant issued for the support of my child. The money which I was charged with stealing was given to me by Mrs Prewitt on condition that I would say nothing of the connection between myself and Mr Prewitt. For what reason Mrs Prewitt gave me that money to say nothing about the intimacy existing between myself and Mr Prewitt I cannot tell but solemnly aver that everything which is hereinbefore set forth is true and hoping Mr President that my humble appeal may be blessed by your clemency—

I am and will always remain
Your most humble & Obt Servt.
                    her
            Elizabeth X Shorter
                   mark
Att: B Milburn.
To His Excellency
Hon Abraham Lincoln
President of the United States

All four judges of the federal court in Washington appended an endorsement to Shorter's letter, telling Lincoln that hers was "a case which deserves Executive clemency." It may have helped that Lincoln had placed all four judges on the federal bench in 1863. Lincoln was also probably moved by the grief of this poor mother who had lost a child. Having lost two children himself, he knew the pain that such a loss caused.

Considering all the evidence on hand, and moved with compassion, Lincoln issued a pardon on November 5, before Shorter could even be sent to prison in New York. On the back of Shorter's letter, Lincoln wrote the following:

Pardon
A. Lincoln
Nov. 5. 1864

Elizabeth Shorter's case may be the fastest pardon granted in Lincoln's presidency. Making that all the more remarkable is the timing. Three days later, Lincoln would stand for reelection to his second term of office.[26]

A Free Black Man in Missouri
Writes on Behalf of a Rebel Soldier

On rare occasions, African Americans wrote to Lincoln on behalf of Confederates. On December 26, 1864, Mrs. Celia Kuykendall of Platte City, Missouri, wrote to Lincoln on behalf of her son, William, who was an officer in the Confederate army. Mrs. Kuykendall said that she had "herd that your message [Proclamation of Amnesty and Reconstruction] offers good terms to any that will quit the rebelian." As she was "now old and infirm and want him to quit the war," she begged Lincoln to "grant him what he asks." Kuykendall enclosed a letter from her son, as well as the following note from a free man of color:

~~Hon Abraha~~
Hon Abraham Lincoln

    I have been living with Mrs Celia Kuykendall for the last three years and have been acquainted with her son W L Kuykendall for Several years and a better friend I never had and I know him to bee a man of his word and as has promised to come home if you will give him a safeguard and pass so that he can leave the state   [I] hereby pray and request you to grant it for we all desire to go to some one of the new Territories and I desire him to come home so that we can go and better our condition   he is all that is wating   I am a free man and have been for eight or ten years and pray you to grant this my first request   I remain yours in freedom. giles morris a f[r]ee Colord man

In January 1865, Maj. Gen. Ethan Allen Hitchcock wrote that these letters were "not sufficiently definite for making any order in the case."[27]

In his posthumously published memoir, William L. Kuykendall recalled a number of his daring exploits during the Civil War era, including his militia service during Bleeding Kansas and his time as a Confederate soldier. According to his memoir, his "old mother" was "arrested and taken to St. Joseph, *where she requested to be booked as a prisoner of war,* and my wife only escaped imprisonment by getting out of the country temporarily on one occasion." Just as Giles Morris told Lincoln, Kuykendall wanted to travel west. In 1865, he went to Colorado "nearly penniless and virtually in rags." He eventually settled in Wyoming, becoming a judge. He spent the remainder of his life in the West.[28]

CHAPTER TWO

Debating Colonization

One of the more controversial aspects of Lincoln's racial policies was his support for colonization. The concept, which had existed since the eighteenth century, had been a popular approach among whites to dealing with racial differences in the United States. Under this scheme, freed slaves would be returned to Africa, or sent to some other region of the world. Proponents of colonization—which included both slave owners and antislavery advocates—saw colonization as a moderate solution to the problem because it would free the enslaved while ensuring that free African Americans would not impinge on the rights or economic opportunities of whites.

For most of early American history, most African Americans opposed plans to send ex-slaves to Africa—rightly seeing colonization as a bigoted scheme intended to rid the United States of people of color. However, following the enactment of the Fugitive Slave Act of 1850, some black leaders, according to historian Wilson J. Moses, began "to reconsider plans for emigration to Africa, Canada, South America, or the West Indies" because life in those places might be safer than in a nation where free men and women could be arrested and enslaved without any right to defend themselves in court. The period from 1850 to 1862, according to Moses, "represented the first peak of black nationalism in the United States"—a period during which some black people maintained that their race could be uplifted only with a return to Africa.[1] While colonization and emigration appear to be very similar, each had a different motive. Black emigrationists distinguished themselves from colonizationists in that emigrationists were motivated by black self-empowerment, while colonizationists sought to rid America of a perceived inferior race.[2]

During the Civil War, there were three primary locations under consideration for colonization. Liberia, on the west coast of Africa, had been a homeland for African Americans since its establishment by the American Colonization Society in 1822. Now a free republic, the Lincoln administration granted diplomatic recognition to Liberia in 1862. Haiti had great promise, since it was the first black republic, having won its independence from France in 1804; however, African American migrants to Haiti in the 1850s had been treated poorly by the local government. Finally, the Chiriquí region of what is now Panama was the settlement Lincoln was most excited about at this time because of its natural coal deposits.[3]

In 1862, Congress enacted several laws that promoted colonization. The April 16 law abolishing slavery in the District of Columbia allocated $100,000 "to be expended under the direction of the President of the United States, to aid in the colonization and settlement of such free persons of African descent now residing in said District, including those to be liberated by this act, as may desire to emigrate to the Republics of Hayti or Liberia, or such other country beyond the limits of the United States as the President may determine." A few months later, the Second Confiscation Act of July 17 authorized the president "to make provision for the transportation, colonization, and settlement, in some tropical country beyond the limits of the United States," of slaves made free by the act who were "willing to emigrate." That same month Congress appropriated an additional $500,000 to assist in the carrying out of these two laws.[4]

Many black leaders feared that such colonization plans would forcibly remove African Americans from the United States. Others believed that they were a step toward deportation. Wrote one critic in the newspaper of the African Methodist Episcopal (AME) Church, the Philadelphia *Christian Recorder*: "We did and still do consider voluntary emigration as simply the stepping stone to *compulsory* expatriation!"[5] In the spring of 1862, reports circulated in the black press that Lincoln or others might force former slaves to leave the United States. In response, Lincoln sent the following letter to John D. Johnson and Alexander Crummell, two African American emigrants who were serving as commissioners from Liberia:

> EXECUTIVE MANSION, WASHINGTON, *May* 5, 1862.
> GENTLEMEN: I have the honor to reply, in answer to your communication of the 1st May, which I herewith return, that neither you nor any one else have ever advocated, in my presence, the compulsory transportation of freed slaves to Liberia or elsewhere.
> You are at liberty to use this statement as you please.
> Yours, very truly,
>
> A. LINCOLN.
>
> J. D. JOHNSON,
> ALEX. CRUMMELL.[6]

Lincoln's letter to Johnson and Crummell implicitly gave his view on the matter—that he would not compel African Americans to leave the United States. In fact, on several occasions Lincoln spoke strongly against compulsory deportation.[7] Still, Lincoln believed that voluntary emigration was a sound policy, and the correspondence he received from both ordinary African Americans and some black leaders seemed to confirm his view. The following letter, from a black émigré in Haiti, shows the enthusiasm for colonization Lincoln heard from some black Americans around the world:

To His Excellency, Abraham Lincoln, President of the United States of America.

Honored Sir,

Excuse, I pray, the liberty I take in addressing one so highly placed as yourself, by intruding upon your valuable time, every moment of which is fraught with business in which the destiny of millions born and unborn, depend; for humbly and respectfully asking permission to thank your Excellency most sincerely for your noble and most judicious efforts in behalf of my unfortunate race and which has resulted in the liberation of the oppressed descendants of africa, hitherto slaves, in the district of Colombia. This act of Justice was aimed at more than thirty years ago, by the efforts of a number of gentlemen and philanthropists, in various shapes, but to no effect; but it has finally been reserved for you, under Divine Providence, to bring this great disederatum to a close: all the praise, all the honor and all the thanks, honored Sir, for such a noble action, belong to you. And when I humbly take into consideration, the conflicting elements by which such a thing of necessity must have been surrounded, — by conflicting interests, diversion of opinions, — no doubt honorable to all, according to the convictions of either party, of right or wrong, superadded by pecuniary interests, the mobile of human actions, the difficulty must have been doubly great and the consummation superlatively grand and glorious for the great american people and disinterested humanity.

Honored Sir, Mr. Jefferson said that "he trembled for his country when he reflected that God was Just and His Justice would not sleep for ever" — What a Sublime thought! And it has been reserved for you and your noble coadjutors to prove that God's Justice has awakened and that the great work of african redemption, whenever it is possible to be done, will be done, through peaceful and legitimate means, alike honorable to the United States as also to the enslaved; that, in the end, both may have cause to bless you, and bless you as the Father of the country and as the benefactor of the africans.

Honored Sir, The house of Burgesses, of the colony of Virginia, remonstrated against George the Third because he continued to send slaves to the colonies, because they foresaw it would be a curse to their descendants; — and has not this curse fallen on the great american people?

Honored Sir, The humble individual who has the honor to address you these lines, is a man of color, born in Fairfax county, near Alexandria, but now a citizen of Haiti. From my earliest youth I was in favor of african colonization and was about starting for Liberia, but finally decided to locate in Haiti and I have no cause to regret my choice individually, yet I am of opinion that the americo-african people, by their habits, language and religion, would be better off in Liberia than here.

I pray Your Excellency to accept my eternal gratitude and may Almighty God preserve your valuable life to see the accomplishment of the great good which has been reserved for you under His Providence.

Permit me, Your Excellency, to subscribe myself, Your most humble & obedient Servant

John B. Hepburn

Port-au-Prince (Haiti) 7th May 1862.[8]

While Lincoln and some Republicans continued to advocate for colonization, they also began to move more forcefully toward an emancipation policy. On July 17, Lincoln signed two important bills into law. The Second Confiscation Act freed the slaves of disloyal masters, while the Militia Act provided for the employment of "persons of African descent" in "any military or naval service for which they may be found competent." Further, the Militia Act granted freedom to these slaves and their families if they belonged to disloyal owners. Finally, on July 22, Lincoln announced to his cabinet that he intended to issue an emancipation proclamation. The war was going badly for the Union during the summer of 1862, though, and Secretary of State William H. Seward warned Lincoln that issuing such a proclamation at that time would look like an act of desperation. Heeding this advice, Lincoln agreed to postpone his plan until the Union won a significant victory in the field. Little did Lincoln know that such a victory would not come for several more months.

In the meantime, Lincoln took steps to help prepare the nation for the momentous transformation that was coming. On August 4, he appointed Indiana minister James Mitchell as his colonization agent. On August 10, Mitchell sent word to black churches in Washington that Lincoln wished to meet with a delegation of African Americans. Representatives of several churches met on August 14, where they selected a group of five men to meet with the president, all of whom were well-educated members of Washington's black elite. Edward M. Thomas, the group's chair, was president of the Anglo African Institute for the Encouragement of Industry and Art and was well known for his personal library and fine art collection. John F. Cook Jr., a graduate of Oberlin College, was the son of the founder of the Fifteenth Street Presbyterian Church, Washington's preeminent black congregation. Benjamin McCoy had established and run a private school before founding the Asbury Methodist Church. John T. Costin was a grand master in the freemasons. The least prominent among the group was Cornelius Clark, a hackman (cabdriver) in Washington, D.C.[9]

Lincoln met with the five delegates on the afternoon of August 14. The president also had a stenographer in the room so that his remarks could quickly appear in the newspapers. (He likely hoped that by showing strong support for colonization, white northerners might be inclined to support emancipation when he announced it soon thereafter.) Mitchell introduced the five men to the president, and after they'd shaken hands and sat down, Lincoln made "a few preliminary observations," informing them that Congress had appropriated funds for colonization, "thereby making it his duty, as it had for a long time been his inclination, to favor that cause." Lincoln proceeded to lecture the five black men on why they should lead their people out of the United States. "You and we are different races," he began. "We have between us a broader difference than exists between almost any other two races. Whether it is right or wrong I need not discuss, but this physical difference is a great disadvantage to us both, as I think your race suffer very greatly, many of them by living among us, while ours suffer from your presence." Lincoln admitted that African Americans were "suffering, in my judgment, the greatest wrong inflicted on any people," but he assured them that under present circumstances they would never become the equals of white Americans. Moreover, Lincoln blamed the presence of African Americans in the country for the war. "But for your race among us there could not be war, although many men engaged on either side do not care for you one way or the other." He continued: "It is better for us both, therefore, to be separated." For African Americans to wish to remain in the United States, he said, "is (I speak in no unkind sense) an extremely selfish view of the case." Lincoln therefore urged this delegation to push for black emigration to Central America. "The country is a very excellent one for any people, and with great natural resources [including coal] and advantages, and especially because of the similarity of climate with your native land—thus being suited to your physical condition." And there, Lincoln told them, "I would endeavor to have you made equals" of the people already living there. The chair of the delegation, Edward Thomas, briefly replied that "they would hold a consultation and in a short time give an answer." Lincoln then concluded, "Take your full time—no hurry at all."[10]

Two days later, Thomas sent two letters to Lincoln:

Washington Augt 16/62

His Excellency The President
Sir
    If it is or will be convenient to your Excellency I Shall hope to have the honor of a *personal* interview with you on Monday Morning at 8 ½ or 9
    I am Satisfied that an interview of a *few* minutes will be requisite to facilitate your object
    I am your Excellenceis
        Obt St
    Edward M. Thomas
    chairman[11]

Washington Augt 16th 1862

His Excellency the President
Sir
    We would respectfully Suggest that it is necessary that we Should confer with leading colored men in Phila New York and Boston upon this movement of emigration to the point reccommended in your address
    We were entirely hostile to the movement until all the advantages were so ably brought to our views by you and we believe that our friends and co-laborers for our race in those cities will when the Subject is explained by us to them join heartily in Sustaining Such a movement
    It is therefore Suggested in addition to what is Stated that you authorize two of us to proceed to these cities and place your views before them to facilitate and promote the object. We desire no appointment only a letter from your hand Saying you wish us to consult

with our leading friends. As this is part of the movement to obtain a proper plan of colonization we would respectfully Suggest to your Excellency that the necessary expenses of the two (or more if you desire) be paid from the fund appropriated.

It is our belief that Such a conference will lead to an active and zealous Support of this measure by the leading minds of our people and that this Support will lead to the realization of the fullest Success, within the Short time of two weeks from our departure the assurance can be Sent you of the result of our mission and that a Success

I have the honor to be your

Excellencies Obt St

Edward M. Thomas   chairman[12]

Edward M. Thomas apparently returned to the White House a few days later bearing a letter of recommendation urging that he should travel to meet "with the leading men of his color in the Northern cities" to persuade them of the soundness of Lincoln's colonization plan.[13] But others were not persuaded by Lincoln's remarks, which had appeared nationwide in the newspapers. In fact, many black leaders were angered by the condescending tone of Lincoln's lecture to the black delegation. Frederick Douglass thought the speech made Lincoln "appear silly and ridiculous, if nothing worse . . . showing all his inconsistencies, his pride of race and blood, his contempt for Negroes and his canting hypocrisy."[14] The black delegation itself ultimately adopted resolutions in which they deemed discussion of colonization to be "inexpedient, inauspicious and impolitic," saying that "we judge it unauthorized and unjust for us to compromise the interests of over four and a half millions of our race by precipitous action on our part."[15]

Several black leaders penned open letters to Lincoln in response to his meeting with the black delegation. In August 1862, a group of Philadelphians published a pamphlet, which they "forwarded to Washington," titled *An Appeal from the Colored Men of Philadelphia to the President of the United States*. This address made a tempered appeal to the president, highlighting the loyalty of the African American community in the United States, as compared with the disloyalty of southern traitors:

In the purity and goodness of your heart, and as we believe, through a willingness to serve the cause of humanity, you have been pleased to hold an audience with a Committee of colored men, brethren of ours—kindred in race.

The object was to acquaint them with the fact that a sum of money had been appropriated by Congress for the purpose of Colonization, a cause which you were inclined to favor, and dear to the hearts of many good men.

Among the prominent reasons given for colonizing us, is the one most common throughout our enslaved country, that of color. Admitting this distinction to be of great disadvantage to us, the cause of many tears and much anguish, as we pass along this rugged life of ours; yet, we believe that most of this prejudice grows out of the Institution of Slavery.

Benighted by the ignorance entailed upon us, oppressed by the iron-heel of the master who knows no law except that of worldly gain and self-aggrandizement, why should we not be poor and degraded?

If, under the existing prejudices, adverse laws, and low degree of general education, a few become respectable and useful citizens, there is truly hope for the many. We pray for a more liberal and enlightened public policy. We regret the ignorance and poverty of our race. We find, however, in this great city a parallel in the white, and however degraded a part of us may be, there is, under the circumstances surrounding each, a deeper degradation still. Our fathers were not, of their own free will and accord, transferred to this, our native land. Neither have we, their descendants, by any act of ours, brought this country to its present deplorable condition. If there is in the heart of any, claiming by virtue of their color and predominance, a desire to persecute and oppress, no such unhallowed motives govern us.

We can find nothing in the religion of our Lord and Master, teaching us that color is the standard by which He judges his creatures, either in this life nor the life which is to come. He created us and endowed us with the faculties of the man, giving us a part of the earth as an habitation, and its products for our sustenance. He also made it sufficient in compass and fruitfulness to provide for the wants of all, and has nowhere taught us to devour each other, that even life itself might be sustained.

Thus, humbly, have we presented our cause in some of its moral aspects.

Permit us, in further response to your generous efforts in our behalf, to present another, and possibly, a more selfish view, embracing pecuniary and political matters, not more important to ourselves than to others.

We know that the problem of American Slavery has been a difficult one to solve; that state[s]men hesitate, politicians ignore, and the people even now evade the serious reality of a most bloody war, caused solely by the dealers in our flesh. We have not sought such a solution, nor asked a sacrifice so great, without being willing to drink of the same bitter cup.

The blood of millions of our race cries from the ground, while millions more are yet enslaved.

They have produced much of the wealth of this country. Cotton, the product of their labor, while it should have proven a blessing to mankind, has well nigh overthrown the Nations dependent upon it, and is now denominated "King."

Thus has the master of the slave enslaved the world. While colonization, in many of its features might be advantageous to our race, yet were all of us to be sent out of the country, the population of the United States would be reduced nearly one-sixth part. It is doubtful whether the people seriously desire a depletion of this kind, however much they may wish to separate from us.

If statistics prove anything, then we constitute, including our property qualifications, almost the entire wealth of the Cotton States, and make up a large proportion of that of the others. Many of us, in Pennsylvania, have our own houses and other property, amounting, in the aggregate, to millions of dollars. Shall we sacrifice this, leave our homes, forsake our birth-place, and flee to a strange land, to appease the anger and prejudice of the traitors now in arms against the Government, or their aiders and abettors in this or in foreign lands? Will the country be benefited by sending us out of it, and inviting strangers to fill our places?

Will they make better citizens, prove as loyal, love the country better, and be as obedient to its laws as we have been? If God has so ordained it, we shall yet be free. In His providence, He may gather us together in States, by ourselves, and govern us in accordance with His laws. Will the white man leave us alone, when so gathered?

We believe that the world would be benefited by giving the four millions of slaves their freedom, and the lands now possessed by their masters. They have been amply compensated in our labor and the blood of our kinsmen. These masters "toil not, neither do they spin." They destroy, they consume, and give to the world in return but a small equivalent. They deprive us of "life, liberty, and the pursuit of happiness."

They degrade us to the level of the brute. They amalgamate with our race, and buy and sell their own children. They deny us the right to gain knowledge or hold property; neither do they allow us to have the avails of our own industry.

They requite our labor by stripes, manacles and torture. They have entailed upon the poor whites of the South a despotism almost equaling that inflicted upon us. By unjust and arbitrary laws they have driven honest white men from their midst, or imprisoned them in their dungeons.

By falsehood and political cunning they have corrupted the politics of the people in all States. Finally, they have rebelled against their Government.

Having set all laws, both human and divine, at naught, what does a just Government owe them in return? Would it be too great a penalty to deprive them of the labor of their slaves, and compel them to earn their own subsistance by honest means; to permit us to be free, to enjoy our natural rights, to have the avails of our own industry; to live with and have our own wives and children; to have the benefit of the school, the church, and salutary laws, that we may become better men and more valuable citizens; to give the slave an opportunity to increase the wealth of the people, while he consumes the more of the world's products? All of this is not too much to ask. We would reciprocate by increasing commerce, and proving to the world that we were worthy of being freemen.

Beyond this, our humble appeal, we are almost powerless in our own great cause.

God, in his providence, has enlisted in our behalf some of the most noble men of the age. May their efforts be crowned with success. In the President of these United States we feel and believe that we have a champion, most able and willing to aid us in all that is right. We ask, that by the standard of justice and humanity we may be weighed, and that men shall not longer be measured by their stature or their color.

That the Ruler over all, in his infinite mercy and goodness, will keep and protect you, and cause your administration to triumph, in justice, over all its enemies, is the prayer of the Colored men of Philadelphia.

[Signed,]
J. C. DAVIS,
REV. JAMES UNDERDUE,
ROBERT ALLEN,
AMOS B. SAYERS,
JOHN C. BOWERS,
JOHN AUGUSTA,
WILLIAM COOPER,
JOSHUA D. KELLEY,
REV. JONATHAN C. GIBBS,
URIAH H. KELLEY,
THOMAS M. DAVIS,
DAVID TROUT,
AND OTHERS.[16]

Others showed less restraint. A New Jerseyian published a hotly worded open letter to the president in the *Liberator* under the headline "A Colored Man's Reply to President Lincoln on Colonization":

To the President of the United States:

HONORED SIR, — As you are awaiting a reply from the negroes of the country to your recent colonization proposition, you will not, I trust, think it strange that an humble person like myself should venture to address you. Not long since, I was highly gratified by the assurance you, sir, are reported to have given President [Fabre] Geffrard [of Haiti], that you will not tear your shirt even if he does send a negro to Washington. This assurance is also very encouraging to me at the present time, as I am unable to see why a native American negro should be more objectionable to you than one belonging to a foreign country. Should I, however, manifest extraordinary stupidity in my remarks, please, sir, to extend your gracious pardon, and be kind enough to attribute all my perversity to the tightness of my hair, which may render my cranium impervious to your most cogent reasoning.

In the outset, good Mr. President, permit me to congratulate you on your good fortune in having a sum of money placed at your disposal in times like these. In this respect, sir, (especially if it is in specie,) you are highly favored above ordinary mortals. Could you now but, also, enjoy the luxury of spending it, for the benefit of those philanthropic coal speculators you refer to, I can well believe that you might feel yourself raised to the highest pinnacle of human happiness.

The simplicity, good sir, with which you assume that colored Americans should be expatriated, colonized in some foreign country, is decidedly rich—cool and refreshing as the breezes of "Egypt," or the verdure of your prairie home. The assertions, however, you do make in favor of your assumption, are worthy of a passing notice. If admitted, they would make sad havoc with the doctrines that have been cherished by the good and great of all ages. Different races, indeed! Let me tell you, sir, President though you are, there is but one race of men on the face of the earth:—One Lord, one faith, one baptism, one God and Father of all, who is above all, and through all, and in all. Physical differences no doubt there are; no two persons on earth are exactly alike in this respect; but what of that? In physical conformation, you, Mr. President, may differ somewhat from the negro, and also from the majority of white men; you may even, as you intimate, feel this difference on your part to be very disadvantageous to you; but does it follow that therefore you should be removed to a foreign country? Must you and I and Vice-President Hamlin,[17] and all of us, submit to a microscopic examination of our hair, to determine whether the United States or Central America shall be our future home?

Pardon me, sir, if I say you betray a lamentable ignorance of a large portion of the country over which, doubtless for some wise purpose, you have been called to preside. You forget Massachusetts, Maine, Rhode Island, —States that are the brightest exemplars of progress on earth—where all men are equal before the law, black and white living together in peace and harmony.

But were all you say on this point true, must I crush out my cherished hopes and aspirations, abandon my home, and become a pander to the mean and selfish spirit that oppresses me?

Pray tell us, is our right to a home in this country less than your own, Mr. Lincoln? Read history, if you please, and you will learn that more than two centuries ago, Mr. White-man and Mr. Black-man settled in this country together. The negro, sir, was here in the infancy of the nation, he was here during its growth, and we are here to-day. If, through all these years of sorrow and affliction, there is one thing for which we have been noted more than all else, it is our love of country, our patriotism. In peace, the country has been blessed with our humble labor, nor have we ever been found wanting in the times that have tried the souls of men.[18] We were with Warren on Bunker Hill, with Washington at Morristown and Valley Forge, with LaFayette at Yorktown, with Perry, Decatur, and McDonough in their cruisings, and with Jackson at New Orleans, battling side by side with the white man for nationality, national rights, and national glory. And when the history of the present atrocious insurrection is written, the historian will record: "Whoever was false, the blacks were true." Would you, then, in truckling subserviency to the sympathizers with this bloody rebellion, remove the purest patriotism the country affords? If you would, let me tell you, sir, you cannot do it. Neither fraud nor force can succeed, but by the fatal ruin of the country. Are you an American? So are we. Are you a patriot? So are we. Would you spurn all absurd, meddlesome, impudent propositions for your colonization in a foreign country? So do we.

I trust, good Mr. President, you will not rend your garments when I tell you that the question of colonization, so persistently thrust upon us by the heartless traders in the woes of a bleeding people, has long been settled by a unanimous determination to remain, and survive or perish, rise or fall[,] with the country of our birth. In our conventions, conferences, &c., again and again, in the most emphatic language, we have declared our utter detestation of this colonization scheme, whatever form it may assume.

In holy horror, disinterested sir, you may hold up your hands at what you choose to denominate the "selfishness" of the unalterable resolution; but pray tell us, is it any more selfish than your own determination to remain here, instead of emigrating to some petty foreign country; and is it as selfish as the desire to exclude us from a country where there is room enough for ten times the present population; or is it, think you, as selfish as the coal traders, and the swarms of contractors, agents, &c., for whose benefit you are so anxious to spend some of the money our liberal Congress has placed at your disposal? If it is selfishness, please, sir, to remember your own plea for the coal speculation, &c., viz.: all persons look to their self-interest.

But say, good Mr. President, why we, why anybody should swelter, digging coal, if there be any, in Central America? In that country where the sun blazes with a fervor unknown in these high latitudes, where a broad-brimmed Panama [hat], a cigar and a pair of spurs are considered a comfortable costume for the natives, why should we, why should anybody dig coal? Do tell. Might we not just as well dig ice on the coast of Labrador? But, say you: "Coal land is the best thing I know of to begin an enterprise." Astounding discovery! Worthy to be recorded in golden letters, like the Luna Cycle in the temple of Minerva. "Coal land, sir!" Pardon, Mr. President, if my African risibilities get the better of me, if I do show my ivories whenever I read that sentence! Coal land, sir! If you please, sir, give [Union general George B.] McClellan some, give [Union general Henry Wager] Halleck some, and by all means, save a little strip for yourself.

Twenty-five negroes digging coal in Central America! Mighty plan! Equal to about twenty-five negroes splitting rails in Sangamon![19]

It was my intention to have shown you, sir, the necessity of retaining the labor of the negroes in the South as freemen,[20] but space will not permit. According to theory, white men can't stand it, can't live *honestly* in the South: we can. Henceforth, then, let this be the motto: "The Gulf States, purged of traitors, the home of the loyal, emancipated blacks!" And then, good sir, if you have any nearer friends than we are, let them have that coal-digging job.

      Yours respectfully,   A. P. SMITH
Saddle River, N.J.[21]

Another strongly worded public letter appeared in the pages of the October 1862 issue of *Douglass' Monthly* newspaper. Its author, George Boyer Vashon, was the first black graduate of Oberlin College in 1844; five years later, he earned a master of arts degree at Oberlin. After studying law for two years in Pittsburgh, Vashon applied for admission to the Allegheny County bar, but his application was denied on account of his race. In 1848 he became the first African American to pass the bar in New York. The following year he embarked on an extended stay in Haiti, where he taught Latin, Greek, and English for thirty months. In 1850 he returned to New York, where he practiced law and then became a professor of belles lettres and mathematics at New York Central College in McGrawville. Following the Civil War, Vashon would serve as president of Avery College in Pittsburgh, as a solicitor for the Freedmen's Bureau in Washington, D.C., and as a professor at Howard University in Washington and Alcorn University in Mississippi.[22] His letter reflects his extensive literary pursuits:

To His Excellency ABRAHAM LINCOLN, President of the United States of America:
HIGHLY HONORED AND RESPECTED SIR, —
      The papers announce, that on the 14th of August you had an interview with a committee of colored men, and addressed them in reference to the propriety of the expatriation of their class. As a

colored man, I am deeply interested in this matter; and feel that under the circumstances, I ought to be excused for the liberty which I take in making answer to you personally.

In the first place, sir, let me say, that I do not put myself in opposition to the emigration of Colored Americans, either individually, or in large masses. I am satisfied, indeed, that such an emigration will be entered upon, and that too, to no inconsiderable extent. Liberia, with the bright and continually growing promise for the regeneration of Africa, will allure many a colored man to the shores of his motherland. Haiti with her proud boast, that, she, alone, can present an instance in the history of the world, of a horde of despised bondmen becoming a nation of triumphant freeman, will by her gracious invitation, induce many a dark hued native of the United States, to go and aid in developing the treasures stored away in her sun-crested hills and smiling savannahs. And, Central America, lying in that belt of empire which Destiny seems to promise to the blended races of the earth, will, no doubt, either with or without federal patronage, become the abiding place of a population made up, in great measure, of persons who will have taken refuge there from the oppression which they had been called upon to undergo in this country.

But, entertaining these views, and almost persuaded to become an emigrant myself, for the recollections of a thirty months' residence in Haiti still crowd pleasantly upon my memory, I am confident that, in thus feeling, I am not in sympathy with the majority of my class, — not in sympathy either with the great body of them. Those men are doubtless aware, that many comforts and advantages which they do not now enjoy here, await them elsewhere. No feeling of selfishness, no dread of making sacrifices, (as you intimate,) detains them in the land of their birth. They are fully conscious of the hatred to which you have adverted, they endure its consequences daily and hourly; — tremblingly too, perhaps, lest the utterances of their Chief Magistrate may add fuel to the fire raging against them, but buoyed up by the knowledge, that they are undeserving of this ill usage, and sedulously endeavoring to perform the various duties that are incumbent upon them, they enjoy, amid all their ill, a species of content, and echo back, by their conduct, your own words [to the black delegation], that "It is difficult to make a man miserable while he feels he is worthy of himself, and claims kindred to the great God who made him." Thus, they have schooled themselves "to labor and wait," in the hope of the coming of a better time. And, this hope is based in the innermost convictions of their religious nature, in the trust which is not to be shaken, that the God who rules the Universe is a God of fixed, and immutable justice, under whose dispensations the proud and defiant ones of to-day become invariably the peeled and broken ones of the morrow; while those who were despised and rejected, find themselves, in turn, the recipients of abundant and overflowing mercies.

These men too, have another reason for clinging to the land of their nativity; and that is, the gross injustice which inheres even in the slightest intimation of a request, that they should leave it, an injustice which must necessarily be, in the highest degree, revolting to their every sense of right. Who and what are these men? Their family records in this land, in almost every instance, antedate our revolutionary struggle, and you, sir, will read in your country's history, unlike the ignorant and rapid reporters, who, from time to time, in their marketless and pen free calumny of a race, detail from our camps the lie, that "the negro will not fight,"—you, Sir, know, that black Americans fighting shoulder to shoulder with white Americans, in the contest which confirm[ed] our nationality, merited and received the approbation of Washington; and, that the zealous and fleet-footed slave of that time, did, for the partizan bands of [Thomas] Sumter and [Francis] Marion, the same kind of offices which the travel worn and scarcely tolerated "contraband" of our days has done for the armies of [Union generals Ambrose] Burnside and [George B.] McClellan. And now, what reward is offered by republican gratitude? Now, forsooth, when the banquet of Freedom has been spread, when the descendants of the men who fought under [British generals William] Howe and [Henry] Clinton, under [Charles] Cornwallis and [John] Burgoyne, have with ostentatious liberality, been invited to the repast, the children of the patriotic blacks who periled their lives at Bunker Hill, at Red Bank, and on many another hard fought field, must be requested, not merely to take a lower seat, but to withdraw entirely from the table.

But setting aside the injustice of a policy which would expatriate black Americans, let us examine for a moment, its expediency. Cicero has declared, in his principal ethical treatise that, "no greater evil can happen to humanity than the separation of what is expedient from that which is right." Let us suppose, however, that he was wrong in thus teaching; and, that the antipathy existing between the white and black races, —somewhat of a one-sided antipathy, by the by—would justify the removal of the latter one from this country. —It might be, indeed, a matter for discussion, whether this antipathy is as extended and as exacting as you allege; whether, instead of being a permanent instinct, it is not rather a temporary sentiment which will gradually pass away, when once its cause—the slavery and wrong imposed upon the descendants of Africa—will have been removed. But, let that pass. Would it be wise, sir, when Denmark and France and England, are looking with envious eyes upon our liberated slaves, and regarding them as important acquisitions to their West India possessions, to denude our southern States of that class of laborers? Has not the experience of our heart stricken armies—an experience which has prompted the yielding up of the spade to the black man, while the musket is withheld from him— sufficiently indicated, that negro cultivators are absolutely required for that portion of the Union?

But, sir, it is not enough, that the policy which you suggest, should be expedient. It must also, be feasible. You have, doubtless, looked at this matter with the eye of a statesman. You have reflected, that, to remove entirely this "bone of contention," demands the expatriation of nearly one-sixth portion of the Union. You have after mature thought, settled the physical possibility of so large an expatriation; and calmly calculated the hundreds of millions of dollars which its accomplishment will add to our national liabilities, —large now, and growing larger daily under the exigencies of our civil war. Have you also considered, that the meagre handful of negroes under Federal rule, constitutes, so to speak, only the periosteum, while "the bone" itself projects over into territory arrayed against your authority, and may yet be employed by unhallowed Rebellion, grown desperate in its extremity, as a vast and terrible weapon for the attainment of its ends? Whether this be a probability, or not, it is clear, that the difficulties in the way of your suggested enterprise are such as entitle it to be termed Herculean. Herculean? I fear sir, that we must glance at another of the pages of mythology to find an epithet with which to characterize it. Africa, in the days of your administration, as in those of the line of Belus may be called upon to witness the retribution dealt out to wrong by the Eternal Powers. The States of this Union, having assassinated in the person of the negro, all the principles of right to which they were wedded, may, like the Danaide; be condemned to expiate their crime; and this scheme of expatriation may prove, for them the vain essay to fill a perforated "cistern which will hold no water."

President of the United States, let me say in conclusion, that the negro may be "the bone of contention" in our present civil war. He may have been the occasion of it; but he has not been its cause. That cause must be sought in the wrongs inflicted upon him by the white man. The white man's oppression of the negro, and not the negro himself, has brought upon the nation the leprosy under which it groans. The negro may be the scab indicative of the disease but his removal, even if possible, will not effect a cure. Not until this nation, with hands upon its lips, and with lips in the dust shall cry repentantly, "Unclean! unclean!" will the beneficent Father of all men, of whatever color, permit its healing and purification.

I have the honor, sir, to be, with all the consideration due to your high office,

Most Respectfully,

Your Obedient Servant,

George B. Vashon[23]

Despite the opposition from black leaders, the Lincoln administration moved forward with its plans. The president placed Sen. Samuel Pomeroy of Kansas in charge of the project, and Pomeroy began recruiting among free blacks in the nation's capital. "Let us plant you free and independent beyond the reach of the power that has oppressed you," he wrote in an address to "the Free Colored People of the United States." By late October, Pomeroy was claiming that some thirteen thousand African Americans had volunteered to go to Chiriquí—which included Frederick Douglass's son, Lewis. However, nothing ever came of this effort. The Central American governments opposed the mass immigration of black Americans, and these diplomatic machinations brought the whole plan to a grinding halt.[24]

On October 27, a delegation of African Americans went to the White House "to express their disappointment in the delay at going to Central America." Many were upset that they were preparing to emigrate but that the Lincoln administration was not moving quickly enough to assist them in

J. Willis Menard.
Courtesy of the
Library of Congress.

the endeavor. Lincoln may have known the leader of the group, John Willis
Menard Jr. of Illinois, and had likely heard him speak in Springfield, Illinois, in 1858, when he gave an "impressive" speech on slavery, "which he
painted in its darkest hues, and gave able remarks in defense of Liberty
and equality."[25]

The delegates brought with them the following note, which appeared in
the *New York Times* under the headline "Memorial to the President from Colored Men":

WASHINGTON, Oct. 27, 1862.

To the President:

SIR: The undersigned, on behalf of their colored brethren, and of
themselves, have called upon your Excellency to learn when we can
take our departure to the land promised us by yourself in the address
made to us in this, your Executive mansion.

We have learned from the Hon. Senator POMEROY, the Agent of Emigration, whom you appointed to conduct us to Chiriqui, that he is ready, his equipment engaged, his provisions for the voyage bought; that a suitable vessel has been found; that the consent of the Government, with its agreement to receive us as citizens with equal rights and obligations, has been obtained; that he only waits your orders to announce the day of sailing, and that he can sail in about one week if the order is given.

Many of us, acting upon your promise to send us as soon as one hundred families were ready, have sold our furniture, have given up our little homes, to go in this first voyage; and now we find that there is uncertainty and delay, which is embarrassing us and reducing our scanty means, until fears are being created that these means being exhausted, poverty in a still worse form may be our winter prospect.

We have seen it stated in the newspapers that you do not intend to let us depart.

We are not willing to believe that your Excellency would invite us to make arrangements to go—would tell us that we could not live prosperously here—would create hopes and stimulate us to struggle for national independence and respectable equality, and when we had made ourselves ready for the effort, in confident belief of the integrity of the promise, that its realization will be withheld.

Congress has placed the power and the means *solely* in the hands of your Excellency, to aid in removing us. *You* began the movement; you appointed Senator POMEROY, in whom not only the colored people, but the whole country have confidence, to see that justice should be done us in our removal. He has said he is ready. We therefore earnestly beg that your Excellency will now give him the explicit orders to sail, before the cold weather sets in to pinch us here; before the storms of winter shall make our voyage a dangerous one.

J.W. MENARD, Illinoistown, Ill.

M. FOSKEY, Washington, D.C.

B. JOHNSON, Washington. D.C.

HENRY JOHNSON, Washington, D.C.

WM. C. BUTCHER, Frankford, Penn.

J. E. WILLIAMS, Middletown, Penn.

H. W. ORSEY, Elmira, N.Y.

WM. A. LAVALETTE, Hornellsville, N.Y.

GEO. W. JACKSON, Hornellsville, N.Y.

Lincoln's private secretary informed the gentlemen that the president "was anxious as he ever was for their departure; that he had placed every thing in the hands of Senator Pomeroy, and that he could not see them then, but would do so in the course of a few days."[26] It is unknown whether those men returned to the White House; however, at some point the following year, some of these same men sent another petition to Lincoln:

His Excellency, Abraham Lincoln.

Sir:

We, the undersigned men of color, beg to represent for ourselves and on behalf of a large portion of our colored brethren, whose convictions, views and sentiments coincide with our own, that, entertaining as we do, a sincere desire to remove to the Republic of Liberia, we do not wish, for various facts and reasons, that the appropriation or any part of it, which Congress was good enough to make, and place in your hands, for our colonization beyond the limits of the United States, should pass through the hands of the American Colonization Society, for that purpose; but, having great confidence in your Excellency, and the Com^r of Emigration, (Rev. James Mitchell), we respectfully ask that you will, through your Com^r of Emigration, make arrangements with parties outside of the Am. Col. Society, for our speedy removal to the said Republic of Liberia.

We are with great respect,

    Yours, &c.

(Signed.)

J. W. Menard, Charles Babcock

M. Foskey   W. A. Lavelette

P. Stafford   Geo. Washington.[27]

Other African Americans also continued to press Lincoln on the colonization issue well into 1863. On March 3, John D. Johnson—the American-born émigré to Liberia who was serving as a commissioner from Liberia—sent the following letter to Lincoln in which he reminded the president of when they had met to discuss colonization in the spring of 1862:

Your Exce^ll

Sir

Some time past, I had the pleasure of an interview, on the subject of emigration &^c at that time you informed me, that you was ready and would be glad to [give] out the money appropriated by Congress for the emigration and colonization of such persons of African Descent as may wish to emigrate to *Liberia* or elsewhere and that if I had any to go, you would grant them all the ade the Law directed.

Now Sir, I have to inform you that on the above, The Revd J. B. Pinney,[28] and my self have become partners in a contract now pending or waiting your pleasure, It has been submitted to Mr [John P.] Usher Sec^t of the Interior who made some little alterations which we agreed to, Mr [Montgomery] Blair Post Master gen^l also informed me that he would favor it, not withstanding he favored Central America,

Mr Pinney and my self have obtained the favor of the New York Colonization society and have some of the best moneyied [men] to back us. We have also those to act as agents for us who have lived in that Country for years as Missionarys   some of them are white

This arraingment seems to be necessary, so as to forward the work.

In order to go among the contrabans, and get them to go any where, we need, Money and agents, Money our friends will let us have, so soon as we complete the contract, which is now in the hands of the Commissioner of Emigration

Now as we have numbers of these peopble waiting to go to the Republic of *Liberia* there to join their friends and families, I pray your Excll that so soon as it meets your pleasure that you will make knowen the same, so I may present this contract for your consideration and signature.

The people need homs Liberia needs emigrants—Therefore so soon as we can get to work, we will benefitt both.

Please inform me of your pleasure in this matter
and Oblige
you Humble servant
J. D. Johnson
325, I. St W.D.C.
special commissioner for *Liberia*
March 3^d '63[29]

John Willis Menard Jr. also continued to press for colonization. In July 1863, he traveled to British Honduras to determine whether it was a suitable location for emigrants. Upon his return to the United States, he sent the following letter to Lincoln:

543 Broome St.
New-York, Sept. 16, 1863.

His Excellency, Abraham Lincoln,

Sir: Having just returned from an exploration of British Honduras, in Central America, with a view to lay the basis of a *permanent home* for myself and those of my colored race who, from unfavorable circumstances in this country, may be disposed to emigrate, I respectfully ask that your Excellency will be good enough to let me report, in pamphlet form, to your Excellency. Should you approve, I will forward some few copies to your Excellency.

I am sorry not to be able to have as many copies printed as I need for general distribution among my race.

I am, Sir, Your Excellency's most obedt. Serv[t]

J. W. Menard.[30]

As late as October 1863, African Americans continued to write to Lincoln seeking to be able to emigrate:

Camden New Jersey Oct 13th 1856 [1863]

To His Excellency Abram Lincoln, President of the United States.

Much Honor[d] Sir

If you will Pardon the liberty I am about to take in addressing one who the nation delights to honor and who (if the persons immediately concerned would be satisfied to receive the desired information from another source) I would not dare approach not even through the medium of the pen. The question which I most respectfully beg leave to ask, is, will persons preparing to go to Africa from this state be entitled to any part of the money appropriated by congress for colonizing persons of African descent; and if so to whom shall they apply, how much shall each individual receive and to whom shall it be paid. If your Excellency will condescend to ~~instruct~~ direct some of your officials to answer the above questions kind heaven will bless you in proportion to the good it may do. I remain your very humble and obedient Servant & subject

B F Brown

In behalf of some enterprising families who desire to go to Africa[31]

Letters like these last few reveal the continued support of a small group of African Americans for colonization and emigration. Lincoln's receipt of this correspondence may help explain some of the president's own continued enthusiasm for the enterprise. However, after a disastrous attempt at colonization on an island off the coast of Haiti in 1863, Lincoln largely moved away from the scheme. "I am glad the President has sloughed off that idea of colonization," wrote Lincoln's private secretary, John Hay, in the summer of 1864. "I have always thought it a hideous & barbarous humbug."[32]

PART II | Commander in Chief

CHAPTER THREE

Recruiting for the Ranks

From the very beginning of the war, African Americans offered themselves to the Lincoln administration as soldiers. Shortly after the firing on Fort Sumter in April 1861, black Philadelphians formed themselves into three companies, but state recruiters refused to accept them as Pennsylvania Volunteers. That same month, "300 reliable colored free citizens" of Washington, D.C., offered their services to the federal government for the defense of the national capital, but they, too, were rejected. By December 1861, the secretary of war, Simon Cameron, wanted to publicly advocate for emancipation and the arming of black men, but Lincoln required him to eliminate such proposals from his annual report.[1]

In April 1862, General David Hunter, commander of the Department of the South, asked the War Department for "50,000 muskets . . . to arm such loyal men as I can find in the country." When the War Department—now under Edwin M. Stanton—did not reply, Hunter decided to take action on his own, "conscripting" all black men between the ages of eighteen and forty-five and declaring all slaves in South Carolina, Georgia, and Florida free. Through coercive means, Hunter raised a regiment known as the First South Carolina Infantry. But many former slaves resisted. Some hid in the woods; others "were taken from the fields without being allowed to go to their houses even to get a jacket." The families of these black conscripts were disturbed by Hunter's methods. "On some plantations the wailing and screaming were loud and the women threw themselves in despair on the ground," one witness observed.

The War Department refused to pay or equip Hunter's men, so Hunter disbanded the regiment on August 9, 1862. Moreover, Lincoln issued a proclamation revoking Hunter's orders freeing the slaves, saying that as commander in chief, the power to declare slaves free was something "which, under my responsibility, I reserve to myself, and which I can not feel justified in leaving to the decision of commanders in the field."[2] (This language may have been a hint that an emancipation proclamation was imminent.)

Meanwhile, on July 17, 1862, Congress and the president enacted two laws that had major implications for the raising of black troops. The Militia Act authorized the president to "receive into the service of the United States . . .

persons of African descent" to labor on behalf of the military, while the Second Confiscation Act authorized the president "to employ as many persons of African descent as he may deem necessary and proper for the suppression of this rebellion, and for this purpose he may organize and use them in such manner as he may judge best for the public welfare."[3] While the Militia Act specified that persons of African descent would join the service for purposes of labor, the language of the Second Confiscation Act seemed to leave the door open to the enlistment of black men as soldiers.

In late August 1862, Rufus Saxton—General Hunter's successor in South Carolina—received permission from the War Department to enlist up to five thousand black soldiers. By mid-November, he had raised 550 men for the First South Carolina; and a few weeks later, Massachusetts abolitionist Thomas Wentworth Higginson became the regiment's colonel. Over the ensuing months, other regiments of former slaves would be raised in South Carolina and elsewhere in the states of the Confederacy.[4]

When Lincoln issued his final Emancipation Proclamation on January 1, 1863, he declared that black men "will be received into the armed service of the United States to garrison forts, positions, stations, and other places, and to man vessels of all sorts in said service."[5] Beginning in 1863, northern recruiters began raising scores of black regiments, the most famous being the Fifty-Fourth Massachusetts Volunteers. Initially, black soldiers were used primarily for fatigue duty—menial labor on behalf of the army—because many white leaders believed that black soldiers would not fight well and that they were physically suited to labor in hot and humid southern climates. But not being allowed to fight was discouraging to soldiers. As one man in the Fifty-Fourth Massachusetts pointed out, "The Regiment is in a state of demoralization. The men are compelled to perform the heaviest kind of Fatigue duty with no pay and impressed by the idea that the officers care nothing for their welfare."[6]

Conservative northern whites urged Lincoln to abandon the policy of enlisting black soldiers, but Lincoln believed that doing so would deprive the Union of the black man's "help, and this is more than we can bear. We can not spare the hundred and forty or fifty thousand now serving us as soldiers, seamen, and laborers." Moreover, Lincoln argued that if black soldiers were willing to "stake their lives for us, they must be prompted by the strongest motive—even the promise of freedom. And the promise being made, must be kept."[7] In all, some 200,000 black men served in the Union army, playing crucial roles at Milliken's Bend near Vicksburg in June 1863, Fort Wagner in Charleston Harbor in July 1863, Olustee, Florida, in February 1864, the Petersburg campaign in Virginia in 1864 and 1865, and elsewhere. Roughly 19 percent of these soldiers came from the free states of the North, while 24 percent came from the border slave states. Fifty-seven percent were recruited in the states of the Confederacy. These soldiers represented approximately 10 percent of the Union volunteers and 21 percent of the black men of military age in the nation.[8] In October 1864, Maj. Gen. Benjamin F. Butler praised the conduct of the black troops under his command who had fought at New Market Heights, Virginia. "In the charge on the enemy's works by the colored division," Butler noted, "better men were never better led, better officers never led better men." And mindful of Northern critics of black soldiers in blue, Butler added, "A few more such charges, and to command colored troops will be the post of honor in the American armies. The colored soldiers, by coolness, steadiness, and determined courage and dash, have silenced every cavil of the doubters of their soldierly capacity, and drawn tokens of admiration from their enemies."[9]

Throughout the war, Lincoln received letters from civilians offering their services to the Union or recommending others for office. The following letters provide a wide array of African American perspectives on military service throughout the war years. They also reveal a great deal about the ways that black men served as recruiters for the Union army, and the various (and sometimes unjust) circumstances under which African Americans joined the service.

A New Yorker Offers to Raise
"Colored Volunteers" for the Union

Letters poured into Lincoln's office in April 1861 offering to raise troops, including this one from an African American man in New York City. Little is known about Levin Tilmon. The 1860 census lists him as a fifty-three-year-old native of Maryland who worked in the Intelligence Office and owned $5,000 in real estate. Even before the firing on Fort Sumter, he wrote to Lincoln offering to assist in the recruitment of black soldiers:

New York   April 8th 1861.

Hon. Abraham Lincoln: — Presdt U.S. —
Dear Sir: —
    In the present crisis, and distracted state of the country, if your
Honor wishes colored volunteers, you have only to signify by answering

the above note at 70 E. 13 St. N.Y.C., with instructions, and the above will meet with prompt attention, whenever your honor wishes them.

Your very Obedient, and Humble Servant.

Levin Tilmon.

It is unknown whether this letter was answered, but it is certain that no black troops were raised as a result of it. It is worth noting, however, that Lincoln retained this letter in his personal papers.[10]

A Former Slave Offers His Services to the Union Cause

John Sella Martin was born a slave in Charlotte, North Carolina, on September 27, 1832. His mother was a slave and his father was their enslaver. When he was six years old, Martin was sold to an "old bachelor" in Columbus, Georgia—forever separating him from his mother and sister. Martin's new master taught him how to read and write, and as a teenager, Martin secretly wrote passes for other slaves to visit their wives on other plantations. Upon learning of this, his master "threatened [him] with severe punishment if he ever wrote another pass for a slave."[11]

Over time, Martin's master went blind, and Martin became instrumental to the man's daily affairs, including business transactions. The two men apparently became close friends, and when the master died a few years later, he made Martin—then eighteen years old—free. Unfortunately, the master's heirs successfully contested the will and sold Martin to a new owner in Mobile, who then later sold him in New Orleans. In December 1855 he escaped from slavery on a Mississippi River steamboat, arriving in Chicago on January 6, 1856. He moved to Detroit, where he began studying to become a Baptist minister. After one lecture, a local newspaper declared him "a prodigy" and "a great man," concluding, "The spirit which manifests itself is one broken loose from bondage and stimulated with freedom."[12]

Martin pastored a Baptist church in Buffalo, New York, until he moved to Boston in 1859. During the Civil War, he toured England speaking on behalf of the Union and emancipation. The London *Morning Star* praised Martin's "anti-slavery labours" and "his wondrous eloquence and power in treating . . . the indignities to which the coloured race are subjected by the boasted 'Southern chivalry' of America." In Britain he helped "to open the eyes of Englishmen to the sinister designs of those who are trying to found a new nation upon the slave whip and the slave copple."[13] Upon returning to America, Martin sent the following letter to Lincoln, enclosing several news-

J. Sella Martin.
Courtesy of the
Library of Congress.

paper clippings—including that from the *Morning Star*—describing his efforts in England:

26 Myrtle St   Boston   July 14, 1862

His Excellency the President

The enclosed extracts will inform you respecting my humble services in England. I am also permitted to refer you to Hon John A. Andrew Governor of Mass as well as to Hon C. F. Adams Minister to England in regard to my work abroad. And I write this to let your Excellency know, that if I can be of any manner of service here, should your Excellency ever think it best to employ my People, I am ready to work or preach or fight to put down this rebellion.

I am your Excellency's Humble Servant.

J. Sella Martin.

Pas. of 1st Independent Baptist Church

Boston.

His Excellency Abraham Lincoln}

P.S. I was in England 8 months and delivered 47 addresses in favor of the "Union."

I send your Excellency only a few of the many News Paper notices of my work in England. J. S. M.[14]

Following the war, Martin moved to Alabama, Mississippi, and Louisiana to see to "the educational wants" of freedpeople. He was elected to the Louisiana state legislature for a brief period in 1872.[15]

A Black Surgeon Requests a Commission in the Army

Born in 1825 in Norfolk, Virginia, to free black parents, Alexander Thomas Augusta wanted to be a doctor. As a young man, he worked as a barber in Baltimore, but when he applied to the University of Pennsylvania Medical College in Philadelphia, he was denied admission on account of his race. Instead, he matriculated at Trinity Medical College in Toronto, where he earned his medical degree in 1856. Augusta practiced medicine in Canada for about six years.[16] Within a week of Lincoln's Emancipation Proclamation, however, he wrote to both Secretary of War Stanton and President Lincoln seeking a commission in the Union army. The letter to Lincoln follows:

> Toronto Canada West Jan 7th/63
>
> To His Excellency Abraham Lincon President Of the U.S.
>
> Sir,
>
> Having seen that it is intended to garrison the U.S. forts &c with coloured troops, I beg leave to apply to you for an appointment as surgeon to some of the coloured regiments, or as physician to some of the depots of "freedmen." I was compelled to leave my native country, and come to this on account of prejudice against colour, for the purpose of obtaining a knowledge of my profession; and having accomplished that object, at one of the principle educational institutions, of this Province, I am now prepared to practice it, and would like to be in a position where I can be of use to my race.

Dr. Alexander T. Augusta. Courtesy of the Oblate Sisters of Providence Archives, Baltimore, Maryland.

If you will take the matter into favorable consideration, I can give satisfactory reference as to character and qualification from some of the most distinguished members of the profession in this city where I have been in practice for about six years.

I Remain Sir

Yours Very Respectfully

A. T Augusta   Bachelor of Medicine Trinity College Toronto[17]

Despite his obvious qualifications, Augusta faced discrimination throughout both the application process and his time in the service. When he arrived before the Army Medical Board in March 1863 to be examined, the president of the board, Meredith Clymer, was surprised to see that he "appeared" to be "a person of African descent." Augusta explained to the members of the board, "I have come near a thousand miles at great expense and sacrifice hoping to be of some use to the country and my race at this eventful period; and hope the Board will take a favorable view of my case." But the board was unmoved. Clymer and Surgeon General William A. Hammond both wanted Augusta's invitation "recalled." Fortunately, Secretary Stanton refused their request and ordered the examination to proceed. On April 1, Augusta passed the board's examination and was commissioned a major in the army. Initially he attended to black soldiers at a contraband camp near Alexandria, Virginia; however, in September 1863 he was appointed surgeon of the Seventh United States Colored Troops (USCT).

Throughout his time in the service, Augusta continued to face violence and intense discrimination from both civilians and fellow officers. He did his work ably and well and eventually rose to the rank of brevet lieutenant colonel, making him the highest ranked African American officer of the Civil War era. In February 1864, he and another black army doctor, Anderson R. Abbott, shocked white sensibilities when they attended a White House levee and were warmly greeted by the president. Following the war, Augusta taught medicine at Howard University in Washington, D.C.[18]

Black New Yorkers Offer Their Services to the Union Army

In mid-March 1863, a delegation of black leaders from Poughkeepsie, New York, arrived in Washington, D.C., for the purpose of tendering the services of some ten thousand black New Yorkers to the Union government. They hoped that Lincoln would appoint Union general John C. Frémont as their commander. The chair of the delegation, Rev. Dr. H. Parker Gloucester, presented the following petition to Lincoln:

POUGHKEEPSIE, Feb. 28, 1863.

Your Excellency, Mr. President:

We, the sons of Freedom, take the liberty of addressing you, through our loyal, patriotic, and tried friend of the slave and Union— thanking you for proclaiming liberty to the suffering millions of our oppressed fellow countrymen, whose groans have ascended to that God who is our refuge and help in time of trouble. We prayed for a deliverer likened unto Moses; for it is said the stone shall cry out of the wall, and the beams out of the timber shall answer it; believing that our prayer has been answered, and that God has raised up your Excellency as a deliverer, and a lamp by which our feet are guided into the paths of liberty. The cause which you have espoused is the cause of human liberty, formidable to tyrants, and dear to the oppressed throughout the world; containing the elements of immortality, sublime as heaven, and as far-reaching as eternity; embracing every interest that appertains to the welfare of the bodies and souls of men, and sustained by the omnipotence of the Lord Almighty.

The proclamation issued by your Excellency, January 1st, 1863, making liberty paramount to slavery, the triumphs of truth over error, liberty over oppression, loyalty over treason and rebellion, republicanism over aristocracy; for the triumphs of these principles our fathers fought and died on Lake Erie, Champlain, upon the Mediterranean, Florida, Schuylkill, Hickory-ground, at New Orleans, at Horse Shoe Bend, Pensacola, Red Bank. Liberty was the sound that rallied our fathers; they adopted the sentiment of our brother, Patrick Henry, which was, "forbid it Almighty God: I know not what course others may take, but as for me, give me liberty or give me death." We are ready to follow the example of our fathers, and rally to our country's call.

We have been called cowards. We deny the charge. It is false. We, through our delegate, offer the service of ten thousand of the sable sons, called the Fremont Legion, to be led to the field of battle; and our motto is: "The Union—one and inseparable." We hope, therefore, that your Excellency will accept the services of the Fremont Legion. For which we humbly pray.

ISAAC DEVOE, President.
REV. JOHN WELLES,
GEORGE ROCK,
WILLIAM JOHNSON,
JAS. A. JACKSON, Sec'y.
CHAS. HERMONG, Cor. Sec.,
REV. JACOB THOMAS,
JOHN A. BOLDING, Treas.,
REV. JNO. DUNGEY, Chap'n.
To his Excellency, ABRAHAM LINCOLN, President of the United States.

Lincoln discussed black enlistment with several other delegations of white and black New Yorkers during the spring and summer of 1863, but New York's Democratic governor, Horatio Seymour, blocked the enlistment of black soldiers in the Empire State. As a consequence, African American men from the Empire State enlisted in regiments from other northern states.[19]

A Servant of William H. Seward's Asks to Be Able to Serve

In 1836, Nicholas and Harriet Bogart, a newlywed couple, began working as servants for William H. Seward in upstate New York—Nicholas as a coachman and Harriet as a housekeeper. Over a period of three decades, Seward developed a great deal of affection for them and appreciated the service they provided to his family.[20] In 1863, Nicholas and Harriet's son, Willis, sent a letter to Lincoln asking for an opportunity to serve in the Union cause. In the letter, he pointed out his connection to Lincoln's secretary of state:

> Auburn   Cayuga County   NY   April 14th 63
> To the Hon Abraham Lincoln
>   Sir   in the Present condition of our country I deem it the duty of Every man to do What lays in his power for the good of his Country   as I am a colored Man Not exactly L[21] Sound   I am refused the rights of A soldier In the 54 Reg Mass Vols   I have been in the Battles of Fort Henry Donelson corinth And With the 51st Ills Vols from their appearance Till General [John] Popes Command of Virginia I have always Traveled in all thir Marchs stood Guard and Taken an active Part in every thing that came along foraging or in Reconnoitering   I am well Drilled in artillery Infantry and I Am A dead shot   i Have Never been sick But once in my Life Have Been Able to take care of myself For 20 years am 34 years old strait as an Arrow can run A mile inside of 5 Minutes and can shoulder 300 lbs and Yet cant be mustered in service   the Defect is that I have been shot in My Left Arm 14 years ago   as to the cupatility [capability?] Of Work I can refer you to the Hon Wm H Seward for whom I Have Worked in 58   I want to get back in The field some way or other   I am dying To get Back   I have been in the Service 16 Months
>   I wish to know if you cant use A word in my behalf to Ensure my Enlistment in A Colored Regiment Should you Conceive Within yourself a favorable Opinion of the Same   Please Direct A Few lines to your unworthy Servt   I am ready in one Hours Notice   I am as well able to go as others that Mustered in Service
>   Write Soon as Possible that I may Be off for the Wars
>   No More At Present
>   Yours With Respect
>   Willis ..A.. Bogart[22]

It is unclear whether Bogart received any assistance from Lincoln. In December 1863, he enlisted as a private in the Twenty-Ninth USCT. On May 8, 1864, he wrote to Secretary of State Seward from Camp Casey, Virginia, telling his former employer, "I am well and in fine spirits." Following the war, Bogart moved to Illinois, where he found himself under arrest for stealing money from a safe. In 1866, he was convicted for larceny and was sentenced to two and a half years in prison. Harriet wrote to Seward on behalf of her son, and Seward in turn successfully petitioned the governor of Illinois for a pardon.[23]

In fact, Bogart did not have a reputation for honesty. In his letter to Lincoln, he claimed to have been present at the Battles of Forts Henry, Donelson, and Corinth, but the Fifty-First Illinois was not at those engagements. When he enlisted in the Twenty-Ninth USCT, he claimed to have been born in England, which is highly unlikely, since his parents worked for Seward in New York when he was born. Later, the Pension Office nearly had him prosecuted for fraud. He claimed that he had received a hernia while in the service when he was thrown by a mule, but his enlistment records showed that he already had the hernia when he joined the service. He also reported to the Pension Office that he had received a "Gunshot wound in left arm/above the Elbow," but army records showed that he had actually been shot by an officer "on account of disrespectful and mutinous language to a Superior officer while under arrest, which has rendered the arm powerless ever since."[24] Letters like this one offer a stark example of how Lincoln and his private secretaries had to sift through mountains of correspondence without much background knowledge of the correspondent and quickly determine whether the requests merited presidential action or even a response.

Lincoln's Valet Petitions for the Appointment of White Officers for a Black Regiment

William Slade had a great deal of influence in Washington, D.C., during the Civil War. As the president's White House usher and valet, he had the third-highest rank among the White House domestic staff, behind only the steward and stewardess. According to Slade's daughter, the president regularly discussed his speeches and political decisions with Slade, even the Emancipation Proclamation. Slade also took on important public roles in wartime Washington. He was active in several black social and political organizations, was an elder at the Fifteenth Street Presbyterian Church, and was a leader

William Slade. Courtesy of the Abraham Lincoln Presidential Library and Museum, Springfield, Illinois.

in the African American community in Washington, D.C., in the areas of military recruitment and the draft.[25]

On April 22, 1863, sixty-seven black Washingtonians sent Secretary of War Stanton a letter asking for the appointment of two white officers—hospital chaplain William G. Raymond, formerly a first lieutenant in the Eighty-Sixth New York Infantry, and chaplain James D. Turner of the Fourth Pennsylvania Cavalry—to recruit black soldiers in Washington, D.C., and Alexandria, Virginia, and to become the commanders of the regiment. In addition to being one of the signatories, Slade also appended this personal note to Lincoln:

> Washington   april 28tt 1863
> His Excellency Abraham Lincoln   President of the United States
> Sir
> The foregoing petition was suggested to me by the Honl Robert Dale Owen[26] and had we not deem'd it of the utmost importance to have it before your Excellency at the earliest practicable moment, I could just as easily have had this paper filld with names, as to have got what we

have, as I beleive to the best of my knowledge, these men are the universal choice of our people and if it is necessary we will increase the List.

Your obedient Servant
William Slade

In addition to Slade, the Washington Union League and Lincoln's own minister, Phineas D. Gurley, along with a number of others, endorsed these appointments.[27]

James D. Turner took an active role in the recruitment of the first black regiment in Washington, D.C., and, according to one newspaper account, "was promised the colonelcy of it by President Lincoln." But his health was failing as a result of the Peninsula Campaign of 1862 and he withdrew his name from consideration for the position. He died in 1864 at the age of forty.[28]

An Admirer of Lincoln's Asks to Be Appointed a Recruiter

Paschal B. Randolph is one of the most unusual characters of nineteenth-century America. Born out of wedlock to a black woman in 1825, abandoned by his white father, and then orphaned at the age of six or seven, Randolph found himself living on his own on the streets of New York City near the notorious Five Points neighborhood. Although he had no formal education, he grew up to become a famous spiritualist.[29]

In 1861, newspapers spread rumors that Randolph would lead a regiment of Native Americans in Wisconsin to "pay its respects to the red tribes mustered by the confederate rebels" in the West.[30] Although this never took place, Randolph became a vocal and active recruiter of black troops following the issuance of the Emancipation Proclamation. In July 1863 in Poughkeepsie, New York, he offered a series of resolutions at a "great Convention of Colored People" in favor of black enlistments. Randolph pointed out that men of color had been loyal and true to the government, and that they held *the balance of power in this contest.* He continued, "We should strike, and strike hard, to win a place in history, not as vassals, but as men and heroes, never forgetting that God, as ever, strikes for the right, ever helping those most who help themselves." The solution to defeating the rebellion, Randolph asserted, could be found "in the shape of warm lead and cold steel, duly administered by 200,000 black doctors."[31]

When Randolph published the second edition of his book *Pre-Adamite Man* in 1863, he dedicated it "To Honest Abraham Lincoln, President of the

Paschal B. Randolph. From *Beyond the Veil: Posthumous Work of Paschal Beverly Randolph* (New York: D. M. Bennett, 1878).

United States, as a testimonial of my gratitude for his efforts to save the nation, and widen the area of human freedom." According to the following letter, Randolph had received permission from Lincoln to do this, which he may have received when he met with Lincoln earlier during the war.[32]

Oct 19th 1863

Sir again, in consequence of the last Proclamation, I solicit authority to raise colored Troops in this State. You will please remember that you gave me permission to dedicate my book "Pre-Adamite Man" to you, and that I came from the Orient on purpose to serve my country. I have, as President of NY State Central Committee, raised many men and sent them to the war. Not one cent have I been paid; not one cent have I asked. I am called eloquent, I want to do all the good I can, and were I not blind of the right eye should long since have been in the Field. Appoint me to recruit Colored troops. Please do this, and let me know what Bounties, pay &c they will receive, and that heaven will bless your great heart, and favor our holy cause, is the belief and prayer of your

    Humble Servant

    P. B. Randolph MD.

5 Tryon Row NY[33]

It does not appear that Lincoln replied to this letter, or that Randolph ever received an official appointment as a recruiter for black soldiers. Following an illness in early 1864, he continued to advocate for Lincoln's reelection. Later—in the third person—he claimed that he went to Louisiana to work on educational issues for former slaves "at the express instance of his friend, President Lincoln." While there he helped establish a school "for colored teachers" named Lincoln Memorial High Grade and Normal School.[34]

A Draftee in Baltimore Requests His Commutation Fee

James Henry Andrew Johnson was born in Baltimore in 1835 and, according to AME minister Alexander W. Wayman, "was reared by [his] Christian father and mother who taught him early to fear God and work righteousness." Johnson was educated by the black abolitionist William Watkins, Sr., and later learned the trade of a barber. According to Wayman, "During his apprenticeship he was brought to the knowledge of our Savior and united with the A.M.E. Zion Church. He soon began to show signs of future usefulness"— meaning, as a Christian minister. During the Civil War, he ran his own barbershop in Baltimore.[35]

In November 1863, Johnson was drafted into the Union army. His letter to Lincoln reveals the consequences of one of the most controversial aspects of the conscription system in the North. The Enrollment Act permitted draftees to pay a $300 commutation fee, which would get them out of that particular draft. Alternatively, a draftee could hire a substitute, which would exempt him from all future drafts. Selling oneself as a substitute became a profitable endeavor during the war, and substitute "brokers" made small fortunes facilitating the enlistment of substitutes. According to Johnson's letter, it appears that the provost marshal of Baltimore, Maj. Leopold Blumenberg, may have been in on a scheme to sell substitutes to draftees.[36]

To The Honorable Abraham Lincoln   President of the United States of America.

    Sir: Excuse me for my boldness, the necessity of the case demands it. I was legally drafted into the service of the United States on the twenty seventh of November 1863; and accordingly notified to report on the 24th of Dec. at the Office of the Provost Marshal Major Leopold Blumenberg. Obediently I did with papers in a legal form claiming exemption on account of physical disability—viz. a sprained ankle of sixteen years' standing, now perceptibly deformed, stiff and unable to endure exercise without pain and swelling. Secondly, *a system that is quickly prostrated by very little exertion in warm weather*; thus, Most Honorable Sir, I have been afflicted from early childhood.

With these pleas and testimony duly given (by upright men although of my own color) I appeared before the Board of Examination for the Third Congressional District, on the aforesaid date (24th inst.) The Major immediately asked me if I was a clergyman: I replied that I was a *preacher*, and gave my papers to the Surgeon. Then my ankle was presented for examination, during which the Major showed much desire for a refusal of my pleas; and indeed urged a conclusion agreeable to his desire. The Surgeon *owned that the ankle was deformed* and hesitated; but finally decided in accordance with the wishes of the Major. Then on examination for the piles (pardon me for the allusion) an acknowledgement was also made of the fact; but as to my periodical nervous condition (upon which great stress could have been laid) and the testimony of it, they received no attention at all.

During these proceedings the Major made some remark about putting "a blue jacket" on me and before my case was decided he wanted to know what I intended to do. So finally a legal exemption was denied me and I was left to do the best I could in my unpleasant situation. But the sequel made the whole case clear. When they discovered that I was conscious that by *their* decision I was in their power, then I was advised *by the Major* to get a substitute; and so consequently I asked him what he charged for them but with apparent unconcern, he replied—"I don't know": nevertheless, the inside man at the door, was prepared to inform aloud that certain parties upstairs, over the Major's Office, had substitutes on hand. With this information, I left the room to find myself a subject for outside men at the door who eagerly directed me to the great substitute depot upstairs. Having obtained three days' grace and feeling like I understood the game, declining to go up as directed, I left the building with one of my witnesses, and afterward, before the expiration of my extended time, by the providence of Almighty God obtained three hundred dollars ($300) and paid it at the Office of the Collector of Internal Revenue, *hoping that under the circumstances related, there might be a chance of its remittance.* I pursue this course—not from an indisposition to assist the Government for my prayers have, and do accord for it—but from the opinion that one man should receive the benefit of the law, as well as another.

Sir, the manner in which they deal with drafted colored men in the Third Congressional District of this State of Maryland, so far as I can ascertain, is not altogether right. Such men are afraid to go to the office with their own substitute. Please remember me.

Most Respect'ly Your Humble Servant

James Johnson as enrolled

Proper Jas. H. A. Johnson No 37 ½ German St. Baltimore Dec. 28th. 1863.[37]

Johnson resisted the pressure to purchase a substitute and instead paid a commutation fee. It is unlikely that he was ever reimbursed. Although Johnson suggested that he was treated this way because of his race, it is likely that most draftees in Baltimore underwent a similar experience. Following the war, Johnson was ordained in the AME church by Bishop Daniel A. Payne. He served in the ministry in many cities throughout the South until his death in 1895.[38]

Black Men from Baltimore Request to Be Treated Fairly

In July 1864, Confederate general Jubal Early launched an attack into the state of Maryland. On July 9, Union and Confederate forces clashed at the Battle of Monocacy, near Frederick, Maryland. Two days later, Early attacked Fort Stevens on the outskirts of Washington, D.C. Present at the battle on July 11 was Abraham Lincoln, who stood atop a parapet to see the advancing rebels.

General Early's invasion caused a panic in Baltimore, where Maj. Gen. Lew Wallace commanded the Middle Department. On July 18, Wallace issued a public letter to "the Loyal Citizens of Baltimore," praising them for taking up arms during the invasion and urging that the city must continue to drill "the national guard of Baltimore." Wallace organized three white regiments to defend the city, but Governor Augustus W. Bradford refused to recognize them as state militia. On July 28, Wallace began organizing the city's black population "into military companies for duty in this city," with black enlistees electing their own noncommissioned officers and the mayor of Baltimore

appointing "experienced white officers." Wallace warned local southern sympathizers: "Secession masters and employers must not interfere in this
business."

Wallace placed Col. Samuel M. Bowman in charge of the program, since
he was "quite popular with the class, and has proven himself their devoted
friend." Unfortunately, Governor Bradford "declined to have anything to do
with the enterprise," since the state constitution did not permit black men
to serve in the militia.[39] Wallace's actions elicited the following protest to Lincoln from a number of black men of Baltimore:

> Baltimore Aug 20 1864
>
> To His Exelencey The pesident of theas uninted States of america
>   sir   it is with Reverence we take this method to inform you of a
> grevance which is growing to a fearful rate amoung the loyal free
> colard people of Baltimore   in the month of July thare was a move-
> ment set on foot to organize the colard men of the wards into milatary
> companeys under the title of melitia under which circumstanc the
> colard men became allarmed called to gather some fiew and appointed
> one rev. S. W. Chase to confer with the military athorities upon the
> subgect   the procedes yor Exelancey will find in print.[40] this was
> followed by an ordor from General Wallace for the organisation of all
> the able bodied men int[o] melitia   the matter was subsequentley
> handed over to Col. bowman who isued ordors for the wards of his
> choice to report to disignated halls   som did but others knowing the
> relation thay bore to the state and Government declined to meet   first
> we knew that the state of Maryland had her mode for calling out her
> melitia which excludes us. that thay had ben called out and the
> emergencey being over tha ware disbanded   during the emergency
> however we volenteared our service to handle the gun also the pick an
> shovel   secondley we know that Congress has made us a part of the
> national force. we now come to the trying part   Squads of colard
> soaldiers accompaned som times by b white men come to our houses
> demand admitance under the authoritey of Col. Bowman. Surtches
> the house Curses our wives our sisters or mothers or if the man be
> found he is made to fall in and martch to the drilling room and thare
> give his name   thare is one instance of a man being Shot at while
> trying to escape   thare are others whare our white inemies go with
> thoas soaldiers for the purpos of Maltreating us. Our ocupation
> sometimes pr[o]hibits us from ariving home before those squads do

compel us to fall in the rank and martch to the drilling room without
supper   all efforts of the people to come to gather in mass meting to
protest aganst it has ben defeated by threts. The Congress of theas
uninted States has made us a part of the National force   then we hold
that we ar subject to the same regulation of the National force   We
have responded to the call by enlistment   We are allso subject to the
draft   the will of the Loyial Colard people of Baltimore citey is as a
part of the National force to be treated no wors then the lawes Demand Governing the National force

And we are shore that the Dignetey of this Government is too Loftey
to Demand a man onley by her Lawful Chanel   Your Exelencey will
pleas Parden the maner in which this Document is lade before you.
Yours with reverance

Loyial Colard men of Baltimore Citey[41]

In response to this protest, Wallace explained that he wanted "to enroll
all the able-bodied colored men of the city, whether free or slaves," but that
he could not do so by asking for volunteers, since so many were owned by
disloyal masters. The measure was a "necessity," Wallace insisted, for "there
must be more troops to defend the city of Baltimore than can always be
spared for the purpose." Wallace admitted that his program was necessarily
"arbitrary," but he maintained that some level of arbitrariness was essential
to fill the ranks because "among the blacks, as with the whites, there are lazy
and trifling people who do nothing without compulsion, and complain when
exerted." Wallace further admitted that "some instances of harshness have
ensued," but he wished the "sufferers" had only come "to me to have their
wrongs redressed" rather than having gone over his head to Lincoln.[42]

Wallace pledged to ensure that the black men "are not abused," and he appears to have released them from service in October.[43] The following month
he established a freedmen's bureau in Maryland to protect freedmen and
women from extortion and ill treatment by their former masters. Wallace
maintained his own bureau until the creation of the Freedmen's Bureau by
Congress in March 1865.[44]

A Michigan Man Asks to Be Able to Recruit More Black Soldiers

Greenbury Hodge was born a slave in Nashville, Tennessee, around 1819. In
Detroit in September 1863, Hodge mustered into the 102nd USCT as a sergeant. His letter, written in August 1864, describes his escape from slavery

in 1844 and his efforts to help recruit Michigan men for the Fifty-Fourth and Fifty-Fifth Massachusetts Volunteers:

Beaufort. South. Carlinah

August. 17 [1864]

President Lincon

i was born in Tenesa an rased a slave in Kentucky Livingston County   my age is forty nine years old last March. I made my escape in 1844 an every since i resided in Michigan detroit   my buisnes was portering an wating on lawyers   i belong to a military compny in detroit three years an when the rebelion broke out an they commence recruting Colered men for Masitusits they came to detroit an i was selected there for to recrut an i help rase the 54 an 55 Masitusits   an i had 22 men there wating transportation an they came and payed up there board an discharge me an the men to an i hung on to the men rather than they should be lost   an i turn in to geting up men for the united states service an i went on so for about two months an i gathered up almost a compny   in o[r]der to keep the men esey i would pay up there bord weakly an give them a litle money saterday nights an i had a lot where i drill the men every day   i had a fifer an 2 drumers hired. Colnel [Henry] Barns [of the 102nd USCT] wrote me an oder one day that he was agoing to Waisington an fore me to save the men until he came back an he would pay the bord   so he came back from Waishington an i turn the men over to him an Capt [Orson W.] Benet [Bennett]   i allways in recruting said com boys not go boy for i expected to go with them an they enlisted very fast   i am now here on Beaufort iland   i had the promice of doing prety much as i pleased   i have come here in the regment an i have not asked permision for to recrut   this regment is now the 3 that i have help rase an i think if i was at liberty i could help rase more   i would like to be detailed out for to recrut as long as you want men. i sold my house an funiture an lot an spent all my bounty for to get up soilders   if you want any father evidence you may apli to lawer jenison[45] an lawer Minard an Midor[46] an mjor Wilcoks[47] an for the regment apli to my Captin an Colinel or Col Barns   the soilders all call me captin it is not very comfortable to have to[o] many in a compny   i left my wife in detroit in one rome she was perfectly satified that i should go to war for to try an help put down the rebelion i am now acting 5 surgent in this regment compny. C. i have had my hea[l]th very good until here resently i had the fever   i could have got

any positon in the regment I wanted but i was short of eduction   i
rremain yours turly
    Greenbery Hodge
    I bleive yet there is help for th widos son

When Hodge died in 1879, an obituary appeared in a Detroit newspaper
under the headline "Capt. Greenbury Hodge: The Old Colored Warrior Has
Gone to His Rest." The article noted that Hodge had "assumed a position in
the front rank among the leaders of the colored element" when he arrived
in Detroit in the 1840s, and that he maintained such a leadership role "up
to the time of his death." But his "celebrity," the article continued, "princi-
pally arose from his military prowess" and his "proficiency in military science." The article predicted that there would "be an immense turn out of
the colored population" for his funeral the next day, "as the old man, with
all his pomp and love of display, was a kindly soul and a great favorite with
his people."[48]

Frederick Douglass Discusses Ways to Free More Slaves

When Lincoln issued his Emancipation Proclamation on January 1, 1863, he
hoped that it would cause masses of slaves to flee their plantations into Union
lines. However, not as many slaves emancipated themselves as Lincoln had
hoped. By the summer of 1864, he was worried that not enough slaves would
become free before the war ended, especially if he lost his bid for reelection.
Much of Lincoln's despair was connected to the military situation. The summer of 1864 was an awful time for the Union, as Ulysses S. Grant's troops
were entrenched around Petersburg, Virginia, and William Tecumseh Sherman's men were stuck outside Atlanta. By August, Lincoln had become convinced that he would lose the presidential election and that the incoming
Democratic president would undo all the gains he had made toward freedom
for African Americans.

In a desperate attempt to free more slaves, Lincoln called Frederick Douglass to come to the White House to discuss a plan. Douglass later recalled
that Lincoln wanted to make the Emancipation Proclamation "as effective as
possible in the event of such a peace." According to Douglass, Lincoln had
said at that meeting, "Douglass, I hate slavery as much as you do, and I want
to see it abolished altogether." Lincoln then asked Douglass to devise a way
to free as many slaves as possible before the inauguration of the next president. According to Douglass, Lincoln was "regretful" that the "slaves are not

coming so rapidly and so numerously to us as I had hoped." This meeting had a profound impact on how Douglass viewed Lincoln. As the fiery abolitionist later explained, "What he said on this day showed a deeper moral conviction against slavery than I had even seen before in anything spoken or written by him. I listened with the deepest interest and profoundest satisfaction, and, at his suggestion, agreed to undertake the organizing of a band of scouts, composed of colored men, whose business should be somewhat after the original plan of John Brown, to go into the rebel states, beyond the lines of our armies, and carry the news of emancipation, and urge the slaves to come within our boundaries."[49] A few days after their meeting, Douglass wrote Lincoln the following letter:

Rochester: N.Y. August 29th 1864

Hon Abraham Lincoln: President of the United States:

Sir: Since the interview with w[h] Your Excellency was pleased to honor me a few days ago, I have freely conversed with several trustworthy and Patriotic colored men concerning your suggestion that something should be speedily done to inform the slaves in the Rebel states of the true state of affairs in relation to them sho and to warn them as to what will be their probable condition should peace be concluded while they remain within the Rebel lines: and more especially to urge upon them the necessity of making their escape. All with whom I have thus far spoken on the subject, concur in the wisdom and benevolence of the Idea, and some of them think it practicable. That every slave who escapes from the Rebel states is a loss to the Rebellion and a gain to the Loyal cause, I need not stop to argue the proposition is self evident. The negro is the stomach of the rebellion. I will therefore briefly submit at once to your Excellency—the ways and means by which many such persons may be wrested from the enemy and brought within our lines:

1st Let a general ag[t] be appointed by your Excellency charged with the duty of giving effect to your Idea as indicated above: Let him have the means and power to employ twenty or twenty five good men, having the cause at heart, to act as his agents: 2[d] Let these agents which shall be selected by him, have permission to visit such points at the front as are most accessible to large bodies of slaves in the Rebel states: Let each of the said agts have power—to appoint one sub agent or more in the locality where he may be required to operate: the said sub agent shall be thoroughly acquainted with the country—and well instructed as to the representations he is to make to the slaves: — but his chief duty will be to conduct such squads of slaves as he may be able to collect, safely within the Loyal lines: Let the sub agents for this service be paid a sum not exceeding two dolls per day while upon active duty.

3dly In order that these agents shall not be arrested or impeded in their work — let them be properly ordered to report to the Generals commanding the several Departments they may visit, and receive from them permission to pursue thier vocation unmolested. 4th Let provision be made that the slaves or Freed men thus brought within our lines shall receive subsistence until such of them as are fit shall enter the service of the country or be otherwise employed and provided for: 5^{thly} Let each agent appointed by the General agent be required to keep a strict acc^t of all his transactions, — of all monies recieved and paid out, of the numbers and the names of slaves brought into our lines under his auspices, of the plantations visited, and of everything properly connected with the prosecution of his work, and let him be required to make full reports of his proceedings — at least, once a fortnight to the General Agent.

6th Also, Let the General Agt be required to keep a strict acct of all his transactions with his agts and report to your Excellency or to an officer designated by you to recieve such reports: 7th Let the General Agt be paid a salary sufficient to enable him to employ a competant clerk, and let him be stationed at Washington — or at some other Point where he can most readily receive communications from and send communications to his Agents: The General Agt should also have a kind of roving commission within our lines, so that he may have a more direct and effective oversight of the whole work and thus ensure activity and faithfulness on the part of his agents.

This is but an imperfect outline of the plan — but I think it enough to give your Excellency an Idea of how the desirable work shall be executed.

Your Obedient Servant
Fred^k Douglass[50]

Fortunately, nothing ever had to come of this plan. Within days of Douglass's penning of this letter, General Sherman captured the Confederate stronghold at Atlanta. From that point forward, Lincoln's reelection was essentially assured, and the outcome of the presidential election in November ensured not only that emancipation would remain a war aim but also that the Thirteenth Amendment would be a priority for Lincoln and the Congress. This meeting and letter are significant, however, in that they show that Lincoln viewed emancipation as more than a mere "military necessity." Freeing slaves at the end of his first term in office would do nothing to help him win the war; he was motivated solely by a desire to expand human freedom in the United States.

A Wounded Soldier Wants to Be of Use to the Service

Elisha S. Robison (sometimes Robinson) was the son of slaves from Ohio. Robison's father, Isaac, became free in 1817 and purchased his wife's freedom for $500 the following year. Raised a Quaker, Robison was thirty-three years old when he mustered into the 102nd USCT in Lowell, Michigan, on October 20, 1863. A few weeks later, on November 5, he was promoted to sergeant.

In February 1864, Robison was shot in camp and lost his right thumb. On November 8, 1864, he applied for a thirty-day furlough to visit his home in Michigan. One of Robison's officers wrote in support of the request, "That he has been unfit for duty the last six weeks on account of a pistol shot wound in the right thumb received at Detroit, & visit his family that are destitute, & have his thumb amputated." Brig. Gen. Rufus Saxton approved the request on November 11.[51] While at home, Robison wrote the following letter to Lincoln:

> Lowell Kent Co. Michigan
> Mr. A. Lincoln Prest. US. Honored Sir
>   Pleas allow me to Explain to you my Condition as a soldier   I Enlisted oct 20th /63 and Enlisted 30 men for the Company to Which I belong and took my Position as 1st Sergt and had good success In gaining the Affections of Both men and officers. On or about the 10th of February /64 While on Buisness for the Company [I] Was assassinated and shot Destroying my Right thumb. And after Reporting to the surgeon He simply bound It up and I have been Excused and Kept In Camp a useless soldier. I think It must be verey Expensive to the Government to Keep men thus, useless to themselves and to the Government, I Do not Want to Earn money In that way, I Enlisted to fight for God and my Country   Sir Being acquainted With you from Historical facts I apeal to you for advice   I Could Do well at Recruiting much Better than Lying Around this way, Pleas Direct to Mrs Julia A. Robison as I shall be with my Regt soon

Yours most truly
Ord Sergt ES Robison
102 USCT
Address My Wife Julia Robison
Lowell Kent Co
Michigan

The Adjutant General's Office received this letter on December 6, 1864. It must have had some effect. In the spring of 1865, Robison was put on recruiting duty in Georgetown, South Carolina. He eventually mustered out with his regiment at Charleston on September 30, 1865. Following the war, he studied medicine at Montreal Medical College and practiced medicine in the Midwest.[52]

Two Black Men Get Arrested for Illegal Recruiting

On October 24, 1864, three black men in Washington, D.C., persuaded another African American man named Philip Richie to go to Camp Casey in Virginia to volunteer in the Union army. They planned to give fifty dollars of the bounty money to Richie and then divide the rest among themselves. Unfortunately for them, the War Department had issued a circular on August 22 that prohibited taking potential recruits out of the city. One of the three men was an unknown driver. The other two, Wesley D. Shields and George Butler, were tried before a "special military commission" on November 5 for illegal recruiting.

At the trial, Shields pleaded not guilty. The only witness in the case, Philip Richie, testified that he went to Camp Casey with Shields and the two other men. "They told me if I did not go with them they would put me in the guard house, and that I would have to stay there till the draft came round," Richie recounted. But Richie further testified that all Shields did was procure passes for them to cross into Virginia; Butler and the other man had done most of the talking and threatening.

In his defense, Shields stated that he was "the first colored man who volunteered his services in the army in Baltimore" and that he was now exempted from the draft, but that he had been recruiting for the Union army since March and that he had only come to Washington to visit his sisters.

Unlike Shields, Butler pleaded guilty, but he explained that he could neither read nor write and that he did not know that Camp Casey was outside Washington, D.C. The court appears not to have believed him, though, since he had lived in Washington for about five years.

The court found both men guilty and sentenced them to six months in prison and a one-hundred dollar fine. Union general Abner Doubleday approved the proceedings and the sentences. From prison at Fort Delaware, Butler sent the following note to Lincoln. Since he claimed at his trial that he could not read or write, it is likely that someone else wrote it out for him.

Millitary Prison Fort Delaware Dec 26th 1864

To his Excellency Abreham Lincoln President of the United States of America

I take the Liberty to address a few Lines to you to make a brief statement of my case   my offence is disobeying orders in this that I took a man out of the district to enlist him not knowing it to be out of the district   and having a Large family to support and this being the first offence of eny kind that I hav commited I hope that you will fiew [view] my case favorable   I am youre most obedient Sirvent

George Butlar

Colored

Upon reviewing the cases, Joseph Holt—the judge advocate general of the army—observed that Shields "appears to have been rather the tool of the man Butler, than actively guilty." But Shields had not asked for pardon, and Lincoln took no action in his case. On January 16, 1865, the president replied to Butler through a subordinate officer "that on an examination of the facts of record and submitted by you, no sufficient grounds are perceived to warrant interference in your behalf." Both men presumably served out their prison sentences.[53]

A Black Minister Seeks to Become a Commissioned Army Chaplain

Francis A. Boyd, a twenty-one-year-old house servant and an ordained minister in Kentucky, longed to become an army chaplain. In June 1864 he met with Col. John Hammond at Taylor Barracks in Louisville, where Hammond promised Boyd that if he enlisted in the service and procured a recommendation from his church elders, he could be appointed a chaplain—but first he would have to enlist. So Boyd enlisted in the 109th USCT on June 23, 1864.

By November 1864 Boyd had not received the promised appointment. (The white officers of the regiment elected a white chaplain instead.) On November 4, he wrote to Maj. Gen. Benjamin F. Butler asking for the appointment he had been promised. "In my regiment I have faithfully filled the post of

Chaplain, and Color sergeant. I have procured a thousand and over six hundred Books, in Cincinnati for the instruction of the Regiment and one hundred and fifty dollars worth of Sanitary goods." He thus asked Butler to confirm his "true calling" by appointing him chaplain of the regiment.

Butler appointed Boyd chaplain of the regiment on November 23, but the officers of the 109th were not pleased with the appointment. On January 5, 1865, Boyd wrote again to Butler (who by now was no longer the commander of the Department of Virginia and North Carolina), informing him that "I have been coolly and contemptuously treated by the Officers of this Regiment" because "predjudices are Dark, and Bitter, and I feel that my life is in peril." In the "name of a long Down trodden and oppressed but truly loyal people," Boyd pleaded with Butler for "protection." Boyd also gathered statements in support of his chaplaincy, such as one from the brigade surgeon, which declared Boyd "capable of doing more good in that Regt. than any White chaplain could do."

In early January 1865, still acting as chaplain, Boyd wrote to the colonel of the 109th asking for a detail of men from the regiment "with axes, to fell Timber, and Build a schoolhouse, to be used also for Chapel purposes" for the "moral improvement, and Education" of the men, most of whom were former slaves.[54]

Between January and March 1865, Boyd sent three letters to Lincoln pleading his case. The first two letters are on U.S. Christian Commission stationery.[55]

> Jan. 12th — 65. 109th U.S.C.I.
> 1st Brig. 2nd Div. 25th A.C.
> Army of the James Virginia.

Mr A. Lincoln
Sir

I have the honor of stating to you that I am the Chaplain, of the 109th U. S Colored Troops, I am a Colored Man, and was appointed to the Chaplaincy, By Major General Butler November 23rd 1864. all the men, Desire me for their chaplain as we are from the same state (Kentucky) and also the Officers with a few exceptions and considering those exceptions, I am induced to write to you for aid and assistance beleiving you to be the patron of universal Liberty with many prayers for your welfare

I subscribe myself
Your most Ob't serv't
Francis A. Boyd
Chaplain 109th U.S.C.I.

On February 16, the adjutant general offered Boyd a position as a clerk. Six days later, on February 22, the War Department revoked Boyd's commission as sergeant, reducing him to the rank of private. An undated notation on Boyd's commission states, "Not confirmed, Appointment irregular." Boyd received word of this action on February 25. That same day he again wrote to Lincoln explaining why he had refused the appointment as a clerk and reminding the president why African Americans looked to him as their "Friend."

Feb 25th 1865.

Mr A. Lincoln
Sir,
    once more I presume to address you as my Friend and protector, I am kept in an agony of suspense, I know not whether I am to stand or fall, on the Evening of February the 16th my commander, sent me to Division Head Quarters, to see General [William] Birney, I did not see the General himself but I saw the Adjutant General, he asked me how I would like to be Clerk, I told him I would not like to be Clerk at all. He told me General Birney, had sent for me, and had power to detail me, I told him General Birney had nothing to do with me, that my case was in the hands of the war Department and unless it revoked my muster in I was Chaplain, and that I could not fill two offices. suppose the war Department, revokes your muster in, will you accept the position of Clerk then, said he. When the war Department, revokes my muster in it will be proper to talk about it, was my response, Suppose the War Department, Declares the whole proceeding null and void, then what will you do was the rejoinder, if the war Department declares the whole proceeding null and void I do not know what I will do. good day Adjutant General, good day Mr Boyd, and I departed. on my return I proceeded to regimental Headquarters, the Colonel, asked me what the Adjutant General said, I related the above conversation to him, and remarked that I did not care about listening to any more such propositions until my case was decided by the War Department, and until my muster in was revoked I was chaplain, and when it was revoked I would be free, that is if it was revoked, our Adjutant, also asked me concerning my visit, when I told him, what passed, and remarked to him, that it was an insult to me, and my race, and that my race, were the only people, who were loyal as a class in the United States. therefore if any among them rose upon their merits, no one

had a right to try, to defraud them out of their office and moreover, I remarked, where predjudice exists let every one keep on his own side of the House. Up to this date, I am in suspense, and I know not whether my appointment is approved or disapproved and I hope you will pardon me for again writing to you, I write to you because, the Colored people, look upon you as their Friend,

Very Respectfully your Obed't serv't
Francis A. Boyd,
Chaplain 109th U.S.C.I.
1st Brig. 2 Div. 25th A.C. [Army Corps]
Army of the James.

March 9th 1865

President Lincoln

Sir   I make a direct appeal to you for justice, I have been terribly injured by the commander of my regiment   it is true my muster into service as Chaplain was revoked by the war Deportment on account of irregularity, but my Colonel has reduced me to the ranks, and is endeovoring to degrade me on account of predjudice alone, I would humbly beseech you if possible, to order me to appear at washington, that I may lay this matter before your excellency in its fullest extent

I am respectfully your ob't se'v't
Francis A. Boyd,
Minister of the Gospel.
in camp of 109th U.S.C.I. in the Field Va.

On May 12, 1865, Boyd wrote to President Andrew Johnson apprising the new president of his ordeal. "I have been offered the position of Hospital steward and orderly sergeant, by the Colonel of my regiment," wrote Boyd, "but I refused to accept it for the sake of the service, because it would look bad to see a man who had been a commissioned officer on his staff and whose only dishonor was the color of his skin, holding the place of a noncommissioned officer." Boyd informed the president that "alarm and distrust exists among the Colored Troops who have witnessed these proceedings," but that Johnson could persuade them "that Justice holds sway" if he would grant Boyd the appointment as chaplain. Then it would be seen "that a colored man, is capable of doing anything under proper instruction that a white man can do."

Four days after sending this letter, on May 16, Boyd was again promoted to sergeant. In November of that year the officers of his regiment elected him regimental chaplain, but because the regiment had fallen below strength, he could not receive the appointment. He mustered out with his regiment in March 1866.

For the next twenty years Boyd sought retroactive pay for the work he had done as chaplain. In 1886, General Butler advocated to the War Department on Boyd's behalf, and in 1888, a congressman from Kentucky introduced a resolution in the House of Representatives to pay Boyd, but these efforts apparently never amounted to anything.[56]

CHAPTER FOUR

Protesting Unequal Pay for Black Soldiers

In late 1862 and early 1863, military recruiters promised black men that they would receive the same pay as white soldiers, $13 per month. Nevertheless, the War Department determined to pay black recruits only $10 per month. On top of that, the War Department also deducted $3 from black soldiers' monthly pay for a clothing allowance, thus bringing their monthly income down to $7. This much-criticized decision was not arbitrary. The Militia Act of 1862 authorized the president "to receive into the service of the United States, for the purpose of constructing intrenchments, or performing camp service or any other labor, or any military or naval service for which they may be found competent, persons of African descent." The law further stipulated that "persons of African descent, who under this law shall be employed, shall receive ten dollars per month and one ration, three dollars of which monthly pay may be in clothing."[1]

Looking at this statute, the solicitor for the War Department, William Whiting, determined that prior to this legislation, African Americans had been excluded from the military service of the United States. Therefore, the only statutory authorization for them was the Militia Act, and it specified the pay they were to receive. As further evidence, Whiting pointed out that in March 1863 Congress authorized African Americans to become army cooks at the same $10 rate. Based on this analysis, Secretary of War Stanton issued a general order on July 4, 1863, ordering his commanders to pay black soldiers the reduced rate.[2]

Many black soldiers refused to accept this diminished pay. "We'se gib our sogerin' to de Guv'ment, Cunnel," said one former slave in Col. Thomas Wentworth Higginson's First South Carolina Volunteers, "but we won't 'spise ourselves so much for take de seben dollar."[3] A sergeant in the Fifty-Fourth Massachusetts Volunteer Regiment wrote home to a friend decrying "all the misery and degradation suffered in our regiment" because of the suffering of soldiers' families. "I cannot any more condemn nor recite our wrongs," he continued, "but console myself that One who is able has said vengeance is mine and I will repay."[4] Some black soldiers protested in nonviolent ways, while others, including members of the Fifty-Fourth and Fifty-Fifth Massachusetts Volunteers, mutinied. Col. Robert Gould Shaw of the Fifty-Fourth even advocated that his regiment muster out rather than receive the diminished pay, since his soldiers had "enlisted on the understanding that they were to be on the same footing as other Mass. Vols."[5]

On November 19, 1863—the same day that Lincoln delivered his Gettysburg Address—Sgt. William Walker, a twenty-three-year-old ex-slave in the Third South Carolina Infantry (Twenty-First USCT) led his regiment to his commanding officer's tent, where he ordered the men to stack their arms while he declared that they "would not do duty any longer for seven dollars per month." Walker's protest had some effect. Within several days, thirteen white officers in the regiment signed a petition calling for equal pay for black soldiers. Nevertheless, Walker was arraigned before a military court for mutiny and a number of other unrelated crimes. He was sentenced to be shot to death.[6] In the wake of this execution, Governor John A. Andrew of Massachusetts penned a stinging rebuke to Lincoln: "The Government which found no law *to pay him except as a nondescript or a contraband*, nevertheless found law enough *to shoot him as a soldier*."[7]

The first test case to come before the Lincoln administration regarding equal pay was that of Chaplain Samuel Harrison of the Fifty-Fourth Massachusetts. Lincoln asked Attorney General Edward Bates for a legal opinion on the matter, and Bates concluded that the Second Confiscation Act of July 17, 1862, "authorized the President to employ as many persons of African descent as he might deem necessary and proper for the suppression of the rebellion, and for that purpose to organize and use them in such manner as he might judge best for the public welfare." Under this provision, Bates argued that Harrison had been lawfully enrolled into the military service and deserved the full pay of an army chaplain, which was one hundred dollars per month plus two rations, as opposed to the ten-dollar rate that the paymaster had offered Harrison.[8]

Lincoln chose not to use Harrison's case as a precedent for other black soldiers, arguing that it was not within his power to change pay rates. Thus, the matter still had to be resolved by Congress. In his December 1863 annual report, Secretary Stanton urged Congress to raise the pay of black soldiers to be equal to that of whites; in June 1864, Congress finally did so. Moreover, the law retroactively offered back pay to any black soldiers who had been free on April 19, 1861, a date that marked the beginning of the war. Part of the rationale of the measure was that those who had been in bondage were also gaining their freedom—which, Congress believed, carried with it a certain value to offset the lower pay. In opposition to the measure, Sen. Henry Wilson of Massachusetts pointed out that distinguishing among African Amer-

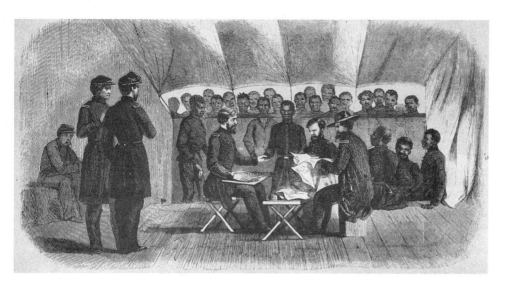

"The War in the South—Paying Off Negro Soldiers at Hilton Head, S.C.,"
Frank Leslie's Illustrated News, August 20, 1864. Collection of the author.

icans based on prewar status would discriminate against the USCT regiments from South Carolina that had a high proportion of former slaves among their ranks—some of the very soldiers who had been protesting for equal pay.[9]

The June 1864 law authorized Attorney General Bates "to determine any question of law arising under this provision," and on June 24 Lincoln asked Bates for an opinion on the matter. Bates replied that the Second Confiscation Act—and not the Militia Act—was what authorized Lincoln to enroll black soldiers, and since the Confiscation Act contained no provisions regarding pay, black troops were entitled to the same pay as other volunteers. Accordingly, on August 1, the War Department ordered that all black soldiers who had been free on April 19, 1861, be given back pay.[10]

Ex-slaves serving in the army—and their white officers—continued to protest the lack of equality offered to former slaves in the Union army, and William Walker's execution became a touchstone in the fight. In a letter to the editor of the *New York Tribune* on August 12, 1864, Col. Thomas Wentworth Higginson of the First South Carolina Volunteers (Colored) pointed to the irony that northern black soldiers were paid the same amount as white soldiers, while escaped slaves who had "been in service and under fire, months before a Northern colored soldier was recruited," might have to "act as executioners for those soldiers who, like Sergeant Walker, refuse to fulfil their share of a contract where the Government has openly repudiated the other share." Moreover, Higginson argued that the "men who enlisted under the pledge were volunteers, every one; they did not get their freedom by en-listing; they had it already." Finally, Higginson pointed out that these men had enlisted trusting that the federal government would uphold its "honor." But now the nation was repudiating the agreement it had made. It would not be until the Enrollment Act of March 3, 1865, that Congress would equalize the pay of ex-slaves serving in the Union army.[11]

One of the most troubling aspects of Lincoln's correspondence with Afri-can Americans is how the federal government's unequal pay policy affected civilians on the home front. Wives, children, and parents who relied on in-come from their soldier kin were often left destitute when those soldiers re-fused to accept the diminished pay that was offered to them. Prices in the North increased by about 100 percent during the war, while wages went up only by 50 to 60 percent.[12] Wages for African Americans likely increased by an even lesser rate.

Black soldiers were tortured by the thought of their families being left des-titute at home. One soldier in the Fifty-Fifth Massachusetts published a let-ter in the *Anglo-African* in April 1864 explaining the perspective of thousands of black soldiers: "Are our parents, wives, children and sisters to suffer, while we, their natural protectors, are fighting the battles of the nation?" he asked. "I have seen a letter from a wife in Illinois to her husband, stating that she had been sick for six months, and begging him to send her the sum of *fifty cents*. Was it any wonder that the tears rolled in floods from that stout-hearted man's eyes?" Another soldier in the Sixth USCT—writing under the pseud-onym "Bought and Sold"—wrote despondently to the *Christian Recorder*, "When I was at Chelton Hill [Camp William Penn] I felt very patriotic; but my wife's letters have brought my patriotism down to the freezing point, and I don't think it will ever rise again; and it is the case all through the regiment. Men having families at home, and they looking to them for support, and they not being able to send them one penny." Sgt. George E. Stephens likewise complained about how this "wrong and insult" from the "Lincoln despotism" had reduced his "estimable wife . . . to beggary, and dependen[ce] upon an-other man."[13]

Hundreds, perhaps thousands, of civilians wrote to Lincoln asking for fi-nancial assistance or relief from their suffering during the war. While most of these letters came from white Americans (including people in the states of the Confederacy), a small number of letters from African American men and women also arrived at the White House. The following correspondence from soldiers and their loved ones give insights into the suffering endured by families who were making great sacrifices for the Union.

A Black Soldier Demands Equal Pay

Raised in Troy, New York, James Henry Gooding moved to New Bedford, Massachusetts, in 1856, when he was nineteen years old. Gooding spent the next four years on whaling ships, returning to New Bedford in 1861. Then, in 1862, he embarked as a cook on a merchant vessel. When Gooding returned home at the end of the summer, he got married and began a family. But the comforts of home would be short lived. On February 14, 1863, Gooding enlisted in the Fifty-Fourth Massachusetts, attaining the rank of corporal. Over the ensuing twelve months he wrote forty-eight letters to the New Bedford *Mercury* discussing his experiences in the army. He also protested the unequal pay of black soldiers in separate letters to Massachusetts governor John A. Andrew and President Lincoln, the latter of which is reproduced here:

Camp of the 54th Mass Colored Regt
Morris Island. Dept of the South, Sept 28th 1863.
Your Excelency: Abraham Lincoln:

Your Excelency will pardon the presumption of an humble individual like myself, in addressing you, but the earnest Solicitation of my Comrades in Arms, besides the genuine interest felt by myself in the matter is my excuse, for placing before the Executive head of the Nation our Common Grievance:

On the 6th of the last Month, the Paymaster of the department, informed us, that if we would decide to recieve the sum of $10 (ten dollars) per month, he would come and pay us that sum, but, that, on the sitting of Congress, the Regt would, in his opinion, be *allowed* the other 3 (three). He did not give us any guarantee that this would be, as he hoped, certainly *he* had no authority for making any such guarantee, and we can not supose him acting in any way interested.

Now the main question is. Are we *Soldiers*, or are we *Labourers*. We are fully armed, and equipped, have done all the various Duties, pertaining to a Soldiers life, have conducted ourselves, to the complete satisfaction of General Officers, who, were if any[thing], prejudiced *against* us, but who now accord us all the encouragement, and honour due us: have shared the perils, and Labour, of Reducing the first stronghold, that flaunted a Traitor Flag; and more, Mr President. Today, the Anglo Saxon Mother, Wife, or Sister, are not alone, in tears for departed Sons, Husbands, and Brothers. The patient Trusting

Decendants of Africs Clime, have dyed the ground with blood, in defense of the Union, and Democracy. Men too your Excellency, who know in a measure, the cruelties of the Iron heel of oppression, which in years gone by, the very Power, their blood is now being spilled to maintain, ever ground them to the dust.

But When the war trumpet sounded o'er the land, when men knew not the Friend from the Traitor, the Black man laid his life at the Altar of the Nation, —and he was refused. When the arms of the Union, were beaten, in the first year of the War, And the Executive called [for] more food, for its ravaging [ravenous?] maw, again the black man begged, the privelege of Aiding his Country in her need, to be again refused.

And now he is in the War: and how has he conducted himself? Let their dusky forms, rise up, out [of] the mires of James Island, and give the answer. Let the rich mould around Wagners parapets be upturned, and there will be found an Eloquent answer.[14] Obedient and patient, and Solid as a wall are they. all we lack, is a paler hue, and a better acquaintance with the Alphabet.

Now Your Excellency we have done a Soldiers Duty. Why cant we have a Soldiers pay? You caution the Rebel Chieftain, that the United States, knows, no distinction, in her Soldiers: She insists on having all her Soldiers, of whatever creed or Color, to be treated according to the usages of War. Now if the United States exacts uniformity of treatment of her Soldiers, from the Insurgents, would it not be well, and consistent, to set the example herself, by paying all her *Soldiers* alike?

We of this Regt. were not enlisted under any "contraband" act. But we do not wish to be understood, as rating our Service, of more Value to the Government, than the service of the exslave. Their Service *is* undoubtedly worth much to the Nation, but Congress made express provision touching their case as slaves freed by military necessity, and assuming the Government, to be their temporary Gaurdian: —Not so with us—Freemen by birth, and consequently, having the advantage of *thinking*, and acting for ourselves, so far as the Laws would allow us. We do not consider ourselves fit subject for the Contraband act.

We appeal to You, Sir: as the Executive of the Nation, to have us justly Dealt with. The Regt. do pray, that they be assured their service will be fairly appreciated, by paying them as american *Soldiers*, not as menial hierlings. Black men You may well know, are poor, three dollars per month, for a year, will suply their needy Wives, and little ones with fuel. If you, as Chief Magistrate of the Nation, will assure us, of our whole pay, We are content, our Patriotism, our enthusiasm will have a new impetus, to exert our energy more and more to aid Our Country. Not that our hearts ever flagged, in Devotion, spite the evident apathy displayed in our behalf, but We feel as though, our Country spurned us, now [that] we are sworn to serve her.

Please give this a moments attention

Corporal James Henry Gooding

Co. C. 54th Mass, Rcgt

Morris Island S.C.

Gooding would not live to see the outcome of this debate. He was wounded and captured at the Battle of Olustee in Florida on February 20, 1864, and died in a Confederate prison camp in July.[15]

Two Destitute Wives Plead for Their Husbands' Pay

When Charles F. Burr and James Jackson enlisted as substitutes for white men in July 1863, the recruiter promised them that they would receive the same pay, bounty, and treatment as white soldiers. Both men mustered into the Third USCT and headed south to Morris Island, South Carolina. But when pay was finally offered to them in September, it was the reduced amount of seven dollars per month. This they refused to accept. On September 27 they wrote to a white officer who had been present when they enlisted. On October 7 this officer, in turn, wrote to Lincoln. "It was stipulated that they were to receive the same monthly pay, the same bounty, the same clothing—be placed on the same footing in every respect as the white men, whose places they were taking," he told the president. "They bound themselves to fulfil their part of the Contract with confidence that the Government would fulfil its part. . . . Can it be possible that these men have been deceived? Is not a contract with a colored man as binding as a contract with a white man?"[16]

Nothing appears to have come of this initial correspondence. But circumstances were getting desperate for their wives. Burr, twenty-five, had been a farmer in New Brighton, in western Pennsylvania, before the war. In July 1863 he was appointed sergeant, but in October he was reduced to the ranks. He and his wife, Matilda, had been married since 1858. She wrote to Lincoln in January 1864, asking for her husband to get paid:

Jenury the 18 1864

mr Abraham lincoln

sir   i with mutch plasur set down to adress you with A few lines to let you know that my husband is in the army and left me hear with A helpless famely and he has not recived any pay and i get no reliefe   i would like to know if you please what will be done   he is in the third u S Colard troops Co K on morris island   his name is Charles Burr   pleas rite and let me know   yours truly
            mattild Burr[17]

Pvt. James Jackson, thirty-five, also of New Brighton, had been married to his wife, Hester, since 1855. These two families must have been close, for the pension records reveal that Matilda had been present at the Jacksons' wedding. It is very likely that Matilda and Hester wrote their letters together:

Jenury the 18 1864

mr abrham lincon

sir   i now set dwon to rite you a few lins to see what can bee dun for my husband   he has bin out for six month and has not got no pay yet and he is sick and i want to know if he cant cum home   i have three small childran and no way for to get a long   he is in the third united states culurd trups on morislund co k   his name is James Jackson   rite soon
            Ester ann Jackson[18]

Unfortunately, these women's husbands would not receive their pay for several more months. The paymaster at Hilton Head reported on February 5, 1864, "that James Jackson refused to accept the amount tendered him, and did not sign the rolls, he like many others, claims the same pay as white soldiers & will accept nothing less, viz. 13. per. month."

Both men survived the war and were honorably discharged on October 31, 1865. Following Burr's death in 1888, Matilda collected a widow's pension until her death in 1920. Following Jackson's death in 1887, Hester likewise collected a widow's pension.[19]

A Soldier Asks Lincoln to Pay Black Soldiers

John H. Harris of the Fifty-Fourth Massachusetts Volunteer Regiment, Co. A, had been born on the Eastern Shore in Maryland and was a thirty-eight-year-old farmer when he enlisted on February 28, 1863. He was promoted to sergeant on March 30, 1863, then reduced to corporal on June 15, promoted back to sergeant on August 31, and then reduced to the ranks on February 16, 1864. Shortly after this second demotion he sent a letter to Lincoln about soldiers' pay:

Morris Island   April 23^d 1864

Mr Abraham Linking   Preasident of the U S of Amarica

you will please Pairdon a humble Soldier for at tempting to address-ing you on a subject that is so vitle to him self and thouse that he is assosoated with   I now at tempt to seake [speak] to you in a humble maner a few words in the be half of the fifty fourth Ridgment of the Mass. volentures who inlised [enlisted] at Read ville mass. in the you yeair of eateen hundere & sixty thee for thirteen dollers and reashens and clothing the same as youther south soldiers wair receaving   it has bin more then forteen mounth sence som of ous have left our hom, to com out and to riesk our lives for the cause of freedom and the Preaservasion of our beloved cuntry   this we don cherfulley that our cildreun & mite enjoy the blesings of a free cuntry and this at a time when it was consederd all most a crim[e] for a colaird man to be seane with a gun moutch more then be allowed him to fight side by sid with the white soldiers   we have had a great meney dificulitis to sir monte [surmount] that youthers have not had   we have labered and fought and a great meney of our noumber have bin slane and youthers have bin mad helplis for Life and our and famileas have sufard but not with standing all that we air still com peled to fight and Laber on, witch we ar willing to do if we cold have our writes that wair Promised ous   but i ned tell you the sufering our wifes and childreans or air o blidge to under go fur the want of the assistence of thir husbans and fathers   we have had no money to them to help them with   we came out heir for the purpos to help to free the Slaves for we saw that god wair a bout to open the prisen hous of boundage and let the oprest go free   with thees Concider ration we came out tl to fight but we mous look to our writs witch god have geaven to all man kind witch we love to[o]   may the write tryump and for that we air dhe terment [determined] to labier for ~~or~~ with all of our hart, we can not duw lest then stend for the write nor can we consider ~~y~~ our selfs contrabands   we did not enli[s]t as soutch   we want to save our famleas from destresed [distress] by our ead [aid]   som way outh [or other?] we nead our pay to get our childrin out of the pore house and to releav our famaley from want   we humboly Preay you to consider our case and great [grant] ~~y~~ our prar in the name of god and humanity that we may be able ~~thouze that~~ to as sis [assist] thouse we love   this we homble pray god may save you and geave you power and be with you throw all of thouze hevea [heavy?] triels that you air oblidge to go th[r]ough and that may he subdue all of your enemis and Bring this our be loved Cuntry through all its therten-ing and preasent calamitys   may she com out of this great Stronger Britter [brighter] and stronger then She ever was and my god greant that she may rest upon the ~~rot~~ rock Crist

you who have don so moutch to kill the monster Slavery   you have dun a ~~g~~ great humaity [humanity?]   may god him self will re waird you   pleas excuse these few lines   no mor from a homble Soldier

J. H. H Co. A. 54th

Mass Vol

Post Cript

Pleas ancer this

Harris was honorably discharged from the service in New York City on August 29, 1865. Nevertheless, the war appears to have taken quite a physical toll on him. Lewis Hayden, an African American leader in Boston, wrote in the early 1880s that since Harris's return, "I have never known him to be well and do not believe he has been able to perform an efficient days work."[20]

The Wife of a New Jersey Soldier Needs Support for Her Family

African American women made a claim to recognition as citizens through the military service of their husbands, as the following letter attests. The correspondent's husband, Benjamin Hinson, was a forty-two-year-old farmer when he enlisted in the Twenty-Second USCT as a private in January 1864. He was shot in the left elbow in Petersburg, Virginia, on June 15, 1864.

Mt Holly July 11 1864

Mr Lincoln,

Sir, my husband, who is in Co. K. 22nd Reg't U.S. Cold Troops, (and now in the Macon Hospital at Portsmouth with a wound in his arm) has not received any pay since last May and then only thirteen dollars. I write to you because I have been told you would see to it. I have four children to support and I find this a great strugle. A hard life this!

I being a col^d woman do not get any state pay. Yet *my* husband is fighting for the country. Very Resp'y yours

Rosanna Henson

Mt Holly N.J.

To his Excel'y

Abraham Lincoln[21]

Private Hinson remained hospitalized until his discharge on April 1, 1865.

Seventy-Four Soldiers of the Fifty-Fifth Massachusetts Demand Their Pay

So many African American men arrived in Boston in the spring of 1863 to enlist in the Fifty-Fourth Massachusetts Volunteers that a sister regiment, the Fifty-Fifth, was formed with the surplus men. Like other black regiments, the men of the Fifty-Fifth Massachusetts were simmering with rage at the racial discrimination they faced in the military. On May 1, 1864, Pvt. Wallace Baker mutinied against Lt. Thomas F. Ellsworth, saying, "I won't stand to attention for you or any other damned white officer." An all-out brawl erupted, and a court-martial sentenced Baker to be executed. He was shot to death on June 18. According to one account, when he was asked whether he was ready for the execution, he exclaimed, "Yes; go and tell your d—d Lieutenant to fire and be d—d, and I'll meet him either in heaven or hell and get even with him."[22]

Less than a month after this affair, seventy-four members of the Fifty-Fifth Massachusetts sent the following petition to Lincoln demanding the full pay they had been promised or saying they would have to resort to "more Stringent mesures":

Camp 55th Massachusetts volinteer Infantry

Folly island   South Carolina

July 16th 18.64

To The President of the united States

Sir   We The Members of Co D of the 55th massechusetts vols Call the attention of your Excellency to our case

1st First We ware enlisted under the act of Congress of July 18.61 Placing the officers non commissioned officers & Privates of the volunteer forces in all Respects as to Pay on the footing of Similar corps of the Regular Army[23]   2[ond] We Have Been in the Field now thirteen months & a Great many yet longer   We Have Received no Pay & Have Been offered only seven Dollars Pr month which the Paymaster Has said was all He Had Ever Been authorized to Pay colored Troops   this was not acording to our Enlistment   consequently We Refused the money   the commonwealth of massechusetts then Passed an act to make up all Deficienceys which the general Government Refused To Pay But this We could not Recieve as The Troops in the general service are not Paid Partly By Government & Partly By State   3rd that to us money is no object   we came to fight For Liberty Jistice & Equality   These are gifts we Prise more Highly than Gold   For these we Left our Homes our Famileys Friends & Relatives most Dear to take as it ware our Lives in our Hands To Do Battle for God & Liberty

4th after the Elaps of over thirteen months spent cheerfully & willingly Doing our Duty most faithfuly in the Trenches Fatiegue Duty in camp and conspicious valor & endurence in Battle as our Past History will show

T[24] 5th therefore we Deem these sufficient Reasons for Demanding our Pay from the Date of our Enlistment & our imediate Discharge Having Been enlisted under False Pretence as the Past History of the company will Prove

6[th] Be it further Resolved that if imediate Steps are not takened to Relieve us we will Resort to more Stringent mesures

We Have the Honor to Rem[a]in your Obedint Servants The Members of Co D

Srgts

John F. Shorter

[Eight sergeants signed below Shorter, followed by sixty-five corporals and privates.][25]

Eleven of the men who signed this petition would be killed in action, while another nine would be wounded while fighting for their country.

Even after the pay issue was resolved in June 1864 for freeborn African Americans, black soldiers continued to face other forms of discrimination. On March 24, 1864, Governor Andrew promoted the first signatory of this letter, Sgt. John Freeman Shorter, and two other noncommissioned officers to second lieutenant. But Union military authorities would not permit them to be elevated to the rank of a commissioned officer because "there is no law

Sgt. John Freeman Shorter. Burt Green Wilder Papers, #14-26-95, Division of Rare and Manuscript Collections, Cornell University Library.

allowing it, they being black men." In response, one member of the regiment wondered, "Do you know of any law that *prohibits* it?" The regiment's white surgeon similarly noted, "There are no finer men or better soldiers in the regiment, but they are looked down upon because of a little colored blood." Finally, on July 1, 1865—well over a year later—the three men's promotion went into effect. Members of the Fifty-Fifth Massachusetts took great pride in this achievement.[26]

New York Soldiers Ask Lincoln for Equal Pay and for the Right to Fight

The following two letters appear to have been written by Nimrod Rowley, a thirty-nine-year-old private in the Twentieth USCT, who had worked as a mason in Elmira, New York, before enlisting in June 1863. The first letter was likely dictated to Rowley by George Rogers, a twenty-nine-year-old laborer who had been born in Baltimore. In the letter, Rogers explains his escape from slavery. The other signatories appear to have served as witnesses. Samuel Sampson was a twenty-nine-year-old farmer from Perinton, New York, and Thomas Sipple was a thirty-three-year-old farmer who had been born in Pennsylvania. Based on the docketing on the back of this letter, it was likely written in early August 1864:

New Orleans   Louisiana   Camp Parpit   1864
My Dear and Worthy Friend
Mr. President.

I thake this oppertunity of interducing myself to you By wrteing thes fiew Limes To let you know that you have Proven A friend to me and to all our Race   And now i stand in the Defence of the Country myself Ready and Willing to oBay all orders & demands that has A tendency to put Down this Rebelion In military Life or civel Life. I Enlisted at Almira state of N. York shemoung County Under *Mr* C. W. Cawing [Capt. Samuel M. Harmon?] Provose Marshall And [when] I Enlisted he told me i would get 13 Dollars Per Mounth or more if White Soldiers got it   he expected the wages would Raise And i would get my pay every 2 Months   hear i am in the survice 7 months And have Not Recived Eney Monthly Pay   I have a wife and 3 Children Neither one of them Able to thake care of Themselfs and my wife is sick And she has sent to me for money

And i have No way of geting Eney money to send to her Because i cant Get my Pay And it gos very hard with me to think my family should be At home A suffering   [I] have money earnt and cant not get it   And I Dont know when i will Be Able to Releave my suffering Family   And Another thing when I Enlisted I was promised A furlow and I have Not had it   Please *mr*. Lincoln Dont think I Am Blameing you for it   I Dident think you knew Eney thing About it   And I Dident know eney Other Course to thake To obtain what I think is Right   I invested my money in Percuring A house an home for my wife and Children And she write to me she has to work and can not surport the Children with out my Aid   When I was At home i could earn from 26 to 28 Dollars A Month   When I Enlisted it told i was to have the same Bunty [bounty,] Clothing and Ration as the Soldier and 325 Dollars wich the 25 Dollars i Never got   I Dont Beleave the Goverment wants me eney how   In fact i mean the New York 20th Rigiment   The Reason why i say so is Because we are treated Like A Parcels of Rebs   I Do not say the Goverment is useing us so   I [do not] Believe the Goverment knows Eney thing About how we are treated   we came out to be true union soldiers the Grandsons of Mother Africa Never to

Flinch from Duty   Please Not to think I Am finding fault with the
rules of the Goverment   If this Be the rules i am willing to Abide by
them   I wonce Before was A Slave 25 years   I made escape 1855
Came In to york state from Maryland   And i Enlisted in the survice
got up By the Union Legue Club   And we ware Promised All satisfaction Needfull   But it seem to Be A failure   we Are not treated Like
me we are soldiers in [and?] coleague Atall   we are Deprived of the
most importances things we Need in health and sickness Both That
surficint Food And qulitey   As for The sick it is A shocking thing to
Look into thire condition   Death must Be thire Dum Doom   when
once thay have to go to the Hospital [they] Never Return Again   such
is the medical Assistance of the 20th Rig n.y   your sarvant under
Arms sincerely
    George Rodgers
    Thomas Sipple Wilmington Delaware.
    Samuel Sampsons
Mr President I Surtify that this I is jest what mr Rodgers sais and my
other frend mr Sipele
    Nimrod Rowley Elmire Chemong CO. N.y
    Pease excuse your Needy Petishners   we most heartly wish you the
intire victory over All Your Enemys. And A spedy sucsess To the Commander in Chief of the Army And Navy   And may Peace Forever Reighn

In the other letter that appears to have been written by Rowley, likely
around the same time as the first, Rowley asks for black soldiers to receive
the same treatment as white soldiers:

                    New Orleans Camp Parpit Louisiana 1864
My Dear Friend and x Pre
    I thake up my Pen to Address you A fiew simpels And facts   We
so called the 20th u.s. Colored troops we was got up in the state of New
York so said By A grant of the President. we Dont think he know
wether we are white or Black   we have not Bin Organized yet And A
grate meney Brought Away without Being Musterd in, and we are
treated in a Different maner to what others Rigiments is Both Northern men or southern Raised Rigiment   Instead of the musket It is the
spad[e] and the Whelbarrow and the Axe cuting in one of the most
horable swamps in Louisiana stinking and misery   Men are Call to go
on thes fatiuges wen sum of them are scarc Able to get Along the Day
Before on the sick List And Prehaps weeks to And By this treatment

meney are thowen Back in sickness wich thay very seldom get over. we had when we Left New York over A thousand strong   now we scarce rise Nine hundred   the total is said to Be we lost 1.60 men who have Left thire homes friends and Relation And Come Down hear to Lose thire Lives in For the Country thy Dwll in or stayd in   the Colored man is like A lost sheep   Meney of them old and young was Brave And Active. But has Bin hurrided By and ignominious Death into Eternity. But I hope God will Presearve the Rest Now in existance to Get Justice and Rights   we have to Do our Duty or Die and no help for us It is true the Country is in A hard strugle But we All must Remember Mercy and Justice Grate and small. it is Devine. we All Listed for so much Bounty Clothing and Ration And 13 Dollars A month. And the most has fallen short in all thes Things   we havent Recived A cent of Pay Since we Bin in the field. Instead of them Coming to us Like men with our 13 Dollars thay come with only seven Dollars A month wich only A fiew tuck it   we stand in Need of Money very much indeed And think it is no more than Just an Right we should have it   And Another thing we are Cut short of our Ration in A most Shocking maner. I wont Relate All now But we Are Nerly Deprived of All Comforts of Life   Hardly have Anough Bread to Keep us From starving   six or 8 ounces of it to Do A Soldier 24 hours on Gaurd or eney other Labor and About the Same in Meat and Coffee   sum times No meat for 2 Days   soup meat Licqour with very Little seazing the Boys calls hot water or meat tea for Diner   It is A hard thing to be Keept in such a state of misery Continuly   It is spoken Dont musel the ox that treads out the corn. Remember we are men standing in Readiness to face thous vile traitors an Rebeles who are trying to Bring your Peaceable homes to Destruction. And how can we stand them in A weak and starving Condition

All four of these men survived the war. Samuel Sampson was discharged for disability in June 1865; the other three men mustered out with their regiment at New Orleans in October 1865.[27]

A Black Chaplain Demands Equal Pay

Jennie Harrison was traveling in Philadelphia with her mistress, a Mrs. Bolton, when she delivered a baby boy on April 15, 1818. Since Jennie and her husband, William, were both slaves in Georgia, their son, Samuel, had the peculiar distinction of being born a slave in the free state of Pennsylvania. Shortly after Samuel's birth, Jennie returned to Savannah and was freed by her owners, along with their other slaves. The slaves were given the option to emigrate to Africa or to remain in the United States. The Harrisons chose to stay.

At some point in the early 1820s, Jennie moved with the Boltons to New York City. Samuel remained with his mother until he turned nine, at which point he was sent to Philadelphia to learn the shoemaking trade from an uncle. At the age of seventeen Samuel experienced an intense religious conversion. He joined a Presbyterian church and decided that he would go into the ministry. Harrison attained some schooling in upstate New York and Ohio before returning to Philadelphia about 1840. In 1847 he moved to Newark, New Jersey, where he worked as a shoemaker and trained for the ministry. Finally, he took a permanent position at a Congregational church in Pittsfield, Massachusetts, which he held from 1850 to 1862.

Following the assault on Fort Wagner in July 1863, Harrison traveled south as a member of the National Freedmen's Relief Association to assist former slaves on the Sea Islands of South Carolina. While there, Harrison preached a sermon to the freedpeople and also visited with wounded soldiers from the Fifty-Fourth Massachusetts.

On August 22, the white officers of the Fifty-Fourth elected Harrison chaplain of the regiment. The following week he returned home to Massachusetts. On September 8, Massachusetts governor John A. Andrew granted Harrison a commission, which Harrison only learned about by reading the newspapers several weeks later. He accepted the commission and prepared to head back to the South, mustering into the service at Morris Island, South Carolina, on November 12. The men of the Fifty-Fourth were pleased to finally have a spiritual leader among them. One black soldier remarked that they had only heard four sermons since leaving the Bay State earlier that year, and "our regiment has felt the need of a chaplain."

When the men of the Fifty-Fourth were finally paid on February 6, 1864, the paymaster at Hilton Head refused to pay Harrison the standard rate for chaplains — one hundred dollars per month plus two rations — because he was "of African descent." Harrison refused to accept anything less and informed Governor Andrew of the situation.[28]

On March 24, 1864, Andrew sent a letter of protest to Lincoln, reminding the president that the Fifty-Fourth and Fifty-Fifth Massachusetts Volunteers were organized "precisely in the same manner as were other regiments of State Volunteers" and therefore should receive the same rights and pay as any other white volunteer regiment. Moreover, Harrison was "an *officer* duly mustered into the service of the United States" who was "filling a *sacred office*" as a chaplain. If Harrison was to be denied the pay that was rightly owed him, "it will be the first time, I believe, since the Christian era, that a man in holy orders, in the Christian Church[,] has by reason of his color, descent or origin been refused the rights, immunities and privileges pertaining to his office and character." Not only was this a violation of the rights of a soldier, but for the paymaster to withhold the appropriate pay was "alike in violation of the rights of the Christian church and of the laws of Congress."[29]

Upon reviewing this letter on April 4, Lincoln ordered Attorney General Edward Bates to "please give me your legal opinion whether the Pay Master should have paid as demanded" and also whether the president could "order him to pay." On April 23, Bates presented Lincoln with a lengthy legal opinion stating that Harrison was a "lawfully appointed and qualified Chaplain" and therefore was entitled to the full pay of any other person holding that office.[30]

On May 3, Lincoln sent a copy of Bates's opinion to the Senate—ostensibly to show his support for increasing the pay of black soldiers. This was cause for celebration among abolitionists. "At last we see day-light," wrote Senator Charles Sumner of Massachusetts to Governor Andrew. Sumner had been having dinner with Secretary of War Stanton when Lincoln burst into the room and said, "I have something good for you"—referring to Bates's opinion. When Sumner informed Lincoln that Governor Andrew had wanted a copy of the opinion, Lincoln replied, "You shall have mine." During the evening Lincoln sent it over to Sumner, who then passed it along to Andrew. "God be praised!" Sumner concluded his letter.[31]

While all of this was going on, Harrison became ill with vertigo and "suddenly became faint and unconcious [*sic*] for a short time." The following day he received a monthlong furlough, and he was compelled to resign his commission on March 8, 1864.[32] He returned home to Pittsfield, Massachusetts, but still had not received his full pay. Exasperated, he sent the following letter to Lincoln.

> Pittsfeild Mass Sep 9th 1864
>
> To His Excellency President Lincoln
> Sir
>   Last March Gov Andrew forwarded a paper to Your excellency; containing the refusal of U.S Paymaster at Hilton Head South

Carolina to pay me as chaplain of the 54th Mass Vols. The usual pay and allowance of chaplains, basing his refusal upon the ground of my being of African descent   Gov Andrews appeal was refered by Your Excellency to Attorney Genl Bates. He reviewed the whole case and gave his decision in my favor since which decision repeated efforts have been made to secure from the Goverment that which is justly due, Which seem to unavailing I have been waiting patiently   I was compelled by sickness to retire from the Army   I was honourably discharged March 14th 1864 in consequence of Physical disability   For three months I was unable to perform any service; My preparation to go into the army compelled me to contract debts for the support of my family which I have not be[en] able to cancle,   because I have not bcen paid for my services by the Government I had to borrow money while in the army of my regi-mental officers   I have not paid them   Major Porter of the US army at Beaufort gave me sixty dollars on these conditions That if he was sustained by the authorities he would pay me all which was my due   If not I was to refund it again as he would have to pay it out of his own pocket   The cheif paymaster at Hilton Head South Caro-lina [said] to me the day I left the department of the South That he had written to Washington in relation to my pay And that it was decided against me or adversely to my claim; consequently the money I recieved from Major Porter I regarded as a loan,   I was mustered into the service Nov 12th 1863 at Morris Island South Carolina   I was discharged March 14th 1864   The whole amt due me is fourhundred and seventy dollars   I suppose that inasmuch as Attorney Genl Bates decided in my favor That sixty dollars is to be deducted from this amount leaving my due fourhundred and twelve dollars   I am in exceedingly embarrassing circumstances which Your Excellency can relieve me from by ordering my pay from the department And thus helping me in this my time of need

I am Your obedient Servant

Samuel Harrison

Lincoln referred Harrison's letter to Secretary of War Stanton on September 15. Stanton, in turn, referred it to the paymaster general of the Union army the following day. Harrison eventually received all the money that was owed him.[33]

The Wife of an Ohio Soldier Asks
Why Black Soldiers Are Not Paid

This letter appears to have been sent to John A. Andrew, the governor of Massachusetts, and then forwarded to the Lincoln administration. The author's husband, William Wicker, was a twenty-eight-year-old farmer in the Fifty-Fifth Massachusetts, who would soon after be wounded at the Battle of Honey Hill, South Carolina, on November 30, 1864.

> Piqua   Miama Co   ohio   Sep 12 1864
> Sir   i write to you to know the reason why our husbands and sons
> who enlisted in the 55 Massichusette regiment have not Bin paid off   i
> speak for my self and Mother and i know of a great many others as well
> as ourselve are suffering for the want of money to live on   when
> provision and Clotheing wer Cheap we might have got a long   But
> Every thing now is thribbl [triple?] and over what it was some thre year
> Back   But it matters not if Every thing was at the old Price   i think it
> a Piece of injustice to have those soldiers there 15 months with out a
> cent of Money   for my part i Cannot see why they have not th same
> rite to their 16 dollars per month as th Whites[34] or Even th Coulord
> Soldiers that went from ohio   i think if Massichusette had left off
> Comeing to other States for Soldiers th Soldirs would have bin Better
> off and Massichusette saved her Credit   i wish you if you pleas
> to Answer this Letter and tell me Why it is that you Still insist upon
> them takeing 7 dollars a month when you give the Poorest White
> Regiment that has went out 16 dollars   Answer this if you Pleas and
> oblige Your humble Servant
>   Rachel Ann Wicker

Hope soon arrived in Mrs. Wicker's mail. In the file with her letter is a copy of a letter to Governor Andrew dated October 10, stating that the 55th would be paid its full amount in compliance with the federal statute equalizing pay.[35]

A Soldier's Wife Asks for Relief during a Time of Great Need

Amos Vincent was a twenty-nine-year-old farmer when he enlisted as a private in the Twentieth U.S. Colored Infantry on December 15, 1863. His wife, Mary Ann, remained at home in Ballston Spa, New York, near Saratoga Springs, with their two young daughters, Emeline (born 1857) and Augusta (born 1859). In much need of financial support, Mary Ann sent an urgent appeal to Lincoln.

Ballstown spa   Sept 28 the 1864

Mr lincoln   kind sir   pleas parden me for intruding upon your time a very litel but sucamstancis ar such that a presumton can bee ovrlookd at such times   my husban is a soaldger in the army   he Enlistid the 15 of last december and has ben gon evar sence and he has not reseaved eny pay since he has bin gon   i am sick and have a family of littel children to tak car of and have no means to car for them with and a solgers wife is lookd upon as some one that nevor wants as long as her husban is in the army alive   i canot get the least bit of help hear   i have tride evry way and evry one tells me if my husban is in your survice i must go to you for asistance   when i was abel to work i don well enought   i am willing to work for my self so that my husban can work for his country   i am proud to bee the wife of a union soalger   i could live on most eny thing so that i could live atall but i canot earn a singel sent   i am sick in bead now as i write and my littel ones are a crying for bread and i have none to give them   but i put my trust in god   i no he does all things well and i donot think he has made eny of his creaturs to let them diy with destatuton   and as evry one has advised me to aply to you for astance i in a humbel maner do so in prayr and beleaving that god will mak menifest to your hart how very needy i am   my husban belongs to the 20 new york regiment of infantry co H of united stats Colord trops   he is in camp Calumetta new orleans in state of loueasana   you will find i have told you the [illegible word][36] of the oficers comanding the regiment that he has not had eny pay nor eny of the regiment   i ask you in the name of our hevnly father to try to give me some releaf for i am needy if evor eny mortil was   do kind and honribel sir pleas lend an ear to my patition for if i was not in the soarist distress i should nevor dar to presume to adress you   but i think one that strives for the good of ther country as you do could nevor let another fello cretur sufer to death that is a doing all thats in ther powr to help put down the rebelon and restore peace and union which i hope through the help of god may sone reign over the land   i will now close praying you to hear my prayr

i am most respectfully your obedant servant

Mrs Mary Ann vinson

My husbans name is Amos vinson

Sadly, Private Vincent died of dysentery at the regimental hospital at Camp Parapet in Louisiana on November 11, 1864. A comrade wrote to Mary Ann informing her that she would soon be receiving her husband's money and belongings, including debts that were owed by other soldiers.[37]

A Wounded Soldier Needs His Pay to Support His Family

On August 19, 1863, William Chandler, a thirty-one-year-old farmer from London, Canada, enlisted in the Eighth USCT at Alleghany, Pennsylvania. Six months into his enlistment, he received a gunshot wound during the Battle of Olustee and was sent to a hospital in Jacksonville. From there, he was sent to Beaufort, South Carolina, and then up to New York.

Wirt Hill   Nov 21 1864

Mr President
Dear Sir
    It is one year ago the 19 Aug Scince I was mustered in to the U,S Service Scince which I had the misfortin to loose my left arm at the battle of Olustee, Flarida on the 20 of Feb   I was voanded [wounded] Slightly in my hip and Severly in my arm and have had my arm amputated and have been in the hospital every Scince   I am home on a furlough   I have never received a cent of pay yet
    Necesity compells me to write to you to see if you can do anything to help me about getting my pay which is due me as a Soldier   My family are Suffering for want of it   I am a poor man and have no way of supporting my family   I was first in the hospital at Beaufort S,C then in August I was sent to New york Harbor Davids Island U,S General Hospital where I have been ever Scince   pleas let me know what you can do about it   I ~~was~~ am in Co. G, 8 U,S Col[d]   if you can do any thing to help a poor Soldier pleas do it and oblige me Your obedient Servent
    William Chandler
write soon
Adress W[m] Chandler
Co G, 8 U,S,C,T
U.S,A, General Hosp
Davids Island New york Harbor
in care of Warren Webster
Asst Sergeon U,S Army in charge of Hospital

Shortly after writing this letter, Chandler was transferred to Central Park General Hospital in New York City. A few weeks later, on January 19, 1865, he was discharged from the service for disability "at his own request."[38]

A Canadian Soldier Requests the Payment of His Bounty

Thomas Pepper was twenty years old when he enlisted in Co. E of the 102nd USCT near Detroit, Michigan, on September 5, 1864. A native of Canada who worked as a laborer, his company descriptive book states that he received a one hundred dollar bounty for enlisting. However, in this letter to Lincoln, Pepper tells a different story.

November the 21st 1864

Mr honerable abraham lincoln

sir   i came in august and was to get $450 dollars bunty and i have not got one cent yet and i dont think)

that i have any bisness in the servis at all   i am the only surport of my mother and i cant sp suport her on nothing   they agreed to pay the money before i left Jackson but they did not do as they agreed)

Therfore i dont consider my self a soldier   if i am to be a soldier [I] want to come in honest a and therefore i beg the most ho[n]erable president to set me free

Dyrect to Beaufort southcarlina company E 102 united states colord trops

rite soon

thomas pepper

to mr abraham lincoln

[P.S.] i rote back for my money and the anser that i got was they did not no any thing about it

It is unknown whether anything came of this letter. Pepper mustered out with his regiment at Charleston, South Carolina, on September 30, 1865.[39]

A Suffering Soldier's Wife Asks for Assistance

Some letters, like this one, arrived with insufficient information about the soldier. As a consequence, nothing could be done for the correspondent.

Thomas Pepper. Courtesy of the National Archives.

Clarendon. Jan. the 16. 1865

mr lincoln Dear sir

i am in trobbell and [do] not know what to do i thought i would write to you my Husband is in the arma but get no pay he is in new orleans the last i heard from him i am sick and [have] no munney my Husband enlistet in pro[vidence] ri in 1863 i dount get no help i have a famley to support i hope the day will come when the black man will have the same write as the white man

Dear brother in crist i look to you as a fother in this f afflixon afflixson may heaven bless you is my prayer it seam as if my cup is full but i look to him ho rull [who rules] all events he will rull all fing [things] well i hope this ware will sease and peas may be restord to this land and cruntry mr lincoln will you tell me if the black man can get his pay men that is fitting for the u[n]ion should have thare pay wharther black or white i have rote to garret smith[40] for help but no

Twenty-Sixth U.S. Colored Infantry at Camp William Penn.
Courtesy of the National Archives.

ancer from him   excuse my riting to you   i reameane your obeadent
sirvent
    Abbie A myers
    in hast   Clarendon orleans county   box 138   ny[41]

A Disabled Conscript Seeks Relief from Injustice

The writer of this anonymous letter was probably a member of the Forty-First
USCT, which was organized at Camp William Penn, near Philadelphia, between September 30 and December 7, 1864. The camp's commander, Col.
Louis Wagner, had been wounded and captured by the Confederates at the
Second Battle of Bull Run in August 1862. In 1863 he was placed in command
of Camp William Penn. The *Philadelphia Inquirer* praised Wagner's "popular-
ity," noting, "he is universally beloved" by his men and "has the confidence

Col. Louis Wagner. Courtesy of Joyce Werkman.

of the officers."[42] Yet on some occasions Wagner clashed with the men who were training under him, as the following letter attests.

Camp wm Penn   cheltan Hill   Pa   Feb 4 1865

Honerble Mr Presadent us

permit me Dear Sir to drop you a few Lines   Dear Sir The 21 of ~~novembar~~ Septembar 1864 I was drafted in The Survis and on The 15 day of october folawing I Landed to The above named Camp in company with 76 men ~~included~~ including my Self and I have Bin here Ever sence and The cause of my Being here So Long is on The acount of my descriptive Role   it cant Be found and my wife is in very Bad Circumstances   I Left hur with 10 dollars and ~~hadent~~ had not pur-

chesed my wintar wood and She must hav sufered this winter   She
has written to me for money Sevral times But I cant gett it to Send
hur   The pay mastar payed of[f] The solders here and I did not gett a
sent of money to Send home   Dear Sir They ar . 8 . pursans here from
Indiana who ar in The Same fix and The Rest of our Company is gon
front and hav got money and Sent it home to Ther familes   Dear Sir
we ar not treated here ~~Lik~~ Like white Solders By no means   we cant
ask Col Wagner one word But what we ar insulted and when a substitut
cums in Camp The Col forses him to giv him his Bounty to take care of
and gives The Solder a Recete for it and very often The ~~pool~~ poor man
Lose it and when such is The case The Col drives The man of[f] and
tells him when he findes The Recete he will giv him The money and
not Before and he keepes it   I am Crippeled and The Dr sed I ought to
hav a discharge But The Col wont concent to it   he Sed ~~Iam~~ I am
playing off and he will not giv me a discharge   Dear Sir I would Like
to know if That is write   if it is I will Say no more   if you ~~Sent~~ Send a
man here you will find my words true
  I Remain Dear Sir your obediant Survent
  Colered Solder

As this letter was sent to Lincoln anonymously, the military could not do
anything about this soldier's predicament.[43]

CHAPTER FIVE

Requesting Discharge from the Service

There is very little scholarly literature on the discharge of soldiers from the military during the Civil War,[1] but letters seeking this sort of aid can be highly revealing. Requests for discharge often discuss citizen-soldiers' rationale for enlisting, as well as the reasons that they and their families believed justified them in leaving the army. Often these letters give detailed accounts of the soldiers' enlistment and mustering in — sometimes including harrowing tales of kidnapping and impressment, which African Americans likened to slave trading. In some of the cases that follow, parents sought the release of their sons (some of whom were minors when they enlisted). In other instances, parents and sons worked together to try to persuade Lincoln to release a soldier from service. Women made maternal appeals to Lincoln, telling him that they needed their sons' financial support to survive. The letters came from high and low. None other than Frederick Douglass sought this sort of assistance from the president — a favor he could curry more easily since he knew Lincoln personally. Taken together, letters seeking discharge give insights into the physical and emotional suffering experienced by families during the war when young men went off to fight.

A Biracial Man Asks for the Release of His Minor Son

Hiram Vail was angry when his sixteen-year-old son, John, enlisted in the Eighth Ohio Infantry without parental consent. John was apparently able to pass for white, since he enlisted in the Union army in June 1861 — well before African Americans were permitted to become soldiers. Against his father's wishes, John went to western Virginia with his regiment. According to Hiram, Capt. William E. Haynes of Co. G sent three armed men to forcibly take young Vail to the front.

In October 1861, John deserted from the army and returned home to Ohio. Throughout that fall, Hiram worked through the court system to seek his son's official discharge. In November 1861, an Ohio judge ordered John released from the army, but the military nevertheless arrested him for desertion. Hiram then wrote to the secretary of war, Simon Cameron, and on December 16, 1861, the War Department ordered the young soldier's release.

Nevertheless, the colonel of the Eighth Ohio refused to comply, claiming that a soldier could not be released while he was under arrest and awaiting trial. At this point, Hiram wrote to his representative in Congress, Warren P. Noble, asking, "Who has got the Power" over his son—the War Department or a regimental officer? By mid-March, Vail still had not received a satisfactory answer, so he penned a letter to the commander in chief.

Vail's opening lines refer to the execution of Nathaniel Gordon, which had just taken place on February 21, 1862. Gordon had been caught off the coast of West Africa kidnapping nearly nine hundred Africans in 1860, and despite relentless public pressure to commute the sentence, Lincoln ordered his execution to be carried out. Gordon was the only slave trader in American history to be executed for his crimes.

Fremont   March the 16: 62

Mrs [Mr.] A Lincon
My Dear Sir
    I heard of the execution of gordon For kidnaping Negros   I want to know if kidnaping is unlawful or if our goverment Will Protect sitizens   if it will I would Like to have my son John M Vail sent home   he was taken unlawfu[lly] From me   he was Proswaded to inlist under capt W E Hanes   I refesed [refused] to Let him go on the [illegible word]   he was not old enf [enough] he was sixteen Last July   the capt armed three men and sent after him and took him away   I persed [pursued] him and took him with A hapas corps [writ of habeas corpus] and the cort Desided that he was not A soldier on the acount he was a miner   But the capt got 2 men [and] throed him on Cars By Force to Grafton Va   my aternis sent the proseding of the trial to your sekretary of war mr caron [Simon Cameron] and he sent A Discharg For John M Vail and sent my Lawyers a copy of it   I recived aleter from cornal Corll [Col. Samuel S. "Red" Carroll] of the Eight ohio rigment Refusing to obey the order   I hav Bin sick all winter   my eldr son is [in] the survs [service] and 2 son and Las [sons-in-law] and 2 Brothes and [I] would Bin thair to[o] if I had Bin well   But my son John dont Want to stay thare   if you peas see to this   I turnd grind stone For you and now I want you to turn For me   I am a sitizen of ohio Free Born and half whit   Peas ancer this as son as you can   Yours Truly
    Hiram Vail
Direct to Freemont ohio

Hiram Vail's appeal does not appear to have worked. His son would attempt to desert two other times before mustering out of the army in July 1864.[2]

A Father and Son Attempt to Deceive Lincoln

Richard M. Smith enlisted as a drummer in the Third USCT on June 26, 1863. The nineteen-year-old shoemaker from West Chester, Pennsylvania, left Camp William Penn, his training site near Philadelphia, without permission on August 12 and, when he returned, "found out that the regiment had left." Smith headed for Philadelphia to try to find the military headquarters, but he was unable to find it. Along the way he met a man "by the name of Aretry Cole & I asked him as a friend where the quarters was he had then been drinking & had several others with him & he told me yes he would shew me so he took me to a 3 or 4 taverns & asked me to drink[.] I told him no I did not drink & instead of taken to the quarters took me as a deserter to wich if I had nown the way to the quarters or camp I would not of been served or probly not have Been taken as a deserter from My Regiment." Smith told military authorities, "i will confess never again to do any thing of the kind."

Smith was sent to his regiment at Morris Island, South Carolina, and was arraigned before a court-martial. He admitted having left Camp William Penn but claimed that it was "not with the intention of staying from the regiment." The court found him guilty not of desertion but of being absent without leave and sentenced him to eight months in prison and loss of pay, and he was sent to Fort Clinch in Florida. After his prison sentence was up, Smith rejoined his regiment on June 26, 1864.[3]

The correspondence that follows was a clumsy attempt at deception.[4] On November 17, Smith wrote a letter addressed to Lincoln but signed it with his father's name and dated it November 28. He then instructed his father to "put an envelop on this and direct it to Hon. Abraham Lincoln Washington D.C." Smith's father apparently did not fully understand the instructions.

Morris Island   Nov 17th/63
Dear father   I am well at present and hope these few lines May
find you the same   Now father no Man has a right to enlist any one
[under] age and particularly if they have a limb or a thumb off   and

I have a letter wrote here for the President and the reason why
I send it to you I want you to please send it on to him for we cannot
get a letter from here to him for the officers opens them and Reads
them if they are for him   and I have wrote it just as if it was from
you and I asked him to write to you to let you know if I can be sent
home again on the account of being under age and My hand
together   just send it as it is and I know a Most that he will have
me sent home for there had been some got out of it this way   and
please to give Me an answer as soon as you get these letters so as
I May know wether you got them or know [not?] & dont keep Me a
freting wether you got them or not   and let Me know whether you
got a letter from Mr Hemphill that I sent you and you look for a
letter from Lincoln and if you get one let Me know imediately
without fail
    Your son   Richard Smith
Directions
Morris Island   3rd Regiment
U.S. Colored Troops
[Written at the top of the letter above the dateline:] put an envelop on
this and direct it to Hon. Abraham Lincoln   Washington D.C

The following letter, in Richard Smith's hand, was included with Smith's
letter to his father. Without thinking, Smith's father, Charles, sent both letters to Lincoln. Smith had accidentally dated this letter from Morris Island,
but he crossed out that line and inserted his family's hometown of West
Chester, Pennsylvania.

> West Chester   Chester Co
> ~~Morris Island S.C.~~
> November 28th 18/63

Hon Mr Lincoln   President of U.S.
Kind Sir
    I am forced to write to you sir about My son who is not of age yet
and whom was persuaded off By some of the recruiting officers of
this place West Chester Chester County Penn and who was taken in
the service against My will and of course without any Examination
for he is not a able Boy and he has not the use of his left hand on the
account of his thumb Being off and his other Disabilities   and
Mr Lincoln By promising I supose a Bounty of 50 Dol^s and when

enlisted and 100 when discharged I suposed was taken off in to the
service on the account of him not being able for such service   Mr
Lincoln I would like you sir at a Convenient time give Me an answer
if I could have him returned home again to Me   he is now in the
3rd Rigiment U.S. Colored Troops Or 3rd Penn Regiment at Morris
Island South Carolina And he has complained of not being well
since he has been out   But Mr Lincoln he has not drawn any
Money Bounty or Monthly Pay and Mr Lincoln at you[r] service sir it
will be of a great accomodation to have him returned to me
again   his Comanding Colonel is Colonel Tillman [Benjamin. G.
Tilghman] 3rd U.S.C.T
    Your Most Obedient Friend &c   Charles B. Smith
father of Richard M Smith of 3rd Reg

Charles B. Smith also sent two letters to Lincoln, written by himself, not
his son.

                      West chester   chester county   PA
to Mr Abraham Lincoln   President of the united States
    kine [kind] Dear and Honorable friend to we pore african
race   Dear Sir   i have corse [cause] to Write to you About a
pore afflicted boy [who turned] 19 years of age [on] october 11th 1863
    He was persaded off by those Recruiting officers of this Place
West chester chester Co PA and taken into the u S service Without
my knowlage   this Boy have not had the Proper use of his left
Hand for 10 years and togather with other afflection in his head
And his thumb on the left Hand is off Down close to the remainder
of his hand to which He often complians of at times in much pain
he also says that he was not examined Before he was taken off into
the service   and now kine Sir may it please your Honour to have
him sent Home to West chester again to me as i have only three
Sons and all of them Warers [warriors] in your Services   and now
Dear and kine sir Will you Please to have him returned Home to me
again as he He is not able for the service   his brothers is able for
the Service but he is not   His name is richard M Smith   his hopes
is altogather in your kiness to release him for he is not able to
Stand it but his other brothers is able to Stand it   and kind Sir I
humley Beg you to have him sent home to West chester chester Co

P A and oblige thy friend   Dear [Sir] please answer my Leter as soon possible
    the Boy aged [Charles] B Smith   the Boys aaged farther
November 27th 1863

West chester   December 5th 1863
to our honorble President   Abraham Lincon
Dear friend   I am forced to call on thee again about my Boy richard M Smith ~~Whou~~ whom was taken off by some of those Recruiters and the Boy not having the use of one of his Hands for the last ten years by reason of his thumb being taken off Down close to the remainder of his hand   the boy is also under age and have been persaded off form [from] his home West chester chester Pennsylvania
    And now Dear Sir i Humbley Beceach you that you will have the boy sent home again as he is not fit for service and oblige me his aged farther
    Charles B Smith

These letters were to no avail. Richard Smith mustered out with his regiment at Jacksonville, Florida, on October 31, 1865.[5]

A Mother Pleads That Her Kidnapped Son Be Released from the Service

James Henry Benson was a twenty-year-old waiter when he enlisted in the Twentieth USCT at Riker's Island, New York, on December 31, 1863. Shortly before traveling to Camp Parapet, Louisiana, Sergeant Benson's mother sent the following letter to Lincoln, which described the unfortunate circumstances of her son's enlistment:

Phila., February 20, 1864
To his Excellency Abraham Lincoln   Pres. of the U.S.
    The following was the cause of a communication between his Excellency Gov. [Andrew G.] Curtin and Secretary Stanton.
    The Undersigned is a poor widow (colored) whose son, James H. Benson, on going to New York to ship, with a shipping agent of this city by the name of Thompson was seized by some six or seven white men, and forced into the 20th Regiment, Co. H, U.S.A., on Rikers Island, New York Harbour, after taking his bounty money.
    The object of this letter is, to see, if your honour could not intercede in his behalf, and procure his speedy release.

An early answer is most respectfully solicited from your Excellency by
Ann Benson
No. 925 Rodman st.,
Phila.,
Pa.

The War Department sent Mrs. Benson's letter to Riker's Island for a report. The general commanding there replied that Benson "seems to be un-
usually intelligent." The letter then traveled to the Adjutant General's Office
and the Provost Marshal's Office for report. Ultimately, however, Benson was
not mustered out until October 1865.[6]

A Black Conscript Seeks Medical Release from the Army

The descriptive book for Co. G of the Thirty-Ninth USCT lists William Jackson
as a thirty-nine-year-old laborer who had been born in Washington, D.C. (in
the petition below he said he was thirty-six). Jackson was mustered into the
regiment at Baltimore on March 31, 1864.[7] His story is recounted in the following petition, which found its way into Abraham Lincoln's hands in May 1864:

The Petition of William Jackson (Colored) humbly shows—

That on Monday the 28th day of March 1864 I was approached by an
officer of the United States Army accompanied by a file of soldiers
while sitting with my family *at my home* in Annarunde [Anne Arundel]
County State of Maryland—

I was asked by the officer my name & age and whether I wished to
volunteer in the army and get the bounty of $400—or to be forced to
go and get nothing—

I replied that my name was William Jackson and my age 36 years.
That I did not wish to enter the army and would not volunteer for any
consideration of bounty because of the del[icate] and uncertain state
of my health, arising from the fact of my having been subject for the
past ten years to constantly returning attacks of Epileptic fits—That I
was totally unfit for military duty and could only expect to drag out a
few months of a miserable existanse—an incubus upon the United
States Government If I was forced to enter its servise

The officer declined to receive my statement, recorded my name at
once upon his book as a recruit, and ordered me to follow him.

With difficulty and by solemnly pledging myself to report to him
that evening at 4 oclock I obtained leave to remain at my home until
the hour for reporting arrived. I immediately went to the two Physi-

cians of my neighborhod Dr^s Waters & Hall one or the other of whom had been attending me for ten years or longer and obtained from each of them the certificates, (annexed herewith as part of this petition) — showing the fact of my having been subject to Epileptic attacks for many years, and of my being incompetant for military duty by reason of this painful and dangerous desease

At the hour named viz 4 oclock P.M. March 28th I reported myself to Capt Read on board the Steamboat Cecil as I had obligated myself to do. I stated my Case and handed him my certificates — he said I looked able to perform military duty and he would not take any certificate to the contrary

I then begged leave to go back to my family and remain all night pledging myself to report next day at 12 oclock. This permission was granted me — The next day at eleven oclock, I reported to the Captain and asked leave to go to Baltimore that morning and seek to obtain an Exemption from the government surgeon before whom the recruits were examined. I pledged myself solemnly (and offered the Captain three or four hundred dollars security from good Union men for the faithful discharge of my pledge) that I would report myself in Baltimore within ten days if I was not exempted   in the mean time I obtained permission and came to Baltimore accordingly on the 29th day of March

I was not allowed to go before the Examining surgeon for ~~several~~ two days but as soon as he would see me I reported to him and was pronounced fit for service and ordered on duty to the Camp near Baltimore where I have ever since [been] and still am detained against my will. I̶

And further that I have never at any time received or agreed to receive any money ~~money~~ by way of bounty or compensation since I have been taken unwillingly from my home and detained in my present situation.

Your petitioner therefore upon the above recited facts prays that he may be discharge[d] from performing service in the United States Army for which he is entirely unfit by reason of his delicate health and peculiar desease

     his
Wm X Jackson
    mark

Balto   April 13th 1864
Subscribed and sworn to before me
   Jno Showacre   J.P.

William Jackson's father, Thomas, also swore before Justice of the Peace Showacre that William's statement was true.[8]

Lincoln was angered by this sort of treatment of African Americans in Maryland. According to his private secretary, John Hay, "The President is in favor of the voluntary enlistment of negroes with the consent of their masters & on payment of the price," but he opposed when the military took "a squad of soldiers into a neighborhood, & carry off into the army all the able-bodied darkies they can find without asking master or slave to consent."[9] Lincoln endorsed William's petition twice. On May 21, 1864, he wrote, "Hon. Mr. [Edwin H.] Webster requests that this man be discharged; therefore discharged—A. Lincoln." Below this, Lincoln specified: "The applicant, William Jackson, is in Co. G, 39th Maryland Colored Troops. AL." The War Department issued special orders calling for Jackson's release as soon as he refunded any bounties that he had received for enlisting. When it was shown that he had received no bounties, he was immediately released.[10]

A Soldier Asks Lincoln to Send Him Some Place Other Than the Army Hospital

Freeman Glasco (sometimes spelled Glascow) was twenty-two years old when he enlisted in the Third USCT on July 3, 1863. A farmer by trade, Glasco had been born and raised in Chester County, Pennsylvania, just west of Philadelphia. He deserted from his training ground at Camp William Penn on July 30, 1863, and returned on September 14. Suffering from chronic diarrhea, he was sent to the U.S. General Hospital at Beaufort, South Carolina, on February 5, 1864, where he remained until he returned to his regiment on July 25. While at the hospital, he wrote the following letter to Lincoln:

> Beaufort South Carolina
> Gen. Hospital No. 6. june 1tt 64
>
> Mr President Lincon.
>   I take this privealage of requesting you to know wether I can not eather be sent to my regement or home under my present situwation for I am now a geting out of heart. I have ben In the Gen. Hospital a going on 5 month and have been exzamons by severl Docters sence here I have been and they say that I will not be able for Drill eny more. I have been [illegible word] for 6 month, and I would wish you to have me sent to my regement or home. I have asked the Docters for to send me to my regement   the Docters would not give me eny sadesfaction of sending me And I thought that I would make this bold attemp to Inform you of my present situwation. If thir Is eny chance for me to

get away from this Beaufort I would be very glad of It. I think that If I am no surves to the regement I would not wish to stay In the Hospital the balence of my time. and If [I] can not be sent home I would to be sent to my regement for this Is the tiesom [tiresome] plase I ever was In. It appers the longer I stay the weeker I get. ~~they~~ I have been In the surves 1 year the 2^{tt} day of july and have hade very good helth and always been able to do my duty untill I met with a misfortion at Batry Crag [Battery Gregg] on Morris Island. I would wish If ther is eny thing that can be don for me I hope you will do It. If It should be for me to go to my regement eny place to get of[f] of this Island. I generly would wish to meat every man upon the level then we can part squer [square]   I must come to a cloes No More at present But I am still willing to do the best I can

    Freeman Glasco. compeny C. 3rd U.S. Col. Troops. Beaufort South Carolina. Gen. Hospital. N° 6.
residense
chesta County Pa.   [circled:] A. L. 5 000
[hand drawn Masonic symbol]

Glasco's request was partially granted. He was returned to his regiment on July 9, 1864, and was honorably discharged on October 5, 1865.[11]

Frederick Douglass Asks a Personal Favor

On the same day that Douglass sent Lincoln the letter related to freeing the slaves (see chapter 3), he also sent a short note regarding his son, Charles R. Douglass (1844–1920), who was serving in the Fifth Massachusetts Cavalry, a black regiment:

> *Private*
> Now, Mr President—I hope I shall not presume to[o] much upon your kindness—but I have a very great favor to ask. It is not that you will appoint me General Agent to carry out the Plan now proposed—though I would not shrink from that duty—but it is, that you will cause my son Charles R Douglass. 1st Sergeant of Company I 5th Massachusetts dis-mounted Cavalry—now stationed at "*Point Look out*" to be dis-charged—He is now sick. He was the first colored volunteer from the State of New York—having enlisted with his Older Brother [Lewis] in the mass. 54th partly to encourage enlistments—He

Sgt. Charles R. Douglass in uniform. Courtesy of the Manuscripts Division, Moorland-Spingarn Research Center, Howard University.

was but 18. when he ~~he~~ enlisted—and has been in the service 18. months. If your Excellency can confer this favor—you will lay me under many obligations

    Again Your Obedient Servant

    Fred^k Douglass

Lincoln endorsed Douglass's note the next day:

Let this boy be discharged.

    A. Lincoln

~~August~~ Sept. 1. 1864.

In accordance with Lincoln's order, Charles R. Douglass was discharged at Point Lookout on September 15.[12]

A Refugee Asks for Her Conscripted Husband's Discharge

William Rouser was thirty-eight years old when he was drafted into the Tenth U.S. Colored Infantry in September 1864. Born into slavery in Rappahannock County, Virginia, Rouser and his family had escaped from bondage earlier in the war and were now living in the nation's capital. Rouser's wife was unable to work and pleaded with Lincoln to discharge her husband:

> Washington D.C.
> September 24th 1864
>
> To His Excellency Abraham Lincoln President of the United States
> My husband William Rouser having been drafted on Tuesday last, in the first Ward in this City, I would most humbly beg to present to your kind consideration the enclosed affidavit of my physician, which shows that I am totally unfit to obtain a living for my young child and myself—also a petition from several persons whom I have known since I have been in this city and who know that it is impossible for me to go out to service or in any way provide for myself and child—thus in the absence of my husband I am thrown upon my own exertions, in order to feed and clothe us—and subject as I am to spasms and convulsions, I can find no person who will give me employment, and no relative or friends to whom I can look for aid or assistance.
> Three years ago my husband left his master in the South, and since that time we have been in this City—
> Praying for your welfare and trusting that you will grant my husband a discharge, for which I would not ask were I able to support myself—I remain Your obdt Servant—
>
>   her
> Julia X Rouser (colored)
>   mark

Rouser's letter and enclosures wended their way through the War Department bureaucracy, but her husband was not discharged from the army until the end of his term on September 23, 1865.[13]

A Kidnapped Substitute Asks to See His Family

Henry Homer was a twenty-eight-year-old farmer from Virginia when he mustered into the service as a substitute at Covington, Kentucky, in July 1864. His letter to Lincoln reveals a complicated story of how he joined the service:

"Avoiding the Draft—Agents of Northern States Engaging Negro Substitutes at Norfolk," *Frank Leslie's Illustrated Newspaper*, September 3, 1864. Collection of the author.

Webster Barracks

Covington Ky. October 1th 1864.

To the President of the United States. Abraham Lincoln
Dear Sir.

As I take the Liberty in writing to you a few lines in stating [to] you the circumstances in the way I was fooled in to the Service and the way I was Sold   I was a making for Norfolk to my home   I was Refugeed ~~to~~ from Norfolk to Lexington Virginia   from there I came off with a Union man to Charleston [West Virginia] and then I was taken from Charleston to ~~Norfolk~~ Ohio   on my way I came across that fellow on the Boat   he was a colored man Selling Substitutes[14]   in the first place he promised me to take me home to Norfolk as he is getting up a Regiment there of Cavalry   ~~int~~ instead [of] him taking me home he was aller time taking me away from home which I told the man I was willing to Journ his Regiment after I get home to see my Wife and family   the

Rascall promised me to take me to my Wife & that he would pay my Expenses & Every thing free so I was taken to Cincinnati   there I was sold & send over the river to Join the Colored Troops and I never got to see that Rascall any more   he was Just send out to buy Substitutes   as I was willing to volunteer and fight for my Country if I only could went home to see my family   & now Your Honer President Lincoln I wish for you to be so kind to do me the gratidute favor as to Release me from this place if you please as I wish to be closer to home   here I am to[o] far away from home intirely for I cant get no forlough and nothing   my home is North Carolina   I d be very glad to see my family again   please transferre me in to any other Rgt you choose so I get closer to home   please Write me an Answer as soon as possible for I am very anxious to hear from you   I spoke to the [missing word?] of my Rgt he told me it would n t do any good so I am writing on my own accord
 I am Respectfully Yours
 Henry Homer
 Calored Man
Please Direct your letter To
Henry Homer   117th U.S.C. Inf   C° A.
Covington. Ky
Webster Barracks

Homer was not permitted to leave the army; he mustered out with his regiment at Brownsville, Texas, on August 10, 1867.[15]

A Soldier Seeks a Discharge for His Comrade

Nothing is known about the author of this letter, Richard Brumbey (possibly Brumbry). Nor can it be known in which regiment the subject of this letter, George W. Jackson, served. (There were several hundred men named George W. Jackson in the U.S. Colored Troops.) Nevertheless, this letter reveals the hope that Lincoln's presidency gave to black Americans, as Jackson prayed for hours in the middle of the night that Lincoln would win the presidential election of 1864. The letter was written on U.S. Sanitary Commission stationery.

Washington   November 10 1864

Mr Mrs President Lincon
 This is the second letter that I have written[16] Mr Presiden[t] so please let this coulloured man a hearing of which is to hour advantage

for you to do so   I was out and spoke this Captin Hitchcok a bout
George W. Jackson and tolde him how useful he was and he was not fit
for survice because he was consumptive and had the rumities [rheu-
matism?] so he was know survice to him selfe nor know one els   one
halfe of him is perished and one leg is drawed and is shorter than the
other so his captin tolde me you would discharge him with out a
wourd or murmer   Mr Lincon he has ben hour main dependance in
giveing us information a bout the plans of those secretts cocieties[17]
with these detestibles secessions and contemptibles Reables   they
surspishion him and they put his name in insted of the other man   so
Mr President this has benn the way so his Captin sayed he would
corrected this so we cante do with out him   this coulloured man will
tell you juste how it is and the other letter you got befor this will tell
you all and will give you all the pure and truthful satisfaction a bout
this George W Jackson   his captin sayed he went by his tent one
munday night and he was prayin at 2 clock in the night for you to bee
Relected for a 3 hours and it wakened all at the Campe wher he
was   he did not stope the next morning   say the Captin[,] George
who will bee Elected   Masar Abraham Lincon   how do you
know   why Captin god tolde me so   why he will bee Elected the
nexte four after this four years   god bless Mr President   and he tolde
the Mcclan men[18] so this is the reason why they put his name and
scratched out[19] one who had benn able to have gone to fight   this has
benn the way so you have the true facts how it he will bee moore expence
to hour Goverment than usefull   but heare he can bee moore good
than anny purson else can do   so heare it is so know juste aske this
coulloured man and he will tell you all a bout the truths moore than can
bee written   so pleas attend to this for it is of importance Preside[nt]
    Richard Brumbey

A notation on Brumbey's letter reveals that by order of the secretary of
war, Jackson could not be discharged.[20]

A British Subject Who Was Forced into
Service Asks for a Discharge

Private William Henry Johnson, a farmer from Canada, enlisted as a substitute in the 102nd USCT on August 11, 1864. (He was a substitute for a
white man named Seligmann Schloss.) In his letter to Lincoln he claimed

that he was forced into the service against his will when he was working in Detroit.

November the 21st 1864

mr honerable abraham lincoln

i thank the lord that i am spard to state to you that i am a man of the brittish subject and was forced to go from Detroit in august last as a substitute)

i have got my papers to show what i am but they did not give me any chance to go to any officer to show them at all but kept me in the barricks u[n]tell i come away)

i dont think there is any justus done to me at all i have a wife an children at home a suffering on the acount of it

i went to detroit to work and there was a colard officer and 5 others that worked me in)

my home is in canada and my family dont no whare i am and it is hard to starve and freeze too   if you pleas to let me go home it will oblige me verry much

William H Johnson to Mr honerable Abraham lincoln

i look to the[e] in the lord to set me free and none other but the[e]   rite soon

Dyrect your letter to Beaufort   Southcarlina

company E   102 united states colard troops

Johnson's appeal was unsuccessful. He mustered out with his regiment at Charleston, South Carolina, on September 30, 1865.[21]

The Mother of a Wounded Soldier Writes to the President

Martin Welcome was twenty-eight years old when he enlisted as a private in Co. A of the Eighth USCT on August 14, 1863. A native of Carlisle, Pennsylvania, he worked as a laborer before joining the service. Welcome appears to have had something of a volatile time in the service. He was promoted to corporal in October 1863 and to sergeant in November, but then was reduced to the ranks on December 4. Less than two weeks later, on December 15, he was again promoted to sergeant; then on February 4, 1864, he was reduced to corporal. On February 20, he was wounded in the left leg at the Battle of Olustee. While recuperating, he was promoted to sergeant on May 1, and he returned to duty on June 4. Welcome was wounded again at the Battle of Chapin's Farm, in Virginia, on September 29, 1864, this time losing the forefinger on his left hand. Following this second injury, his mother, Jane, wrote to Lincoln asking for his discharge:

Carliles   nov 21 1864

Mr abreham lincon

I wont to knw sir if you please wether I can have my son relest from the arme   he is all the subport I have now   his father is Dead and his brother that wase all the help that I had   he has bean wonded twise   he has not had nothing to send me yet   now I am old and my head is blossaming for the grave and if you dou I hope the lord will bless you and me   if you please answer as soon as you can if you please   tha say that you will simpethise withe the poor   thear wase awhitie jentel man [a white gentleman] told me to write to you   Mrs jane welcom   if you please answer it to

he be long to the eight rigmat co a u st colard troops   mart welcom is his name   he is a sarjent

Unfortunately for Mrs. Welcome, the chief of the Bureau of Colored Troops replied on December 2, 1864, that "the interests of the service will not permit that your request be granted." On April 1, 1865, Welcome was again reduced to the ranks; he mustered out with his regiment as a private on November 10, 1865, at Brownsville, Texas. He would suffer pain from his injuries for the rest of his life.[22]

A Kentucky Soldier Wants to Care for His Family

George Washington, a farmer from near Louisville, Kentucky, was forty-four years old when he enlisted as a substitute in the 123rd USCT for one year on October 5, 1864. Three weeks after mustering in, he was appointed sergeant. In December, he wrote to Lincoln to ask for a discharge so that he could help his family:

December 4th 1864

Mr Abrham Lincoln

I have one reqest to make to you that is I ask you to dis Charge me for I have a wife and she has four Children   thay have a hard master one that loves the south hangs with it   he dos not giv them a rage [rag] nor havnot for too yars   I have found all he says let old Abe Giv them close   if I had them I raise them up but I am here and if you will free me and hir and heir Children with me I can take cair of them

She lives with David Sparks in Oldham Co Ky
My Woman is named Malindia Jann my daughter
Adline Clyte and
Malindia Eler and
Cleman Tine and
Natthanel washington   and my name is George Washington
ħ heir in Taylors Barrecks and my famaly suferring   I have sent forty
dollars worth to them cince I have bin heir and that is all I have and I have
not drown [drawn] any thing cince I have bin heir   I am forty eight
years my woman thirty three   I ask this to your oner to o blige yours &c
    your un [own] Gratful Servent
    George washington
Taylors Barrecks Co B   123 Rig

Washington's request was not granted. He mustered out with his company
at Louisville, Kentucky, on October 16, 1865.[23]

A Mother Seeks Her Son's Discharge

Armor Bass was eighteen years old when he enlisted in the Twenty-
Seventh U.S. Colored Infantry on March 7, 1864. He had been born to a free
black family in North Carolina but had moved with his family to Xenia, Ohio,
in 1861, where he worked as a laborer. His military service record shows that
he was sick and in a military hospital in October 1864, but that he had returned to active duty by November. During his illness, he must have written
a letter home, for his mother soon thereafter sent a letter to Lincoln asking
for his discharge:

Xenia Dec the 7th 1864

President Lincoln Esq
Dear Sir
    I drop you these few lines Concerning my son who in [is?] in the 27
Regiment 9th Army Corps Conpay F Colord   Armer Bass of this plase   he
was under age and ran away from me   if he was a healthy boy I would
give him up freely but the doctor sayed that he was consumptive   he was
sunstruck on the 30[th] of July at the Battle of Petersburg and he has not ben
well since   I wish you would see to him geting a discharge if you please
please answer this as soon as you rec[j] it   I shall expect him in the Cours of
three weeks for I think that you will send him   Your's most Obe[di]ant
    Alcia Bass

Bass served out his enlistment and was honorably discharged in September 1865. After the war, he married and worked in a waterworks department in Bellefontaine, Ohio. When he died in 1907, his obituary stated that he would be mourned by his surviving family members "while a host of friends, both white and colored, bow in a last tribute of respect."[24]

Family Members Seek to Find Out about Their Loved Ones

Relatives of Union and Confederate soldiers often endured long and difficult periods during which they did not know whether their loved ones in the army were dead or alive. Correspondence between the battlefield and the home front was often infrequent and irregular, leaving family members to wonder and worry. After major engagements, civilians checked casualty lists in newspapers (which were often inaccurate) or traveled to battlefields to scour the scarred earth in search of a familiar face. In some cases, northerners wrote to Lincoln asking if he could tell them the whereabouts of their soldier kin.

In this first letter, a sibling of a soldier named Charles Brown of the Fifty-Fourth Massachusetts wrote to Lincoln about her and her siblings' concerns:

> To oure much Beloved President we Wright Greeting
> We wish to obtain information of oure Beloved Brother who enlisted in the 54th collard Rigement, this last Fall and was Stationed on Galloupes Isiland [Gallops Island in Boston Harbor] for a Short time and then was Removed South and we parted from him there and Since we can obtain no information of the Rigement whatever   if you would oblige us by Sending us a line to Middleton Mass you would Greatly oblige you humble friend and Releive many anxous harts   if we could asertain whare the Rigement was we could write to him and if he is still liveing could here from him   oure Brothers name is Charls Brown   this is from you wel Wisher
> Lucy Freeman
> Middleton   December 1st
>   Mass
> and May God in Mercy Bless you

Three men named Charles Brown enlisted with the 54th Massachusetts, although one was transferred to the 55th. All three men survived the war.[25]

This second letter involved Thomas Patton (aka Payton or Peyton), a forty-three-year-old coachman from Philadelphia who had enlisted in the Twenty-Fifth USCT in February 1864. At Fort Pickens, Florida, Patton was "injured in [his] left side . . . by a piece of Plank in the line of duty" on August 24, 1864, but he was still listed as present on his company muster roll through April 1865. Nevertheless, his wife had not heard from him for a long time (she said two years, but he had only enlisted a year before), and she wrote to Lincoln seeking information:

Philada, March 7th 1865

Hon Sir

My husband Thomas Patton C° H. 25th regiment U.S Colored troop left here nearly two years ago and I have never heard from him since his step brother Henry Harris of C° B.. 45th regiment has never been heard only through report that he was dead   we have been waiting for a long while to see if we would hear from them   not wishing to trouble your honor hope has left us and we are compelled to write to you to know if you have any account of them.

I have the honor to remain Your Obedient Servant

Sarah Patton

Please direct to the care of Peter Kelly 511 South 6th St

On June 11, 1865, Patton was sent to the U.S. General Hospital at Fort Barrancas, Florida; he was discharged for disability in September.[26]

CHAPTER SIX

Navigating Military Justice

Civil War soldiers could be tried in several different types of military courts. Field officer courts, regimental courts-martial, and garrison courts-martial could try minor offenses and were limited in the types and severity of punishments they could mete out. More serious offenses, including capital cases as well as those involving officers, were tried by general courts-martial. General courts-martial could range in size from five to thirteen members. A simple majority could find a defendant guilty, and two-thirds could sentence death. All but one of the letters in this chapter were written by men who had been tried and convicted by general courts-martial.

The most recent analysis of general courts-martial cases involving African American defendants found that "black soldiers enjoyed high standards of fairness and due process when facing general courts-martial." According to historian Christian Samito, "While endemic racism in the Union army tainted the disciplinary process on other levels, the records reveal that officers on general court-martial panels wrestled with providing fair judicial process to black defendants while maintaining discipline so that African American soldiers received equal treatment and justice in cases involving capital-level crimes." From his examination of the records, Samito concludes that the white officers presiding over cases often sought ways to grant leniency to black soldiers who were convicted of various crimes—particularly since those who were protesting injustice were often justified in their complaints (for example, many black soldiers mutinied when they were not given the same pay as white soldiers, as they had been promised when they enlisted).[1]

Participating in trials by court-martial played a significant role in the political socialization of African Americans during the Civil War era. Ira Berlin and the editors of the Freedmen and Southern Society Project concluded that the process of bringing black soldiers into the military justice system helped teach ex-slaves how to live under the rule of law. Military justice introduced African Americans to formal judicial procedures—they could testify against whites, cross-examine witnesses, and appeal convictions through the military chain of command. If they believed themselves wrongly convicted, they could even petition the secretary of war or Lincoln.[2] As such, their experiences in military courts "helped prepare them for civilian life in a society at least nominally ruled by law."[3]

Four Black Soldiers Ask for Equal Pay and to Be Allowed to Fight

The Fourteenth Corps d'Afrique was organized at New Orleans in August 1863 and was stationed around the city as part of the Union defenses. In October 1863, the regiment was transferred to the District of West Florida, and in April 1864, it was redesignated the Eighty-Sixth USCT. Like many other black soldiers, the noncommissioned officers of this regiment asked for equal treatment as white soldiers.

> Barrancas West Fla Pensacola Bay
> Jan 16th 1864
>
> Honorable Abraham Lincon Presedent of the united States
> Sir
>   we the undersign non commissioned offerciers So called and Your Most humble Servant off The fourteenth Regiment Corps de afrique we ask off You to gain information wether we Ar to have the Same treatment bestowed on ous As all off the Regtiments that is now fighting In the field to bestow [restore?] the union as it was
>   Please Your Honor   we inlisted to fight For our country and for the laws off the Land   we have tryed to do so ever sence we Have been in the Service and that has been Six Months, and ever Sence we landed on this peninsula we have done our utmost in pretecting goverment property   Thare has not been a call for defending The cause that we ar fighting for Sence we Have been on this peninsula that we refused To do,   thay tell ous for working quality we ar fare surperior to all the white regtment and for fighting we will never faulter From that
>   Please Your Honor   sence we have Been on this peninsula for the defence off The Navy Yard we have thowing up breats Works [been throwing up breastworks] from the bay to the buyio and all off the fettuge duty is preformed by this regiment and the grand out post is preformed by ous   also the line off pickets Exstend for nine Miles
>   Please Your Honor   when we inlisted in the united States Service the understanding was that we Should recieve the Same pay and rattion as the white Soldiers   we have the Same felling For our Wifes and Chrildrens at home and we Study the wellfare off them as much so

as the white Soldiers,   the majoyity off the Men in this Regtiment have familys in New orleans and from letters recieved here Thay ar in a Starving condistion   thare are Some four or five oderly Sergant that have wife In the North how is Exspecting to derived off ous something to live on   we cant seport Them on Seven dollas per a month—

Please Your Honor

all we ask for is Justist Bestowed on ous and thare Shant be one Star on the Glourious banner off liberty that wont Shine out Brightly over all off the patriots Fighting to montaining your most just law

Please Your Honor we dont looke for Eney better treatment than the white Soldiers but the Same   the cannon and Rifles ball have not a bit off respects off person in action   our lives is as Sweet to ous as it is to them that recieves thirteen Dollars per month

Please Your Honor

when you called for Soldiers off african desent I John. H. Morgan the writeter off this letter was in the western army off the united States in the capacity off A Servant   I left and went home to Cincinnati to inlist to fight for My Country   Me and My Nefphew thought our Serviceses would be more needed in this department   as soon vickburg and Port Hudson was takeing⁴ we come to New Orleans to inlist in army off the Gulf   of [if?] Congrees has passed a law to pay the black Soldiers Seven dollas per Month I would like transferd to a northing regiment—

Please Your Honor

for drill this regiment Can not be exceled for the time that we have Been in the Service,   thare ar five off the first Sergents that can read and write and can Preform all off the dutys off a Sergent—

Please your Honor

this letter is from the sergants Fourteenth Regtment Corps de Afrique   Writting by John. H. Morgan   first sergant   Company K

Wᵐ J Barcroff   first Sergent   Cᵒ H.

William. D. Mayo   first Sergent   Cᵒ D

John Talor   first Sergant   Cᵒ A

Your most humble and obidients Servants⁵

The harsh sting of injustice may have taken a toll on at least two of the signatories of this letter. Sgt. William J. Barcroft, a twenty-three-year old barber from New York City, was later found guilty of saying that "there were colored people enough in the city of Mobile to take it" and that he and his comrades "would kill every white son of a bitch in the city, or that he would lead them to hell." On another occasion, Barcroft struck one of his white officers in the face and threatened to shoot him.[6]

On May 8, 1864, Sgt. William D. Mayo, a forty-three-year-old native of Washington, D.C., refused the orders of a superior officer to have his company clean part of the regimental grounds. Mayo was placed under arrest but left his quarters without permission. He then gathered together eight or ten privates from his company and paraded them to regimental headquarters, telling them "that he loved his men and would live by them & die by them, and would stand no such work from any Captain and would never go into a fight with Captain [John A.] Miller and would not soldier under any Captain in the Regt."

Mayo was arraigned before a general court-martial and found guilty of disobedience of orders. The court sentenced him to be reduced to the ranks; to have his chevrons, buttons, and other insignia cut off; to be drummed out of camp; and to be imprisoned at the Dry Tortugas at hard labor for the remainder of his enlistment. Mayo arrived at the Dry Tortugas on September 24, 1864.[7] About two weeks later, he wrote the following letter to Lincoln:

> Fort Barrancas 1864
> Florida Oct 7
>
> To The Honerable Abrham Lincon
>   I your Partishener W^m D Mayo 1st Sarg^t C^o D. 86 cullard Infentry of L.A. will now state to you the condishons I am in being confined in the Provost Guard House under the sentanc of A Genl Cort Marshal held hear on the 8^inst of Aug last   this centence being to serve a turm of one year and 9 months hard Labour without pay on Torturgas Island   the charges bein aganst me is 1st disobediants of Orders which I can proove I am not guilty of by over 25 of the same Reg^t   charge 2^d Breach of Arest which I plead guilty to under those surmstances,   thare was a Private John Vier suffering punishment in the way of Riding a Wooden Horse   the word came to me that he had falen from the horse dead   I was excited and Humanity hurid me to his asistince at once not remembering that I was under arest untell My Capt ordred me back to my quarters which I returned to amediatly   charge 3^d Mutinus conduct in that I W^m D Mayo gathered some 6 or 8 men and said I would not serve under Capt Miller enny longer which they faild to proove and which I can say before God and Man I never uterd   one thing more I will draw your attention to is I was denyed the privaleges of having some 25 witesness who I could of Prooved my entire

inocences by and alowed but 2 only   thare being two comishend
Officers against me I was suposed of course to be guilty. under this
unlawfull and unjust punishment I can but Apeal to your Honner for
Justice in this case   in a pucenarury point of view I say nothing
however I will say one thing   I am getting towards 50 years of age and
my Wife is over fifty and Goverment will hav to suport [her] while I am
redy willing and able to as enny good Loyal man can   I hav ben always
bn faithfull and don My Duty as a Souldier should and concequenuly
I want Justice don me in return by hir   when I was sent to the Guard
house I was deprived of My own private property   I had the Army
Regulations that I bought and paid for with mis own money, and
charged me with reading that which a Nigar had no buisness to know.
now Dear Sir I Apeal to a Greate Man a man that is governing this
Nation to govern the Justice and punishment that is delt out to one of
its Faithfull subjects

 I Remain Your Obediant Servent

 W^m, D, Mayo 1st Sarg^t C^o D, 86 Cullard Infantry
Barrancas Florida

It took military authorities several months to locate a record of Mayo's
trial. Finally, on May 13, 1865 (a month after Lincoln was assassinated), an
officer replied to Mayo stating that "an investigation into the merits of your
case . . . shows no grounds to justify the exercise of Executive clemency in
your behalf." Mayo remained in prison until he was released by order of the
War Department in December 1865.[8]

A Deserter Asks for Clemency

On the night of October 5, 1863, Corp. John Johnson of the Fifteenth Corps
d'Afrique (later designated the Ninety-Ninth U.S. Colored Infantry) deserted
from his regiment at Brashear City, Louisiana. A former slave who had actually been born in Baltimore, Johnson was eventually discovered at the Louisiana plantation where he had formerly been enslaved, and on January 16,
1864, he was returned to his regiment as a prisoner.

At Johnson's trial for desertion, which commenced on February 6, the only
witness was a white officer from Johnson's company who testified that Johnson "had been complaining of illness for quite a while and had requested several times to return home to be cured." The officer also stated, however,
that Johnson seemed "discontented" because he had been promised promo-

tion to sergeant by an officer in another company, but the promotion had never happened. When asked about Johnson's intelligence, the witness replied, "I believe him to be nothing extraordinary as regards intelligence," but he was "sufficiently intelligent to understand the penalty of desertion." The witness also claimed that at one time the Articles of War—the laws defining desertion and other military crimes—had been read every Sunday morning, but "lately they have not been read so often."[9] Finally, the witness testified that Johnson had a wife at his old plantation and that he appeared "quite well" when he was arrested.

Johnson offered no evidence or defense and never cross-examined the witness. He was found guilty and sentenced to be reduced to the ranks and imprisoned at hard labor for ten years without pay. Upon reviewing the case, a superior officer reduced the sentence to five years. From prison, Johnson sent the following letter to Lincoln:

> Fort Jefferson   Florida
> August [illegible character] 13th 1864
>
> To Mr lincoln   Dear sir
> I wish to state my case to you   I am hear in prison in fort Jefferson and was cortmarshell as a desirter and it was sumthing knowd nothing about   that is for to leave the Righ [regiment] for good   it is sumthing I never thought of   I went away from the righment because I was sick   stade untell I got well and I went and give myself up to them for the sake of giting Back to the rigment a gaine   but littel did I think that it wase that much harme   I told them that I did not leave for good and thay never red no Laws [the Articles of War] to mee   and I was so glad to get back to the righment and then thay courtmarshell mee and I never knowd that It was any harme for aman to leave the army to get well when he wase sick   thay put mee in prison   I like to be a souldere very well becouse when I listed for i did not [receive] any money   I listed for to trie to be a servist to the united states and I wish to go back againe to the righment againe as I com out for a souldere   so I wish you to parding me whare I am wroung though it wase veary well that thay put me in prison for it made me know sumthing about souldering that I never would have knowd about souldering   I have no more
> John Johnson
> Comp A   15 Lousiana Volingtares
> Cor d Africans

On September 10, Lincoln's private secretary John G. Nicolay referred Johnson's letter to the judge advocate general. The Bureau of Military Justice wrote a report on the case, but unfortunately one-third of the paper is missing. It is unknown exactly how Lincoln responded to Johnson's letter; however, Johnson remained in prison until September 1865, and he mustered out in April 1866.[10]

A Sergeant Incites Mutiny and Threatens a Superior Officer

By the spring of 1864, Sgt. Adam Laws of the Nineteenth USCT had become angry at how the soldiers in his regiment "had been abused by their officers, struck down in the ranks, struck in the breasts with the butts of muskets, and it was time there was a change." Laws declared that black soldiers "were *men*" who were "fighting for their country," and they deserved to be treated as such. Eventually the disaffection felt by the men erupted in protest, and Laws was arrested and court-martialed for his role in it.

Laws was charged with inciting a mutiny on April 17 at his regiment's camp near Baltimore and saying that "the Government had swindled them [black soldiers] and lied to them — that they didn't even pay them the beggarly seven dollars a month"—and that if black soldiers refused to fight, there would not be enough other soldiers to force them. Laws was also accused of leading his comrades in attacking a black sutler in their camp and destroying his wares, claiming that he was a "rebel" and a "traitor" who had threatened to raise five thousand troops for the Confederate army.

A few days later, on April 23, the regiment left its camp near Annapolis and halted near a railroad line, where Laws purchased a few pies from "some hucksters" on the side of the road. Col. Henry G. Thomas of the Nineteenth USCT saw Laws away from the regiment and ordered him to return into line, but Laws had paid for the pies with a five-dollar bill and was waiting for his change. Laws replied that he "would go when he got ready and not before."

When Colonel Thomas responded that Laws would be arrested for disobeying orders, Laws allegedly retorted, "God damn you don't you lay your hand on me[;] if you do it will be the last man you will ever put your hand on." Laws then grabbed "a large club" and swore that "he had been imposed upon long enough receiving no pay" and that if the enlisted men of the regiment would get their arms and "only stand by him there were not men enough in the Division to put them down." After being arrested, Laws allegedly threatened his colonel again, saying, "Damn you, you shall suffer for this." For these actions, Laws was charged with threatening a superior officer.

At his trial in August, Laws pleaded not guilty to all of the charges and specifications. Colonel Thomas testified that Laws had been absent without leave on the morning of April 23, and that when he returned to camp "he commenced dancing about and shouting, behaving in a very unseemly and disrespectful manner . . . swearing and making a disturbance." However, other witnesses contradicted Thomas's testimony, stating that Laws had not been AWOL and that other soldiers had also stepped out of line to purchase things from the hucksters. Moreover, they claimed that Thomas appeared to have shoved Laws, and that Laws did not have a club but a walking stick.

The court found Laws not guilty of inciting mutiny and threatening a superior officer, but guilty of conduct prejudicial to good order and military discipline. It sentenced him to six months at hard labor at Fort Jefferson in the Dry Tortugas. The commanding general approved the proceedings of the trial on August 31. From prison, Laws sent the following letter to Lincoln:

Oct. 7th /64
Castle Williams.

President.

Dear sir.

I have been arrested, and sent to castle Williams and the case i will state to you. My Colonel Henry G. Thomas, ordered me to my company one day. When i was buying something to eat i started to go to my company and he followed me and drew his Sword to strike me   i turned around and told him not to strike me   i went on to the company and he sent a file of men and had me arrested and i have been coartmarchled and my sentense i have never heared   i know not What it is But i would ask you for Pardon. i have been a soaldier that has always done my duty   i have never so mutch as missed one Roll call, and my Parents look to me for suBsistense   they are old and grey headed and not able to help one another   i am their onley suport they have   sinse i have been in Prison they have suffered   i would sooner serve the Balence of my time for half Pay than to see them suffer While i am in Prison. dear sir, if you Please think of my poor old grey headed Parents   not for my selfe that i weep but for those who cannot help then selves.

Nothing more at Pressent but I still remain a heart broken Soldier ready and willing to take my arms up again and stand in the defense of my country

O grant me that Priveledge if you Please
Most Obiedient Soldier
Adam Laws.
1ˢᵗ Sargent, Co. D.
19ᵗʰ U.S.C.V.

On October 11, Lincoln's private secretary, John Hay, referred Laws's letter and the case file to the judge advocate general of the army, Joseph Holt. Holt summarized the trial proceedings for the president, pointing out that the lieutenant commanding Laws's company considered him "the best soldier in the regiment," who was "always a good soldier, and very respectful to his officers." Normally Holt would recommend whether or not Lincoln should issue a pardon, but in this case Holt left it to Lincoln "to determine whether the ends of justice have been satisfied by his confinement since the commission of the offence in April 1864."

Upon reviewing the case in January 1865, Lincoln ordered that Laws be released from prison and restored to duty. Laws returned to his regiment as a private but was promoted back to sergeant on July 31, 1865. He mustered out with his regiment at Brownsville, Texas, on January 15, 1867.[11]

A Black Soldier Asks for Release from the Guardhouse

James T. S. Taylor, a twenty-three-year-old laborer from Charlottesville, Virginia, was drafted into the Second USCT in August 1863. While at the front, Taylor kept the readers of the New York *Anglo-African* newspaper abreast of the movements of his regiment. In January 1864, he told them that the regiment "received a most favorable and kind reception from the citizens, both white and colored," when they passed through Philadelphia and New York. A few months later, however, the men of the Second USCT received a different reception when passing through a southern city. "They looked at us with as much wonder as though it was the first sight they ever beheld," wrote Taylor, "and the last one they ever expected to see in this world." Taylor also impressed upon his readers that the men of the Second USCT were eager "to strike a blow at rebeldom" and to fight "for liberty and freedom to the oppressed of our native land." Taylor's positive attitude and literary abilities must have made a positive impression on his superior officers, for on November 10, 1863, he was promoted to commissary sergeant of his regiment.[12]

While stationed in Florida in the summer and fall of 1864, Taylor was caught stealing rations from the subsistence stores and selling them to a local baker named Moffat. The officers of the Second USCT confronted Taylor, but he "denied having sold any rations very stoutly." When they "pressed" him on it, however, he confessed and told them that the $500 he had received "was in the hands of a colored citizen of Key West." The officers recovered the money and arrested both Taylor and Moffat. Moffat was held over for trial in the federal district court in Florida, whereas Taylor was arraigned before a military court. Lt. Col. John Wilder noted that Taylor "has the merit of giving up the $500 which probably he might have effectually concealed."[13]

While awaiting trial, Taylor sent the following letter to Lincoln:

Head Quarters 2nd: U.S. Infantry Col^d
Fort Taylor Key West Fla: Nov. 15th 1864.
A Petition To Mr. A. Lincoln President U.S.A. —
To your excellency from A Non Commission Officer in the colored Service. In Jestification to my self I cannot help from Appealing to you for some assistance under existing Circumstances. I should have Refrained from Acquainting your Distinguished honor and high Abilities with this affair, but as I enlisted in the U.S. service in Washington D.C. — I cannot have no better Source to apply for aid than to ask A favor from your Hands. and even urgent necessities in Behalf of myself compels me to do so, particularly at the present time. I was Appointed Regular Commissary Sergeant for the 2nd: Regiment U.S.I.C. Nov. 25th. 1863. by the Sanction and approval of Gen. [Silas] Casey whilst the Regiment was Organizing at Camp Casey Virginia near Washington D.C. — I continued in that capacity till the 6th. of this month when I was taken from the post Commissary here in Key West and confined in Fort Taylor for selling Subsistence stores to A citizen which A large po[r]tion of the citizens here have permission from the Commanding General to purchase Government store for thir own use. however I never Received any Orders from my Superior Officer not to do the same and All the Funds which I Received from time to time were refunded by me to our chief Officer Lt: Col. Wilder now in command at Fort Taylor. I am very Desirous of being Releaved or Release from this Imprisonment and captiverty being permitted if possible to seek A higher branch in the service which I think would only be Jestice, as I haveing left my home in Charlottesville Alb. *Co:* Virginia two years Ago to Avoid the Rebel service my Journey was All

most imparellel in Deluding the Rebel pickets and finally Reaching the union lines in safety. I reported at the Head Quarters: of Gen: [Alexander] Hays witch ware at Union Mills Va. Immediate on the Orange & Alexandria R.R:—the General Retained me and those Accompanied me at his H^d: Qurs: two weeks During which time I give him All the Information respecting the enemy and whereabouts that I know of. if my humble Appeal be Granted the favour would be thankfully Received and I hail with Joy that this may meet A favourable Consideration on your part. I am Sir your humble soldier.

    J. T. S. Taylor.

    2nd: U.S. Infantry Colored[14]

While the circumstances are unclear, Taylor does not appear to have ever gone to trial, and he was released from prison on March 2, 1865. Even while he was being detained at his regimental headquarters, he continued to send letters to the *Anglo-African*. In one letter, dated January 2, 1865, Taylor advocated for "equal privileges" for black soldiers, maintaining that African American men should be given the opportunity to lead black troops as regimental officers. "This spirit certainly does not agree with that manifested by the President in his different proclamations," wrote Taylor. "Are we still to be deprived of all those rights and privileges which, by our sacrifices, we justly merit? This nation had to be taught some very severe lessons by Providence before they would even let the negro have a musket, and now, not until equal rights are given us as soldiers, will the God of all Wisdom lead the nation to a victorious triumph and a lasting peace."

Six weeks after his release, on April 18, Taylor married Eliza DeLancey, a woman he'd met while stationed at Key West. Following Taylor's discharge in 1866, the couple moved to Charlottesville, Virginia, where they lived for much of the remainder of their lives. Taylor achieved a certain level of prominence in the postwar period and in 1867 was elected to Virginia's state constitutional convention. He remained active in politics until his death in 1918.[15]

A Soldier Convicted of Attempted Murder Asks for Pardon

At about 3 P.M. on February 8, 1864, Pvt. James Castle of the Fourteenth Rhode Island Heavy Artillery, an African American regiment, was serving as a sentry at Fort Esperanza on Matagorda Island, Texas, when he called for someone to stand in his place so that he could relieve himself. The other members of the guard expected Castle to return in a little while, but he did not. About four hours later, members of his regiment heard a pistol shot nearby and they found Castle outside camp in a state of intoxication. He was immediately arrested.

Castle was court-martialed and charged with conduct prejudicial to good order and military discipline, assault with intent to kill, and alarming the camp by the discharge of firearms. He pleaded not guilty.

At the trial, which took place on April 21, several witnesses testified that Castle had left his post claiming to be sick but that he never returned. Two black soldiers from the Second Engineers Corps d'Afrique who lived next door to Castle's washerwoman further testified that Castle had caused trouble with them on two consecutive nights. According to Pvt. Prince Sheldon, Castle had showed up at Sheldon's tent on Sunday, February 7, and left "a bottle of Whiskey laying on the floor." When Sheldon asked Castle to leave, Castle allegedly "said he did not care a damn he would come here when he pleased." According to Sheldon, Castle appeared again the next night—February 8— and started another altercation, saying, "By God he would put two balls through me, he wheeled around and pulled his pistol out of his pocket and shot at me, that ball missed me and he shot again and this ball struck me on the wrist." Unlike the other witnesses, Sheldon testified that Castle was probably sober.

Castle was found guilty and sentenced to imprisonment for ten years at hard labor with a ball and chain at the Dry Tortugas, and to forfeit all pay. He began petitioning military authorities for pardon almost immediately. On May 1, 1864, while still in Texas, he sent the following letter to Lincoln:

> metgora Iland Pass Cove valey Texas
> may the 1th
> Dear sir   I wish to in forme you of my bad situashen   I wasas A privet in the 14 rodiland Colard rigment   on the 8th of genreyway [January] I was on gard At the fort expranze [and] taken sick with A griping Pane in my stumek   [I] cald for the corple of the gard And wase realeave [and] went to my tente   [I] stade their Aboat half A nouer [an hour] got no beter left my tent To get some white oke barke to make some tea   I was told that it god for me   I cold not git None   I went to the 2th louisna rignent   was Toald that whisk and red peper was good for me   I got A bottle of it to the settlers [sutlers]   I went from their to wasch woommen whitch was Betwene the tow camps by A crick to her hose Where I had some close [and] hask hur for them   she told me to set [sit] down they wood be redey soon   I told hur that

I was sick [and] hask Hur to make me some hot whiskey and Put some peper in it   she did so   I drink A teacup full   A woomem of culler came in Asked me for some of the whiskey   I tolder Hur to take it   she did so and went in Hur one house or hut   in about ten minet A man came in wheir I was [and he] ask me if That was my bottel   I told him it was   He told me that he did want now one To fetch whiskey around their   I must go away or elce he wood nock me away   I Toald him that I came their to git my Close and not to quarl and was not In his house   he sed he did not care for That I must go   he drow A stick on me   At the time I drow my revolver [and] told him if he hit me I wood put A hole Thro him   I went out of the dore   he folerd me   I fird over his sholder twice as Near as I can gess   did not try to hit Him   I fird to ceap him from harmeing me then run to the camp   being Excited doant now what I sead when I Came to camp

I wase arrected soon after put in dubl Irens cep thre 3 months and cort marcle Fond gilty   I had no witness [because] the tow weman was gone to new orleans   they give me ten years ball and chane   I inlected [enlisted] or came with the recuting oficer From chatthem canaday west [Chatham, Ontario, Canada]   [I] have A mother their [and] I am hur onley suport   [my] father Is dead   I beg A faver of you to parden me for my mothers sake   if I not she will fall one the town for she hase no sport

James Castle

Upon reviewing Castle's letter and the trial transcript on May 27, Judge Advocate General Holt wrote that the proof at the trial "was very conclusive" and that Castle had provided "no mitigating circumstances" in his letter. Holt therefore recommended against any remission of the punishment. A white officer similarly wrote on July 1 that this "is a *hard case* he has given me more trouble than any other man in the Regt. He has often threatened to kill his officers." Castle's request was denied.

From prison at the Dry Tortugas, Castle sent another letter to Lincoln some time in November 1864:

To His Excelance Aberaham Linken   Preseandent of the uni states
    Der sir   I wish to infrme you of my present sicuashun   I am A prisener at fort jefercon For ten years Csharge of salt [assault] and Temt [attempt] to kill and leaving my post At fort ~~jefere~~ Expranzy texas   on the 8 of jenury I Cald for the Corple of the gard while I was On post   he came I told him I Was sick with A pane in my stumick

and I wanted to go to The rear [and] he reavedle [relieved?] me   I
went To the rear was taken worse went To the dekters tent ask for the
Dockter   I was told he was gone to The other end of the iland   [I] went
To my tent lade down [but] got now Better   was told that red peper
And brandy was good for me   I got up and wen[t] to the setlers of The
seckent louisna ingeners [engineers] and got it   went from thir to my
Watcher woomens witsh was betwene The two campes to git some
clean Close   while thir tow colard solgers Of the seckent louisna came
in the Hut [and] sed to me that I must go A Way from the place   [They]
sed some of Ouir men had mad some noise their The night before   Ɨ I
told them That I node nothing about it [and] that I had come for my
close [and] that Was All   the weemen told them the same that I had
yoused them Like A gentleman ever since They had bin washing for
me   They sed that thay thy had made up thir minds to not Let our
men come around thir eney more that I had better git Away [and] if I
did not they wood Throw me in A crick witch Was in frunt of the house
Or hut   I drowed my revolver And shot twice [two words crossed out]
one ball wetn [went] over one sholder The other A fleach wonde [flesh
wound] in his Arm   I was cort marshel [and] got Ten years   the two
weeman wir sent to new orleans before my Trile came of[f] sow I had
now Witness   I belong to the 14 rodiland Colard rigment   I have got
A mother That is poor [and] I am hur onley support   she is old and
doant live in this Cruntry   she is in cshatam canada West
    Please your Excelance to parden Or releace me from arrest—
    Jame W. Castle

Castle persisted. On December 22, 1864, he sent another letter (written
in another hand) to Secretary of War Stanton, further explaining the situation. According to this letter, the officer in command of Matagorda Island
"sent the [washer] woman away to New Orleans so that they could not appear on the trial in my defence, & I was not tried until *3 months afterwards*,
held in double irons, & close confinement all the time."

Upon reviewing the case again in January 1865, Judge Advocate General
Holt's Bureau of Military Justice reported "that without more satisfactory evidence of merits than the mere assertions of the prisoner, which are totally in
conflict with the facts testified to at the trial, mitigation of punishment cannot be recommended." Lincoln therefore again chose not to act in this case.

But Castle would not give up. In August 1865, he appealed to President
Andrew Johnson and included a statement from twelve of his guards at Fort

Jefferson that he "has been ready and attentive to his duties & we consider him worthy of executive clemency." In September Judge Advocate General Holt recommended that in light of "the reformation promised by his good conduct during the imprisonment he has undergone of seventeen months," Johnson might mitigate his sentence to five years and "without further punishment with ball and chain." Johnson, in fact, went several steps further. He ordered the prisoner's release in February 1866, and Castle walked free on March 14.[16]

A Former Servant of Ulysses S. Grant Asks for Pardon

Franklin Smith was twenty-six years old when he enlisted as a private in the Twenty-Eighth USCT at Indianapolis on Christmas Eve 1863. On July 17, 1864, he was arrested for causing a mutiny near the tent of an officer of the Nineteenth USCT. According to the charges against him, Smith had "created an uproar, by loud cursing and swearing" at his camp near Petersburg, Virginia. When he was ordered to be quiet, he stripped off his clothes "as if to fight" and swore at the officer, saying, "God damn you, I am on my own ground, and you have nothing to do with me" and "The damned son of a bitch if he touches me I will knock his damned head off."

At his trial, Smith pleaded guilty to the charges against him and was sentenced to imprisonment for the remainder of his enlistment and forfeiture of all pay. He was sent to Fort Delaware. From there, he sent the following letter to Lincoln:

> Fort D[e]lawar[e]
> October the 29 1864
>
> President Lincoln   Sur
> I apeal to your Great orthority For gustes [justice] As i am one of the Colerd Soldiers of Compny B 28 USA Colard troupes   I was at play when a Liutenet that had not Eny Straps on trid to put me in the Guard house
> And I resisted him not knoing That he was an oficer   I didnot Think that I was doing eny Thing rong   tharefore I hop That you will look at my Case and if posibel repreve me, If you pleas
> Franklin Smith
> I am A poor frendlis Boy put hur and my money All taking away from me   I weighted om Lieutenent Genreal Grant 2 years   he no my Cariter [character] af enyone does

Smith's letter passed through several hands in the executive branch of the government. Docketing on the back of the letter and elsewhere in the case file reveals that several people took note of his service to Ulysses S. Grant. On July 14, 1865, Secretary of War Stanton remitted the unexpired period of Smith's sentence.[17]

A Scuffle with a White Officer Leads to an Arrest

On August 8, 1864, the buglers of the Third U.S. Colored Cavalry were summoned to regimental headquarters, but one of them, David Washington (sometimes spelled Washiton), a twenty-five-year-old teamster from Mississippi, was absent. Capt. Andrew Emery of Co. B later learned that Washington had gone into downtown Vicksburg. When Emery confronted Washington the next day, he "denied being absent, and said that he could prove it by other boys." But Emery claimed that rather than go gather his proof, Washington instead went to the colonel of the regiment "and complained . . . that I had abused him and that I had had him tied up for a number of hours without cause." (Tying up black soldiers by their thumbs so that they were forced to stand on tiptoe was a cruel, painful, and humiliating punishment that black soldiers resented because of its reminiscence of slavery.)

When Washington returned to the company, Emery told him that he would "tie him up," but Washington retorted "that he would not be tied up but would go and complain again to the Colonel." At that point Emery tried to tie Washington up. According to Emery, Washington "struck at me and resisted a good deal until I was obliged to call for help." Lt. Joseph R. Randall rushed to the scene and helped Emery tie up Washington, but thirty or forty-five minutes later they discovered that somebody had cut him down. Angry about what had transpired, Washington then left camp. Two days later he was discovered back in Vicksburg. He was arrested, put in jail, and court-martialed for insubordination and desertion.

At the trial, Washington claimed that Emery had struck him "before I pulled away from him," but Randall countered, "I do not remember that I saw the Capt. strike you[;] you made considerable resistance and cause[d] considerable of a struggle before you could be arrested."

In his defense, Washington claimed that the adjutant of the regiment had sent him down to Vicksburg to get a watch, but he did not have any proof to present to the court. Washington called one defense witness, Corp. Allen Kelley, but Kelley's testimony did not do much to help Washington's cause.

When he asked Kelley whether he had seen the captain jerk him to the ground and strike "me in the face at this time with a revolver," Kelley replied, "I saw the Capt. jerk you down in the struggle, I did not see the Capt. strike you, the Capt. did not have his revolver until after you commenced resisting violently when he called for it."[18]

The court found Washington guilty of both charges and sentenced him to one year at hard labor and loss of all pay and allowances. From the military prison at Vicksburg, Washington sent the following letter to Lincoln:

Vicksburg miss November the 26 /64
to the Mr. A. Lincon Presedent of the U S A

Dear Sir itestifie that David Washiton a Bugler of co B thurd US Colerd Calalry My Capt fell out with me fer what I dont know he struck me [and] I came up to the courthouse and reported him Genl. Slomkum [Henry W. Slocum] made me stay at the courthouse untill my capt get hear it was too days be fore my capt come up the capt he then come up frome campt and reported me feradeserter I was put in geail on the 7[the] of August 1864 I am put [in] prson fer twelve month all lowents [allowances] and pay stoped the cort says it can not do me enny good as my cpt reported me as a dezerter and Genal. Slomkem was not hear at time of my tryl if he had bin hear I wood came clear I am agood solger all ways has done what is right my cap[t] drew apistole on me iam will[ing] to do what right yet my [illegible word][19] will so to I drop thes fewlines asking fer Jested [justice] I ought not to be in prson if I had Jested done me I am a colerd man I have no edication I dont know nothing at all abought law I am willing to do all I can for you as [a] solger or a man if you pleas doe all you can fer me pleas let me hear from you

I am respectfully yours
David Washiton
in Vicksburg miss in prson

In December 1864, the War Department replied to Washington that the secretary of war found "no sufficient grounds for interference" in the case. At some point Washington was transferred to Gratiot Street Prison in St. Louis, from which place the War Department released him in September 1865.[20]

A Murderer's Wife Asks for Mercy for Her Husband

Alfred H. Chapman was twenty-nine years old when he enlisted in the Twenty-Seventh USCT at Columbus, Ohio, on February 11, 1864. Chapman had been born in Ross County, Ohio, and worked as an engineer. He was appointed first sergeant in Company D but was reduced to the ranks on August 24. He was promoted to corporal a few months later, on October 21. On the evening of November 12, Chapman was in the cook's tent near Petersburg, Virginia, distributing rations when twenty-year-old Private Randolph Burr entered and asked for bread. Chapman told Burr that he'd already gotten his rations. When Burr replied that he had not, Chapman called him a "damned liar" and told him to leave the tent. When Burr refused, Chapman shot him with a musket. The bullet entered Burr's chest and passed through his stomach. When an officer arrived at the scene, Chapman denied having shot Burr. But the officer then found the wounded Burr at the doctor's tent and learned about the argument that had precipitated the shooting. Burr died in the predawn hours of the following morning.

Chapman was arrested and court-martialed for murder. At the conclusion of the trial, he claimed that Burr "had always quarreled about his rations" and that "he would come and get rations and hide them away, and then come after more; and that Burr had threatened to knock him in the head with a club." Nevertheless, the court found Chapman guilty and sentenced him to be hanged.

On December 9, 1864, Chapman's wife, Martha, sent a letter to Union general Ulysses S. Grant, asking that her husband's sentence "be suspended and unexecuted until such time when she can be more fully hea[r]d, on behalf of her said husband." She asked this on behalf of herself and her "six small and helpless children." As Martha was unable to write, the letter bore her mark rather than a signature. In support of her request, the mayor of Chillicothe and three other men signed her letter. That same day, she sent the following letter to Lincoln. Curiously, the letter to the president was written in a different hand and was not signed with her mark.

Chillicothe. Dec 9th 1864.

To His Honor the President of the U.S.

It is with great trepidation, I intrude on your Excellency, to ask your clemency in behalf of my husband Alfred H. Chapman, Sergeant, Co D, 27. U.S.C.T. Liut, Frank K. Larabee, Commanding Co. — who has been Court-Marshaled for killing one of his comrades, while under the influence of liquor.

I would humbly beg of your Honor, to commute his sentence if it is in your judgement possible. He has always been considered an inoffensive person; his own worst enemy; he would drink too much   I know nothing of the particulars; only the sad situation in which he is placed.

Again I would beg your Honor to give another instance of the mercy, for which you are so b[e]loved by others as unfortunate as your humble servant

Martha Chapman

Chillicothe

To the President of the US.

PS. your excelency   he is at camp near petersburg South side railroad. Alferd H. Chapman your excelency, Soon as you get this pardom him if you please for fear he Be dead

While it is not entirely clear what happened, Chapman appears to have escaped from confinement at the headquarters of the Third Division, Twenty-Fifth Army Corps, in March 1865.[21]

A Bounty Jumper Seeks Pardon for Desertion

Born free in Cincinnati, Ohio, Isaiah Price was a twenty-five-year-old barber when he enlisted as a private in the Fifty-Fifth Massachusetts Volunteer Regiment on November 30, 1863. A few months later, in February 1864, Price was granted a brief furlough, but when he did not return to his regiment at its expiration, he was labeled a deserter. In May, Price appeared at Gallops Island in Boston Harbor, where he attempted to enlist as a private in the Fifth Massachusetts Cavalry (possibly under the alias William Johnson). Someone there recognized him as having belonged to the Fifty-Fifth Massachusetts, and he was placed under arrest for desertion.

On Thursday, June 9, 1864, a court-martial convened at the Draft Rendezvous on Gallops Island, and Price was arraigned for desertion. The first specification described the circumstances surrounding his furlough and arrest. The second specification stated that he enlisted as a private in the Fifth Massachusetts Cavalry without being discharged from the Fifty-Fifth Massachusetts. Price pleaded guilty to both specifications but not guilty to the charge. He chose not to call any witnesses but made the following address to the court: "Five of us enlisted in Boston, for infantry some of them did. They asked me what I wanted to go into Infantry or Cavalry. I told them I would go into Cavalry. Those other fellows all went into 55th Mass Infty and

I guess he put me down for that too. After I did not go into the Cavalry I suppose he put me down for Infantry. I wanted to go in the cavalry in the first place. That is all." With this the court found Price guilty of desertion and sentenced him to be shot to death by musketry. Upon reviewing the case, Maj. Gen. John A. Dix mitigated the sentence to imprisonment at the Dry Tortugas for the remainder of his enlistment with loss of all pay.

While confined at Gallops Island, Price's conduct was "very good, with a few exceptions." As a consequence, he was permitted to walk freely about the camp and was required to do "little hard fatigue duty, but has served as barber for the Provost Guard." On October 31, 1864, Price sent a petition to General Dix, claiming that his confinement "is daily causing a severe injury to his health" and asking for the papers from his trial to be forwarded to the commander of the post where he was confined. Two months later, Price sent the following letter to Lincoln. The letters to Dix and Lincoln are in different hands, and Price's enlistment record is marked with an "X," indicating that he was likely illiterate.

Please preuse this letter through before casting it aside

Ca[s]tle Williams
New york harbour   Jan 11[th] 65

to Abe Linclon   Presrd

Sir—as I am fifteen hundred miles away from home and have no friends to attend to my case nor any officers to aid me I thought I would appeal to you to see if you would not do something for me in regard to my case   I enlisted in Nov. 64 for the 55th Mass. colered vol.   after I had been enlisted about a month I received a pass from Brig'd general, Devans [Charles Devens] on Long island boston harbour Mass. for twenty four hours and as I had not been home for six months before I whent home and failed to return at the specified time untill nearly two months had expired   when I returned I was asshamed to go back to the island so I whent to some men who I thought where friends to me [and asked them] what I had best do to keep from punishment   they told me I had better reinlist in the 5th Mass. col. Cavalry   so bing ignorant in regard to military affairs so I done as they advised thinking it would be best for me and returned to the island   they arrested me in may 64 on a charge of desertion and reinlisting   they tried me about the first of june and kept me waiting my sentance eight months when my sentance was to serve the remainder of my time at Dry Tortugas which time amounts to one year and eleven months and all pay stopped. I think it is pretty hard   I would not care so much for myself but I have a wife and two little children in Cario, Ill,   my wife has no way to get along for she cant draw any state aid fro [for] she lives in Cario, Ill, and I enlisted in Boston   the children bing small she cannot leave them to go out to work   she has to go out and gather up her washing and do it at home the best way she can,   she keeps writing to me for money and I have none to send to her and times are awful hard with her. I threfore appeal to you to do some-thing for me and [my] family and I will be thankfull and prove my gratitude by being faithfull to you and contry herafter for I am no bounty jumper. I would be thankfull if you would but let me reinlist and would serve you three years faithfully and try and be a good soldier. Sir President I know that it is taking a great liberty in sending to you on subject but I appeal to you as a last resort and trust you will view my case as liently as possible and show some mercy to me and my family for you are my only hope   I have written one letter before but the writing was so poor that I did not send it but I thought I would send this one. Sir would you please answer this and let me know the worst and ease my anxious heart   I know it is asking a good deal but pardon the liberty I have taken in so doing   hoping you will veiw my case favorably   I re[m]ain Yours Respectifully

   Isaiah Price
Castle William
Governors island
N.Y harbour

On January 16, Lincoln's private secretary John G. Nicolay referred this letter to Judge Advocate General Holt. Upon reviewing the letter and court-martial case file, Holt wrote, "It is probable that the prisoner is a 'bounty-jumper,' and it is not believed that he is entitled to any further mitigation of punishment." He remained in prison at Fort Jefferson, Dry Tortugas, until February 21, 1866, when the unexpired portion of his sentence was remit-ted and Price was released from prison.[22]

A Young Black Soldier Refuses to Be Arrested

John Pool was eighteen years old when he enlisted in the Fourteenth Rhode Island Heavy Artillery, a black regiment that came to be known as the Eleventh U.S. Colored Heavy Artillery. The company descriptive book listed Pool as having "African" complexion along with black hair and black eyes. Prior to joining the service in Providence, Rhode Island, on August 27, 1863, Pool had worked as a laborer in New York.[23]

In June 1864, Pool was court-martialed for conduct to the prejudice of good order and military discipline, and showing contempt and disrespect to a superior officer. He had refused arrest after he'd left the guardhouse at Fort Esperanza at Matagorda Island, Texas, without permission on March 29, 1864, shouting, "I will be damned if I let any white officers arrest me." When Lieut. Charles H. Potter tried to tie him up, Pool exclaimed, "I will be damned if I let any white officer tie me. Lieut. Potter is a damned Coward, if I had one of those Bayonets I would stick it through him. You dare not shoot any one you are too big a Coward." Pool pleaded guilty to the charges and specifications except for the words that he would have stuck Potter with a bayonet. At the trial, Lieutenant Potter and another white officer testified that Pool had been intoxicated when the incident took place. Pool offered no testimony or explanation. The court then found him guilty of both charges and specifications and sentenced him to hard labor for the duration of his enlistment, the loss of all pay then and thereafter due him, and a dishonorable discharge from the service.

Pool was sent to Fort Jefferson at the Dry Tortugas. From there he mailed the following letter to Lincoln. He likely did not write this letter himself as his enlistment record contains his mark in place of a signature. The letter was written on Fort Jefferson stationery.

Fort Jefferson, Tortugas, Fla., January 20 1865
To his excelncy Abraham Lincoln Presedent of the U.S. of A.
Mr President.

I have the honor to call your attention to the consideration of my court martual and the charges and specifycation connected there with.

I enlisted in the state servise on about 29 day of August 1863 as a vollenteer for the 14 Rhode Island Hev. Arty know [now] known as the 11 U.S. Hev Arty (Colored)   we enlisted as state troops and where assuered by Gov. James Y. Smith of the Gov. of the state of Rhode Island that we would not be required to leve the state and should receive the some [same] pay and allowenc as all other troops of like Arms of servise   we entered the servise with that assurance and exspectted that all would be right   the first breach of promas that we ware call upon to do was that of leveing the state howevr we did not utter a murmer   we went forth exspecing to me [meet?] what ever the grate monester war had in store for us   we as souldiers exspected fetigue and hardship and even death it selfe if it was required at our hand   everything whent along quietly untill some where about the 30ᵗʰ of march 1864 when we was offered pay at seven dollars per month of which I and the most of Battallion refused   we was call up in line and marched up by companies to receive our pay   some took there pay   I and a number of others refused the pay on the grounds that was the second breach of promas thay had tryed to subject us to. I knew what the U.S. was paying colored soldiers at that time but as we was garrenteered the same pay and allowence as other troops of like arms of servise we exspectted that the state would make up the defitienty [deficiency] and having some money at the time we wanted to wate for our pay untill the will of our Gov. could be known.

not knowing but that we where contending in a civeral [civil] maner for our rights we exspecetted when the will of the Gov. could be known we would receive justice and stated the facts in a polite maner to our supperior offices which immediately ordered us under arrest and refered charges against us of exciting mutenny and disobediance of orders of which I was tryed and sentence herefor the period of two years   know [now] sir I humbley repeal to your honor if we have been justly delt with. if in your judgement we have not I most respectfully request that my sentenc may be repreaved and I return to my duty which I so willingly vollenteered mysulf   should you comply with my request you may rest assuered that I will ever be fond [found] at my duty as long as life and health last or tts untill the grate monester war cloud has banish from of this far [fair] continent.

Very respt your obt servt

John Pool

Co. "C." 14. Rhode Island Hev Arty Coled.

Upon reviewing Pool's case, Judge Advocate General Holt stated that his eight months of confinement seemed to be sufficient punishment for his drunk and disorderly conduct. In March, Pool was ordered to be released from prison and restored to duty.[24]

One Imprisoned Soldier Appeals to the President on Behalf of Another

Jack Morris was twenty-one years old when he enlisted in the First Louisiana Native Guards (later designated the Seventy-Third USCT) at New Orleans in September 1862. In October 1864 he was sentenced by a court-martial to two years' imprisonment at hard labor at the Dry Tortugas for stealing and deserting his post. Unable to write, a fellow prisoner wrote the following letter to Lincoln on his behalf. The writer of the letter, Samuel Roosa of the Seventieth USCT, had previously been recognized by one of his superior officers for being "an excellent penman."

> Fort Jefferson Turtugas Fla. Jenuary 24ᵗʰ 1864 [1865]
> Sir I have the honor to respectfully call your attention to a few remarks which I hope may receive your libral consideration.
>   I am a prisener here at fort Jefferson turtugas fla. I was sentence here for the short period of six months I will not mention the injustice I received at the discretion of my court martrial. for I have but such short period to remain here that I deem it hardly nessessary to enter into the merits of the case. but I shall speek inbehalf of a great number of poor but patriocic colored soldirees who have become victoms to a cruel ponishment for little arror. I will attemp to state in bref the circumstences connected with the case of Jack Morris of Co. "F" 73ᵗʰ U.S. Colored Infy. who enterd the U.S. servise on the 27ᵗʰ day Sept 1862 and was errested on the 27ᵗʰ day of June 1864. and sentenced. on about the 20ᵗʰ day October 1864 at Morganza. having served some two years allmost fathfully without even as much as being once ponish in the lease. He was trie and held to answer the charge of leveing his post he had often been told by his officers he said not to leve his post the consequence of which he know not he having call siveral times for the corporal of the guard but without responce with respects to you sir It being case of necesity he thought that it would not be a killing circumstance as much as he did not go out sight and hearing of his post he was absent but five minits and when he returned the corpral ask him where he had been he told him after which he was poot immediately under arrest. and received a sentence of two years hard labor at this post he is a man of famely and has not had no pay sinc he has been in servise but once and then he received but few months pay at seven dollars per month which of couse couldnot efford his famely

much releaf. I am well awere that every breach of military regulations which officers or soldiers are guilty of is ponishable at the discretion of a propper court martrial but I do say and appeal to your honor that there aut to be a liberal consideration and allowance made for ignorence   the person refered to enfect [in fact] most all of the colored troop recruted in this department with few excepttion are egnorent men who know nothing more then the duties of hard labor and as slaves was held for that perpose and where not permtted to even as much as hendle there masters book. much less having the privelage of reading or even allow the use of a small elementry speling book and of corse are as total egnorent of the regulations as a poor while efrican is of gramer or elgebra. I appeal to your honor and most respectfuly request in the name of him who has at his command the destination of all nations that his sentence may be repreved. he says he dont mind the ponishment that he is receiving here but he would like to be where his servis-eses may be of some use to the contry and the proceeds of which may be used for the support of his famely which is in great need of it   in this department it is different from the most of the military post   the famely of the (colored) soldiers perticularly the poor who are depending upon there husband for support   the most of the inhabitince perticular the welthey portion are so prejudice against the famely of colored soldiers in the US servise that thay wont even give them employment for no prise to sustain if posible the old hipocrittical idea that free colored people wont work and of cours the soldiers families have to suffer   in other states infact in most of the northern states there is releaf fonds but here there is none, and if the only support are taken away by death or any other cause thay must suffer and that severely. for I have been and eye witness to a grate many cases not only deprved of there homes on the a/sc^t [account] of little means of pay there house rent but baught at abased by passes by insulting words such as (now you see what the yenkees will do for you had you not better stay with your masters.) the soldier seeing his famely subject to such crual ponishment and ill treetment does feel some what discuraged when he is ill treeted by thoes who is his only relience is for justice and his present existence for I have never have saw a more solom lot a priseners then I saw here from like circumstances   (all thay have to say that the yankes treat me more woser then the rabs)   for my part I cant complane   I have had evry respect shown me since I have been in the servise with but few exceptions   I even was allowed while under arrest as a freehold cittizon of the state of New York to cast my vote on a ritten form for that perpose for the first time for the candidate of my choise and as we hale the election of the fondor of the proclamation of emencipation we as poor priseners with undanted patriocism to the cause of our contry look foward towards washing[ton] to here something in behalf of poor priseners   we know that your four years of administration has been as berdensome as it has victorious and no dought you have but lettle time to listen to the grate many pleas that comes through such scorce   we do feal as union soldiers that we may ask with that positive assureanc that we will be herd   all we can say that we are sory that we have become victoms to a millitary crime and do senserely repent and ask to be forgiven   we cant do no more   where we to remain here 5 years we should be know less sory then we are know. Very respectfully your humble & obt servt

 Samuel Roosa

On February 26, 1865, Morris sent a letter to the commander at Morganza (where he had committed his crime), stating, "I am sory of ever have committed a crime or a military offence if I should remain here five years I would be no less sory then I am know not on the account of the work we have to perform because we dont have very hard labor but because my poor famely is suffering for a daily support." He wrote that he was willing "to return to my regiment and do my duty as a true and patriotic soldier." Morris was eventually released in November 1865 by order of the War Department.[25]

An Accused Deserter Appeals to Lincoln for Release

On February 11, 1865, William J. Nelson, a twenty-four-year-old from Cincinnati, wrote to Governor John Brough of Ohio from the guardhouse at Todd Barracks near Columbus, Ohio, describing the ordeal of his enlistment in the Twenty-Seventh USCT and subsequent imprisonment for desertion. Shortly after writing this letter, Nelson was transferred to the military prison at Wheeling, West Virginia, and then to Baltimore. From there he sent a nearly identical letter to Lincoln.

 Baltimore Maryland Guard House february 22th 1865
To His Excelency and most hily honored President   to you I look and beg of you to look at my case and take compashion on me   I have bin ronged out of my Writes   a man came to my residence in mercer County ohio and told me that he had authority to get up volenters and

that he Was paying $200 dollars for one year and I thought that I would go for one year so I Went With him and then he made me drunk and sold me to another man for a substitute and did not give me any money atall   and I had marryed a Widdow With eight children Who are depending on me for support and I am a poor colord man havent enything for them to live on except by my labor   and I am in the gard house and cant do enything for them and they have had me ever since the 28 of last month and my family is suffering   in the first place they carryed me to Johnsons island then to camp Delaware[26] and then I found out that I Was sold as a substitute and they tryed to make me be mustered in as a substitute and I Would not   then the soldiers told me that I Was right and they could not hold me and that if I Was to get out and go home that they Would not nor could not disturb me   and so the guards let me out of the camp and I Went home and stayed fore months and then a man came and taken me and put me in prison and they have had me ever since   now to your honor I beg to look on me and see in to my case   I Was born on Walnut hills near Cincinnati ohio and Was sold in tiffin ohio   I never was out of the State till I was taken a prisncr   now I beg your majestys honor to take compashion on me if you please   I am glad that I have the honor of being your Excelency Servant

    William Joseph Nelson

The outcome of Nelson's case is unknown, but his letter nevertheless says a great deal about how a free man of color dealt with a troubling situation. His language reveals how he thought about the unscrupulous methods adopted by some military recruiters—that their practices resembled those of slave traders who bought and sold African Americans for their own (the recruiters' or slave traders') benefit. Also of significance, he took actions on his own to try to gain his freedom, working to win the sympathy of military guards who released him from custody, apparently without formal proceedings. In short, Nelson struggled to solve his own problems and wrote directly to Lincoln only after he had exhausted all other options.[27]

PART III | Chief Citizen

CHAPTER SEVEN

Appealing for Equal Treatment

On May 19, 1864, Abraham Lincoln met with Mary Elizabeth Wayt Booth, the widow of Maj. Lionel F. Booth, a white officer who had fallen in battle when Confederate forces under Nathan Bedford Forrest overran and captured Fort Pillow, Tennessee, on April 12. This particular assault is infamous today because the rebels massacred black Union soldiers who were trying to surrender. At the meeting, Mrs. Booth tried to persuade Lincoln that the wives and children of black soldiers who fell in battle should be provided for through the pension system in the same way that the widows and children of white soldiers were, even though they had not ever been *legally* married. Following the meeting, Lincoln sent a brief letter to Charles Sumner of Massachusetts, telling the senator that Mrs. Booth "makes a point which I think very worthy of consideration which is, widows and children *in fact*, of Colored soldiers who fell in our service, be placed in law, the same as if their mariages were legal, so that they can have the benefit of the provisions [made] the widows and orphans of white soldiers." Lincoln added, "Please see and hear Mrs. Booth." Sumner pursued the matter, and in early July Congress passed a bill extending pension benefits to the widows and children of black soldiers who died in battle or as a result of a wound or disease contracted in the military service. Lincoln signed it into law on July 4.[1]

Lincoln's letter to Sumner offers important insights into one of the most frequently quoted lines from his second inaugural address — that the nation ought "to care for him who shall have borne the battle, and for his widow, and his orphan."[2] Clearly when Lincoln spoke those words on March 4, 1865, he envisioned caring for not only white families but also black ones. In fact, Lincoln had been thinking about racial equality for some time. In the aftermath of the infamous 1857 *Dred Scott* decision, he argued that black men and women deserved the equality embodied in the Declaration of Independence. And at Gettysburg in November 1863, he argued that the war was being fought to prove "the proposition that 'all men are created equal.'" Just what that equality would look like would take time to settle, but in these letters, black men and women wrote to Lincoln calling for guarantees of freedom and equality under the law. In several of the instances that follow, Lincoln dialogued with the correspondents in person, and those conversations helped shape his thinking about what equality would entail.

A Soldier's Mother Asks for Retaliation against Confederate Soldiers

After Lincoln issued the Emancipation Proclamation, Confederate authorities pledged to execute or reenslave black soldiers (and their white officers). The Lincoln administration could not simply say or do nothing. On July 30, 1863, Lincoln issued an Order of Retaliation, calling the Confederate policy "a relapse into barbarism and a crime against the civilization of the age." In response to the policy, Lincoln pledged "that for every soldier of the United States killed in violation of the laws of war, a rebel soldier shall be executed; and for every one enslaved by the enemy or sold into slavery, a rebel soldier shall be placed at hard labor on the public works and continued at such labor until the other shall be released and receive the treatment due to a prisoner of war."[3]

The day after Lincoln issued his Order of Retaliation, an African American woman, whose son was fighting in the Fifty-Fourth Massachusetts Regiment, sent a worried letter to the president (she would not likely have been aware of the order yet). The letter, which follows, reveals the unique concerns that black families faced when they sent their sons off to fight:

Buffalo   July 31 1863

Excellent Sir

My good friend says I must write to you and she will send it   My son went in the 54th regiment. I am a colored woman and my son was strong and able as any to fight for his country and the colored people have as much to fight for as any. My father was a Slave and escaped from louisiana before I was born morn [more than] forty years agone[4]   I have but poor edication but I never went to schol, but I know just as well as any what is right between man and man. Now I know it is right that a colored man should go and fight for his country, and so ought to a white man. I know that a colored man ought to run no greater risques than a white, his pay is no greater his obligation to fight is the same. So why should not our enemies be compelled to treat him the same, made to do it.

My son fought at Fort Wagoner but thank God he was not taken prisoner, as many were   I thought of this thing before I let my boy go but then they said Mr. Lincoln will never let them sell our colored solders for slaves, if they do he will get them back quck he will rettally-ate and stop it. Now Mr Lincoln dont you think you oght to stop this thing and make them do the same by the colored men   they have lived in idleness all their lives on stolen labor and made savages of the colored people but they now are so furious because they are proving themselves to be men, such as have come away and got some edica-tion. It must not be so. You must put the rebels to work in State prisons to making shoes and things, if they sell our colored soldiers, till they let them all go, and give their wounded the same treatment. it would seem cruel, but their no other way, and a just man must do hard things sometimes, that shew him to be a great man. They tell me some do[5] you will take back the [Emancipation] Proclamation, don't do it. When you are dead and in Heaven, in a thousand years that action of yours will make the Angels sing your praises I know it. Ought one man to own another, law for or not, who made the law, surely the poor slave did not. so it is wicked, and a horrible outrage, there is no sense in it, because a man has lived by robbing all his life and his father before him, should he complain because the stolen things found on him are taken. Robbing the colored people of their labor is but a small part of the robbery their souls are almost taken, they are made bruits of often. You know all about this   Will you see that the colored men fighting now, are fairly treated. You ought to do this, and do it at once, Not let the thing run along meet it quickly and manfully, and stop this, mean cowardly cruelty. We poor oppressed ones, appeal to you, and ask fair play.

   Yours for Christs sake
   Hannah Johnson

Johnson's letter speaks to the tenuous nature of freedom during the Civil War era and the fears that many African Americans had that the Union gov-ernment would not adequately protect African American soldiers. On the bottom of Johnson's letter, a (presumably white) woman named Carrie Co-burn added, "Hon Mr Lincoln, The above speaks for itself."[6] Dozens of men named Johnson served in the Fifty-Fourth Massachusetts, and it is unclear which one was Hannah Johnson's son (he also may have had a different surname).

Following the Battle of Fort Pillow on April 12, 1864, Lincoln polled his cabinet to determine how he should respond to the massacre. Several cabinet members called for the taking and execution of hostages, while others said that innocent Confederate POWs should not be executed but rather only the perpetrators of the crime. In the end, Confederate authorities began treating black soldiers as prisoners of war, and Lincoln never acted to kill Confederate hostages, since in Lincoln's words, "Blood can not restore blood."[7]

A Black Virginian Asks Lincoln about the Status of His Rights

The Civil War brought about great uncertainty throughout the states of the Confederacy as black and white people vied for power and a sense of control over their daily lives. In this letter, an African American man from Virginia asks Lincoln for insights into what he will be able to do on the land where he lives—land that had presumably belonged to a rebel family:

Washington D.C
Jany 22[d] 1864

Mr Abraham Lincoln
Dr Sir

Some Reckon and others guess But what I wish to know is this, what do you mean to do with us, Col[d] population   are we to suffer and our enemies reap or can we *Reap* now   I was brought up a farmer and if I can have a hut in my own native land and a little help that will suffice me, then I have a family you *know* well   do the best you can and oblige yr obt Servant

Ed. D. Jennings

NB

My address near Warrenton Springs Fauq[r] C° Va (come up)

Lincoln retained this letter in his personal collection of papers but he does not appear to have responded. It is possible that Jennings may have personally delivered this letter to the president at the White House because he wrote it in Washington, D.C., and put "come up" at the end, indicating that he had traveled from Warrenton to Washington.[8]

A Mother Asks for Equal Treatment for Her Son

James S. Weir, an eighteen-year-old farmer from Buffalo, New York, enlisted in the Fifty-Fourth Massachusetts on November 26, 1863. His parents, Rev. George Weir Jr. and Nancy M. Weir, were prominent "colored citizens" in upstate New York. In 1862, Nancy published a hymn in the *Liberator* commemorating the emancipation of slaves in Washington, D.C. In it, she praised God for permitting the slaves to be freed, while asking God to bless "the Nation's honored Chief! / Thy servant may he be, / Who wisely has advised relief, / Columbia's soil to free."[9] A few months after her son mustered into the army, Nancy wrote the following letter to Lincoln explaining her family's hardships and the injustices her son was facing:

Rochester   Monday   feb. 8th 1864

To Honorable A Lincoln

    Sir   it is with a deep sense of my Duty that i attempt to forward a few lines to inform you sir of the Circumstances Connected with my Sons Enlisting in the 54th Mass Regiment

    he is as good a young Man I will venture to assert as Can be found though blonging to the "so Called infortunate" Colored race   feeling for the government Hearing her Cries of Distrees in the great Struggle for national life I Consented for him to go to the Rescue not Heeding the Consequences. my self & 7 seven Chrildren was depending on Him [and] My Husband an aged Minister of the gospel   it was assured my son he would receive $300.00 Bounty as other men that would enable us to live without suffering if He returned No More   But After Enlisting the United states pay Master refused to give Him one cent   so he went to the battle field with sorrow of heart be Cause of the Helpless ones dependent on him   we see drunkards be Cause of their white hue Receive that wich is Due to All equally   I truly Beleive sir that you are not in favor of injustice in this Matter   I Humbly Ask if it is in the order of your Administration that he might be restored to us again if his services is not worth as Much as other Mens. for the people of Color are praying day & night for your hands to be supported[10] untill this great struggle proves victorious on the side of the Union

    James S. Weir is on Morris Island S.C.   Co. D.   an answer is solicited By the Mother of J. S Weir

    I am most respectfully yours Humble Servant

    Mrs Nancy M. Weir

Residence   No 24 gregory St

Rochester   NY

NB. will your Honor please Accept a copy of My Composition that i will send that have been Circulated & sung 3 of [or?] 4 years freely

Almost a year later, Nancy again wrote to Lincoln about her son's bounty:

Rochester Jan 9th 1865.

Hon. Abraham Lincoln
Sir

Pardon me for my boldness   nothing but the keenest necessity has Compelled me to make a petition for any part of my sons Bounty as it was promised him at his Enlistment   he Come under the $402/00 Bounty of wich 75 00 was promised him at his Enlistment the rest in forty dollar sums from time to time after reaching the place of destination[11]   he left good buisness with no other motive than to serve his Country & as a good Christian supposed his bounty would Keep his dependant Mother with 9 in family from distress but his disappointment has Caused him much grief on account of our adverse Circumstances. Grocers with whom in times past we have dealt hundreds of dollars with & supposed was our friends but since the Election would have sold me out in 6 days but the Constable of our ward is a union man & would not   we had to mortgage my sewing Machine and house hold goods for 60 days for the sum of $72 00 costs making it 80 00   the sixty days will expire on the 13th day of febuary next 1865

I humbly beg sir if I Can obtain any part of it that I may receive such if information

Very respectfully
Mrs Nancy M. Weir.
James S. Weir. Acting Corporal
54th Mass. Voll[s] Co. d.   Colored
S.C.
General Fosters division

Unfortunately for Mrs. Weir, the Adjutant General's Office replied that Weir was not due any federal bounty because he enlisted prior to July 20, 1864. Instead, she ought to apply to Massachusetts authorities for a bounty (a government clerk mistakenly thought she was writing from Rochester, Massachusetts). James Weir served until August 20, 1865, when he was honorably discharged. He returned home and lived with his family until 1867 and later worked as a railroad conductor in Detroit.[12]

Louisiana Creoles Appeal for the Right to Vote

New Orleans was the most ethnically diverse city in America during the Civil War era, home to citizens of French, Spanish, African, English, and other backgrounds. Unlike any other place in the South, a vibrant, wealthy free black community existed in New Orleans at the beginning of the war. These men possessed a number of important political rights, including the ability to buy and sell property, make contracts, inherit and leave an inheritance, sue and be sued in civil court, testify against whites in criminal cases, and not be testified against by slaves. At least twenty-three of these elite free blacks owned slaves, and at the beginning of the war, several of them loaned significant amounts of money to the Confederacy.

After the Union occupation of New Orleans in April 1862, the elite free black population of the city began pushing Union authorities for the right to vote. Initially they showed little interest in advocating for universal black manhood suffrage, believing that their "industry and education" gave them "all the qualifications necessary to exercise the right of suffrage in an intelligent manner"—unlike black men who had recently been held in bondage. As one black newspaper explained, in the debate over extending the franchise to African American men, people should not "confuse the newly freed people with our intelligent population."[13]

In March 1864, two free men of color—E. Arnold Bertonneau and Jean Baptiste Roudanez—traveled to Washington, D.C., to petition for the enfranchisement of black Louisianans who had been born free before the war so that they could participate in the reconstruction of Louisiana. This first petition captured their belief that they were equipped to vote, whereas the masses of slaves and ex-slaves were not. The petition carried roughly one thousand signatures, including those of a number of black men who had fought in Andrew Jackson's racially diverse army during the War of 1812. They presented it to Lincoln at the White House on March 3:

> To His Excellency Abraham Lincoln   President of the United-States, and to the Honorable the Senate and House of Representatives of the United States of America in Congress assembled:
>   The undersigned respectfully submit the following,
>   That they are natives of Louisiana, and Citizens of the United-States; that they are loyal citizens, sincerely attached to the country and the Constitution; and ardently desire the maintenance of the National Unity, for which they are ready to sacrifice their fortunes and their lives.

E. Arnold Bertonneau.
Courtesy of Thomas
Bertonneau.

That a large portion of them are owners of real-estate, and all of
them are owners of personal property: that many of them are engaged
in the pursuits of commerce and industry, while others are employed
as artisans in various trades; that they are all fitted to enjoy the
privileges and immunities belonging to the condition of citizens of the
United States, and among them may be found many of the descendants of those men whom the illustrious Jackson styled "his fellow-
citizens" when he called upon them to take up arms to repel the
enemies of the country.[14]

Your petitioners further respectfully represent that over and above
the right which in the language of the Declaration of Independence
they possess to liberty and the pursuit of happiness, they are supported by the opinion of just and loyal men, especially by that of

Edward Bates, attorney General, in the claim to the right of enjoying the privileges, and immunities pertaining to the condition of citizens of the United States;[15] and to support the legitimacy of this claim, they believe it simply necessary to submit to Your Excellency, and to the Honorable Congress; the following considerations which they beg of you to weigh in the balance of law and justice.

Notwithstanding their forefathers served in the army of the United-States in 1814–1815, and aided in repelling from the soil of Louisiana a haughty enemy, over confident of success, yet they and their descendants have ever since, and until the era of the present rebellion been estranged and even repulsed, excluded from all rights, from all franchises, even the smallest, when their brave fathers offered their bosoms to the enemy to preserve the territorial integrity of the Republic.

During this period of forty-nine years, they have never ceased to be peaceable citizens, paying their taxes on an assessment of more than fifteen millions of dollars.

At the call of Gen'l [Benjamin F.] Butler, they hastened to rally under the banner of Union and Liberty, they have spilled their blood, and are still pouring it out for the maintenance of the Constitution of the United States; in a word they are soldiers of the Union, and they will defend it so long as their hands have strength to hold a musket.

While Gen. [Nathaniel P.] Banks was at the siege of Port Hudson, and the city threatened by the enemy His Excellency, Gov. [George F.] Shepley called for troops for the defense of the city, and they were foremost in responding to the call, having raised the first regiment in the short space of forty eight hours.

In consideration of this fact, as true and as clear as the sun which lights this Great Continent; in consideration of the services already performed and still to be rendered by them to their common country, they humbly beseech Your Excellency and Congress to cast your eyes upon a loyal population awaiting with confidence and dignity the proclamation of those inalienable rights which belong to the condition of Citizens of the Great American Republic.

Theirs is but a feeble voice claiming attention in the midst of the grave questions raised by this terrible conflict, yet confident of the justice which guides the action of the Government, they have no hesitation in speaking what is prompted by their hearts, "We are men, treat us as such."

Mr. President and Honorable members of Congress: the petitioners refer to your wisdom the task of deciding whether they, loyal and devoted men, who are ready to make every sacrifice for the support of the best Government which man has been permitted to create, are to be deprived of the right to assist in establishing a Civil Government in our beloved State of Louisiana, and also in choosing their representatives, both for the Legislature of the State, and for the Congress of the Nation.

Your petitioners aver that they have applied in respectful terms to Brigadier General Geo. F. Shepley, Military Governor of Louisiana and to Major Genl N. P. Banks commanding the Department of the Gulf, praying to be placed upon the Registers as voters; to the end that they might participate in the reorganization of Civil Government in Louisiana, and that their petition has met with no response from those officers, and it is feared that none will be given, and they therefore appeal to the justice of the representatives of the Nation, and ask that all the citizens of Louisiana of African descent, born free before the rebellion; may by proper orders be directed to be admitted to be inscribed on the Registers, and admitted to the rights and privileges of electors:

And your petitioners will ever pray:

J. B. Roudanez

Arnold Bertonneau

Delegates of the free Colored population of Louisiana
New-Orleans La: January 5th 1864.
[Roughly 1,000 signatures follow. The first twenty-eight belonged to veterans of the War of 1812.][16]

While in Washington, D.C., the two men wrote a new memorial asking for the right to vote for all black men in Louisiana, which they may have presented to Lincoln at a second White House meeting on March 12. Charles Sumner of Massachusetts introduced both petitions on the floor of the U.S. Senate on March 15:

To His Excellency Abraham Lincoln President of the United States, and to the Honorable the Senate and House of Representatives of the United States of America in Congress, assembled.

Your Memorialists respectfully show that they are loyal Citizens of Louisiana of African descent, born free.

That they have been appointed a committee by the signers of the accompanying Petition, to which this memorial is supplementary for the purpose of presenting the said Petition and of urging in person, the, as your Memorialists believe, just claims therein contained.

That your Memorialists desire to present for your favorable consideration the following statement and prayer in addition to the accompanying Petition, namely

That, whereas it may be urged that the United States has no authority to change the laws and Constitution of the State of Louisiana, as to the qualification of voters at State elections, this has already been done by the authority of the United States in respect to white Citizens of Louisiana employed in the military and naval service of the United States as will more clearly appear by what follows.[17]

That the Constitution of Louisiana Title 2 Art. 12 excludes soldiers, seamen, or marines in the army or navy of the United States from the right of suffrage.

That by General Order N° 24, from Head Quarters Department of the Gulf, Major General N. P. Banks ordered, that the Citizens who had volunteered for the defence of the Country in the army or navy and who were otherwise qualified voters, should be allowed to vote in the election-precincts in which they might be found on the day of election; thereby enfranchising those who were by the Constitution and laws of Louisiana disfranchised.

And your Memorialists further show that the constitution and laws of Louisiana have been altered by the authority of the United States in other respect and more particularly

That by the Proclamation of Major General N. P. Banks dated New Orleans January 11th 1864 it was declared that the officers chosen in the election then approaching, should constitute the Civil Government of the State under the Constitution and laws of Louisiana except so much of the said Constitution and laws as *recognize, regulate, or relate to Slavery*.

And your Memorialists further show that though in their accompanying Petition they have only asked the right of suffrage for those Citizens of Louisiana of African descent born free before the rebellion, yet that justice and the principles for which they contend require also the extension of this privilege to those born slaves, with such qualifications as should affect equally the white and the colored Citizen, and that this is required not only by justice but also by expediency which demands that full effect should be given to all the Union feeling in the rebel States, in order to secure the permanence of the free institutions and loyal governments now organized therein.

And your Memorialists pray that the right of suffrage may be extended not only to natives of Louisiana of African descent born free, but also to all others whether born slave or free, especially those who have vindicated their right to vote by bearing arms; subject only to such qualifications as shall equally affect the white and colored Citizens.

And your Memorialists will ever pray

J. B. Roudanez

Arnold Bertonneau

Delegates of the free Colored population of Louisiana

Washington, March 10th 1864.[18]

While meeting with Lincoln, the president said to Roudanez and Bertonneau, "I regret, gentlemen, that you are not able to secure all your rights, and that circumstances will not permit the government to confer them upon you. I wish you would amend your petition, so as to include several suggestions which I think will give more effect to your prayer, and after having done so please hand it to me." One of the men replied, "If you will permit me, I will do so here." Lincoln then asked him, "Are you, then, the author of this eloquent production?" "Whether eloquent or not," came the reply, "it is my work." Lincoln and the Louisianans then sat down side by side and amended the document. According to one witness, "The Southern gentlemen who were present at this scene did not hesitate to admit that their prejudices had just received another shock."[19]

Meeting with these Creole leaders from New Orleans clearly had an important effect on the president. On March 13 — the day after the possible second meeting — Lincoln sent a letter to Michael Hahn, congratulating him for his recent election as governor of Louisiana. The majority of Lincoln's letter, however, consisted of a "private" suggestion — that Hahn consider extending the franchise to "some of the colored people . . . for instance, the very intelligent, and especially those who have fought gallantly in our ranks." Such voters, Lincoln continued, "would probably help, in some trying time to come, to keep the jewel of liberty within the family of freedom." This was the first time that a sitting president suggested extending the right to vote to any persons of color.[20]

North Carolina Slaves and Freedmen
Petition for the Right to Vote

About a month after Lincoln's meetings with Roudanez and Bertonneau, a delegation of ex-slaves and free blacks from North Carolina came to Washington to petition Lincoln for the right to vote in their state. The leader of this group, Abraham H. Galloway, had been born into slavery in coastal North Carolina in 1837 but escaped to Philadelphia when he was about twenty years old. Early in the Civil War, he worked as a spy for Union general Benjamin F. Butler, and by the spring of 1863 he was at the center of Union recruiting efforts in North Carolina. In April 1864, Galloway made his way to Washington, D.C., where he personally presented a written petition to Lincoln. Joining him were a merchant and farmer named E. H. Hill; two barbers, Clinton D. Pierson (sometimes spelled Pearson) and John R. Good; an older minister named Isaac K. Felton; and a baker named Jarvis M. Williams. Four of the six men had been born into slavery.[21]

The men were astounded when they were welcomed through the front door of the White House. Reverend Felton later remarked that it would have been considered an "insult" for a person of color to seek to enter the front door "of the lowest magistrate" in North Carolina. Should such a thing occur, Felton said, the black "offender" would have been told to go "around to the back door, that was the place for niggers." But not so with Lincoln at the White House. The visitors were escorted to Lincoln's office, where each man shook the president's hand. They then presented their petition to him:

> *To His Excellency the President of these United States:*
> WE, the colored citizens of North Carolina, composed alike of those born in freedom and those whose chains of bondage were severed by your gracious proclamation, cherishing in our hearts and memories that ever to be remembered sentence, embodied in the Declaration of Independence, that "all men are created free and equal," being well aware that the right of suffrage was exercised, without detriment, by the colored freemen of this State previous to 1835, and that some of the Northern States, most advanced in arts, sciences, and civilization, have extended that right to the colored citizens with eminent success and good results, do most earnestly and respec[t]fully petition your Excellency to finish the noble work you have begun, and grant unto your petitioners that greatest of privileges, when the State is reconstructed, to exercise the right of

Abraham H. Galloway. From William Still, *The Underground Rail Road: A Record* (Philadelphia: Porter and Coates, 1872).

suffrage, which will greatly extend our sphere of usefulness, redound to your honor, and cause posterity, to the latest generation, to acknowledge their deep sense of gratitude. We feel proud in saying that we have contributed moral and physical [words illegible] to our country in her hour of need, and expect so to continue to do until every cloud of war shall disappear, and your administration stand justified by the sure results that will follow. Feeling sanguine of the success of this our petition, and that you will, with pleasure confer upon us this inestimable boon prayed for, we, with the most profound respect, remain, yours, respectfully, in behalf of the people,

ABRAHAM H. GALLOWAY,
CLINTON D. PEARSON,
JOHN R. GOOD,
ISAAC K. FELTON,
JARVIS M. WILLIAMS.

Lincoln told his visitors that he "had labored hard and through many difficulties for the good of the colored race, and that he should continue to do so." He gave them the "full assurance of his sympathy in the struggle the colored people of North Carolina are now making for their rights," and told them that he "would do what he could for us." But as voting "was a matter belonging to the State it would have to be attended to in the reconstruction of the state." Still, the president said that he "was glad to see colored men seeking for their rights," especially since "this was an important right which we, as a people, ought to have." When their conversation concluded, Lincoln again shook each man's hand. Reflecting on their experiences, the North Carolinians were moved by how Lincoln had received them. John Good said that Lincoln "received us cordially and spoke with us freely and kindly."[22]

A Maryland Slave Desires to Be Free

The Emancipation Proclamation only freed slaves in areas in rebellion because Lincoln believed that the Constitution protected slavery in the loyal states. As a consequence, slaves in Maryland remained in bondage after Lincoln issued his famous edict. In 1864, an enslaved woman in Maryland wrote to Lincoln to ask about her status and her rights:

> Belair Aug 25th 1864
>
> Mr president
>
> It is my Desire to be free. to go to see my people on the eastern shore. my mistress wont let me   you will please let me know if we are free and what i can do. I witte [write] to you for advice. please send me word this week. or as soon as passible and obligde
>
> Annie Davis
> Belair Harford County, M D.
> Belair Harford Co[23]

Fortunately for Annie Davis, freedom soon came to her state. In fact, Lincoln had been working behind the scenes for months to promote emancipation in Maryland. In October 1864, voters in Maryland ratified a new state constitution that officially abolished slavery. Soon thereafter, when a large gathering of African Americans came to celebrate outside the White House, Lincoln told them, "It is no secret that I have wished, and still do wish, mankind everywhere to be free. And in the State of Maryland how great an advance has been made in this direction." As of November 1, 1864—when the new state constitution went into effect—Annie Davis was free.[24]

A Pennsylvania Soldier Wants the Same Rights as White Men

On November 18, 1864, Zachariah Burden enlisted as a substitute for one year for a drafted man named Joseph H. Parker in Indianapolis, Indiana.

A native of Ohio, the twenty-nine-year-old farmer trained at Camp William Penn near Philadelphia before being sent to join the Eighth USCT in Virginia. Although his military service record contains no indication of his being sick, Burden sent the following letter to Lincoln:

Feb the 2 1865

Mr Abebrem Lenken the Presdent of the ñŧŧ u.s. stats

I will rite you A fuw Lins to let you now that I am not well and i Can not rite to Day for i am siCk but i am in Good hops that you will rede this   i have ben sick Evy sence i Come her and i think it is hard to make A man go and fite and wont let him vote and wont let him go home when he is sick   we had Boys her that Died that wood gout [get] well if thy Could go home   thy Can Come back as well as A whit man   i hope you ~~hope~~ will give us some pleser of our life   give us A Chene [chance?] of A man   i will rite no more this time   i Dont wont you to get mad with what i say for i Dont mene any harme   rite soon if you pleze and let me no how you feel   so No More this time

stat of Vargenne [Virginia] in Cit of Johne [?]

To A Lenkin

[P.S.] my wife is left A long and no helf [health or help?] and thy wont let me go home   Derect you letter to City Point 8 Reg u.s.C.T.   25 Corps 2ⁿ Briggad 2nd Divsion Com. B   Derict to

Zack Burden

Burden mustered out with his regiment at Brownsville, Texas, on November 10, 1865. Following the war, he lived in Indiana, Oklahoma, and Kansas. For the rest of his life he suffered from an injured foot, which he claimed was the result of having worn a shoe that was too small while he was a soldier.[25]

CHAPTER EIGHT

Soliciting Aid for Christian Ministries

In eighteenth-century America, black and white northerners routinely worshipped together in church, although the houses of worship were usually segregated by race, and black members generally could not vote on church business. Within the churches themselves the leadership was almost always white, and African American parishioners typically had to sit in "Negro pews," which often did not even allow a view of the pulpit. Between 1791 and 1820, black northerners increasingly began worshipping in separate black churches. According to historian Richard J. Boles, such institutions "provided social, political, and leadership assistance [to African American Christians] that very few, if any, predominantly white churches provided."[1] Black churches, in other words, permitted African American clergy to lead their flocks, while the laity did not have to endure the stigma of sitting in segregated, second-class pews. Of equal importance, black ministers believed that they could reach unconverted people of color more effectively than could white clergy. And perhaps most importantly, these congregations became key players in various black social reform movements, particularly abolitionism.

By the mid-nineteenth century, separate African American churches and fraternal organizations were at the center of the black community and black activism, and black Christian leaders sought holistic improvement in their congregants' lives. As such, they believed that their ministries needed to tend not only to African Americans' spiritual well-being but also to their economic needs and social concerns. Spirituality within black churches, according to historian James Oliver Horton and sociologist Lois E. Horton, was a "this-worldly faith" that minimized the distinction between the sacred and the secular aspects of people's lives. The Hortons continue, "In carrying out their sacred ministries, black churches provided opportunities for spiritual worship and guidance, political forums, social and family aid associations, and facilities for community meetings, cultural preservation, entertainment programs, and education and training. For black ministers and congregations, working against slavery and promoting civil rights were also important ways to fulfill their Christian mission."[2]

It was within this context that many African American religious leaders met with or wrote to Abraham Lincoln. Black pastors saw themselves as spokesmen for their communities, delegated with certain authority to speak on behalf of the poor and downtrodden among them. The leadership they had developed within black churches during the antebellum period had prepared them for some of the unique challenges of the Civil War. Thus, they actively sought opportunities for more African Americans to serve as chaplains, hospital stewards, or missionaries among black soldiers and ex-slaves. Based on their past experiences, they believed it was important for black pastors and missionaries to work with the poor in the black community, and they looked to the federal government for assistance in these endeavors.

Black Ministers Ask for Permission to Minister to Black Refugees

On August 21, 1863, a delegation of eleven black ministers of the American Baptist Missionary Convention went to the White House to ask Lincoln for financial assistance. The leader of the group, Leonard A. Grimes, had been born free in Virginia in 1815 but had, from an early age, done what he could to help the enslaved. In the 1830s he was imprisoned in Richmond for assisting fugitive slaves. After moving to Boston, he was said to have helped "hundreds of escaping slaves" on their way to Canada in the 1840s and 1850s. During the Civil War he worked to recruit African American soldiers, including some for the Fifty-Fourth Massachusetts Infantry.[3] Upon reaching the White House, Grimes presented the following note to one of Lincoln's secretaries:

> Washington D.C.   Aug. 21st 1863
> To his Exilancy, President Lincoln
>   Your petitioner would, respectfully beg an inter view of a few moments, for a deligation of Ministers of the Gospel, now in session in the City of Washington, as the "American Baptist Missionary Convention,["] and if an interview should be granted please name the hour.
>   Yours most respectfully
>   L. A. Grimes of Boston Mass
>   Pres. American Bap. Miss. Convention
> His Exilency

Rev. Leonard A. Grimes. Courtesy of the Library of Congress.

Pres. Lincoln
[On the next page:]

Leonard A. Grimes	of	Boston Mass
Sampson White	"	Philadelphia Pa.
Edmund Kelley	"	Newbedford Mass.
Noah Davis	"	Baltimore Md.
Saml Madden	"	Washington D.C.
W^m E Walker	"	Trenton N.J.
Wm Williams	"	Baltimore Md.
Albert Boulden	"	Washington DC

Collen Williams	"	Georgetown D.C.
W^m J Walker.	"	~~Was~~ Fredericksburg Va.
Danl G. Muse	"	Washington DC[4]

According to a newspaper report, Lincoln "made some interesting remarks" during the meeting and then granted the delegation's request. He penned a brief note, stating, "To-day I am called upon by a committee of colored ministers of the Gospel, who express a wish to go within our military lines and minister to their brethren there. The object is a worthy one, and I shall be glad for all facilities to be afforded them which may not be inconsistent with or a hindrance to our military operations."[5]

One of the ministers at the meeting, Edmund Kelly, brought the following note, along with a newspaper clipping of an article he'd written—"The Colored Man's Interest in the Present War"—and images of his children. Kelly had been born in bondage in 1818 to an enslaved woman and an Irish immigrant. When he was six years old, his mother was sold away. In the 1830s Kelly was hired to a primary school teacher, where he bribed young children into teaching him how to read. He later became a Baptist minister and saved up $2,800 to purchase the freedom of his wife and four children. As a free man, he authored several articles on behalf of his "deeply wronged race," one of which he sent to Lincoln with the following letter:

Respected Sir
    The enclosed is a copy of my first out of five appeals to the colored People of the U.S. to come forward after your recent call upon them. the 2nd is a Pamphlet prepared for a Guide of Christian-relation to thier duty God—their Country—and themselves & my views of the future destiny of this Country—also a bill of my exercises in different parts of the Country, & would be pleasd to have one or more recitation in Washington & vicinity
    you[r]s truly   E. Kelly—
    of Newbedford Mass—
Aug 21, 1863

During his lifetime, Kelly gained a reputation as "a successful minister, pastor and evangelist" who "leans upon God and praises him for his goodness and love." For many years he pastored a church in New Bedford, Massachusetts. One of Kelly's sons, William D. Kelly, fought with the Fifty-Fourth Massachusetts, while another, John D. Kelly, returned to Columbia, Tennessee, after the war to serve as the principal of a "colored public school."[6]

JOHN H. KELLY,
The Scriptural Reciter,
Born November 14, 1852

JANE E. W. KELLY,
The Scriptural Reciter,
Born February 6, 1854.

John H. Kelly and Jane E. W. Kelly, children of Rev. Edmund Kelly. This image was enclosed in Kelly's letter to Lincoln. Courtesy of the Library of Congress.

A Minister Asks Lincoln to Appoint More Black Army Chaplains

Jeremiah Asher was born free in Connecticut in 1812 — the grandson of an African man who had been kidnapped at the age of four on the Guinea coast and brought to America as a slave. In 1840 Asher began shepherding a new black Baptist church in Providence, Rhode Island. After nine years there, he became the pastor of Shiloh Baptist Church in Philadelphia, where he would remain until December 1863. In the wake of John Brown's failed raid on Harpers Ferry in 1859, Asher told his congregation that he would pray for Brown, then added, "If the cause of human freedom will be served by Brown's death, then I want him to die." This remark led his congregation to groan audibly.[7]

Rev. Jeremiah Asher. Courtesy of Joyce Werkman.

In September 1863 Asher sent the following letter to Lincoln, urging the appointment of black chaplains, presumably for the regiments that were training just outside Philadelphia at Camp William Penn. Having worshipped in predominantly white New England churches as a young man, Asher knew the benefits of having African American spiritual leaders among USCT units.

Philadelphia
Sept 7th 1863

To his Excllency Hon Abraham Lincoln   President of the United States
Dear Sir

In behalf of the Colerd Clergy and Churches of Philadelphia I write to ask you if there is any Law of Congress Prohibiting the appointment of Colerd Chaplains to the Colerd Regiments of United States Volunteers.

The Soldiers are anxious to have Colerd Ministers as their Spiritual Teachers   Applications have been made at the war Department but have not been considered   if there is no Legal obstruction will you be Pleased to use your influence in this matter and thus oblige the Colerd Regiments who are anxious to have Religious instruction and the Colerd People in general who ever have been and ever will be Loyal Subjects to the government   Thus your Petitioner will ever Pray

I have the Honor to be your most obedient Servant

Jeremiah Asher Pastor of the Shiloh Church 1013 Rodman St[8]

On November 1, 1863, twenty-six officers of the Sixth U.S. Colored Infantry signed a petition requesting that Asher would become their regimental chaplain, and by December Asher was on his way to Yorktown, Virginia, to join the regiment. Throughout his time in the service he exhibited a genuine concern for the spiritual welfare of his men. When the Sixth moved northwest toward Petersburg in May 1864, Asher reported that "our opportunities for holding service while in the field are usually much fewer than when in winter quarters, but we have managed to hold service with but two exceptions each Sabbath since we have been in our present location. The exceptions were when the regiment were in the trenches." On June 13, he added, "The last month has been one of constant excitement and fatigue. The men have been working on the fortifications day and night, not excepting the Sabbath."[9]

In September 1864, Asher again lamented the lack of religious instruction among the troops: "The number of sick and wounded collected in the hospitals from the different regiments is quite large. I had supposed that they had been favored with the preaching of the word," he wrote, "but I was informed by one who had been there from the beginning: he told me they never had a sermon preached to them since they had been there." While the soldiers were stationed near Petersburg, he thought that it would "be well for one of our chaplains to spend some time with them."[10]

In addition to caring for the spiritual needs of the Sixth USCT, Asher worked diligently in North Carolina recruiting new soldiers for the regiment. On one occasion, he wrote, "The last month has been one of constant excitement and fatigue." He eventually ran himself ragged. The regimental surgeon wrote on July 21, 1865, that Asher was "suffering from the effects of remittent fever and that *a* change of location is necessary for his recovery and *to prevent loss of life*." The surgeon's recommendation for a thirty-day rest for Asher was approved that same day, but unfortunately Asher contracted typhoid fever and died six days later, on July 27. One observer noted that he died, in part, from "over exertion" while attending to his duties. A month after his death, the American Baptist Missionary Convention praised his "marked and highly useful" life, saying that against the wishes of his congregation, "he felt impressed to share a part in the fortunes of his country." He was the only African American chaplain to die while in the service during the Civil War.[11]

"Colored Odd Fellows" Invite Lincoln to Their Anniversary Celebration

In the fall of 1863, the Grand United Order of Odd Fellows in America, a black fraternal organization, planned a large celebration in Washington, D.C., for its eighteenth anniversary. In anticipation of the event, three leaders from the organization—John A. Simms, John F. N. Wilkinson, and Thomas Cross—met with Lincoln to ask for police protection against potential violence. They presented him with this letter:

> *Washington City, D.C.*
> *September the 23d, 1863.*
>
> TO HIS HONOR, THE PRESIDENT OF THE UNITED STATES OF AMERICA.
>
> The Annual Moveable Committee of the Grand United Order of Odd Fellows, in America, composed of colored men, will hold their annual convention in this city, commencing October the 7th. At the adjournment of which the order will celebrate the occasion by a public parade and demonstration, in Israel Church, Capitol Hill. The committee on behalf of the convention most respectfully ask the protection of the civil and military authorities of the city on that occasion.
>
> We remain most respectfully,
> Your obedient servants.
> John A. Simms,
> Thomas H. Cross,
> John F. N. Wilkinson, Committee

The president replied with a short note, which was likely written on the back of the committee's letter:

While I think it probable that the protection sought within will not be needed, it is altogether proper that it should be given, if needed, and I doubt not, would be given without any direct interference of mine.

A. Lincoln.

September 23d, 1863.[12]

The preceding correspondence was sent to the *Christian Recorder*, the newspaper of the AME church, to be published. A few weeks later, Simms, Wilkinson, and Cross sent Lincoln this invitation:

Hon

Sir   you are most Respectfully invited to attend the celebration of the G. U. O of OF in America, at Isreal Church "Capitol Hill" Friday 9th instant at 1 ½ oclock

Respectfully yours &C &C

John A Simms

Jno. F. N. Wilkinson

Thos Cross, Comttee

To His Excellency

The Hon A. Lincoln

President

Washington   Oct 8th / '63[13]

Lincoln was unable to attend the celebration—the invitation arrived just one day before the event, and he already had a cabinet meeting scheduled. However, he did provide police and military protection for the three hundred celebrants and twenty thousand spectators. He also retained the invitation in his private collection of correspondence.

Black New Yorkers Seek Federal Funds to Elevate Their Race in Africa and America

On November 5, 1863, James Mitchell, Lincoln's commissioner of emigration, arranged for a "short interview" between Lincoln and the officers of the African Civilization Society. Founded by the black Presbyterian minister Henry Highland Garnet in the 1850s and incorporated in the state of New York on May 5, 1863, the society sought to bring about "the civilization and Christianization" of people of African descent around the world. It also hoped to help end the transatlantic slave trade by bringing "lawful commerce" to

Africa, and to ensure "the elevation of the condition of the colored population of our own country and other lands."[14]

At four o'clock in the afternoon on November 5, Lincoln met with five representatives of the African Civilization Society, all of whom were prominent African Americans from Brooklyn. Among them, George Washington Le Vere was the pastor of St. Paul's Congregational Church in Brooklyn. Henry M. Wilson, a graduate of Princeton Theological Seminary, had been a Presbyterian minister in New York since the 1840s and became a proponent of emigration in the late 1850s. And Richard H. Cain, a native of Virginia, had attended Wilberforce University in Ohio and gone on to become a preacher and then bishop in the AME Church. After greeting the president, they presented him with the following petition:

An Address to the President of the United States.

Washington DC   Nov 5th 1863.

Mr President

The present Delegation in whose name I now speak, are men who love and fear God. We have often earnestly prayed, that he alone would choose your changes; suit you to circumstances: bless you, and direct you, and all your associate counsellors. We deem it a great privilege at this time to be permitted to submit the fact; that our society is fully organized and with one exception: quite prepared to develope our great scheme of modern civilization and christian benevolence; or as it is more fully expressed: in Art[icle] *Second* of The Constitution: ["]The object of this society shall be, the civilization and christianization of Africa; and [of the descendants] of African ancestors in any portion of the earth where-ever dispersed; also the destruction of the african slave trade, by the introduction of lawful commerce into Africa, the promotion of the growth of cotton, and other products there whereby the natives may become industrious producers, as well as consumers of articles of commerce; and generally the elevation of the condition of the coloured population of our own country and of other lands."

Our field of operation is as wide as the world. We have the requisites for its proper cultivation, except money. Of this important medium we are quite destitute.

Our faith in the living God amid the great and peculiar events transpiring under the present administration prompts us to beleive that your Excellency was raised up in the wisdom of Jehovah to reform

Rev. Richard H. Cain. Courtesy of the Library of Congress.

this great nation and deliver millions of captives, just as trully and certainly as Moses (once an exiled Hebrew) was to deliver God's ancient covenant people the Jews from Egyptian bondage   As Representatives of the African civilization society we hereby greatfully acknowledge your many timely services recently rendered a suffering portion of our race in this land. Your acts have so fully demonstrated the Problems of national mercy and righteousness that we cannot tell in which they exell. Mindful of the account which we are to render to both God and man, we here submit the singular fact; that this is [the] only Institution of the kind on our Globe managed wholly by coloured Gentlemen. We beleieve ourselves to be the proper, if not the only legal applicants for suitable portions of the funds; so wisely and liberally appropriated by the present Administration: For the benefit of certian portions of coloured people in this land as well as other parts of the earth.

The Society is universal in its tendences and designs, and under a fourfold *Idea* in due time we hope to be able to give civilization, the Gospel, Science and commerce to our people where-ever they may need them.

In order that we may at once enter upon, and continue this work without interruption we earnestly pray that the President of these United States may find it in harmony with a good conscience, and most excellent judgement, and within his Executive discretion to place the sum of ~~Five~~ $5000 or more Dollars to the credit of the African Civilization Society; with such arrangements that we may draw on the proper Department, for Similar amounts as the progress of our work s[h]all require the same.

All of with is most Respectfully Submitted

George. W. Le Vere

Peter S Porter

William Anderson

Richard H. Cain

Henry. M. Wilson Secretary[15]

According to news reports, Lincoln "gave them a patient hearing, and said he would bestow upon their written communication due consideration." Around the time of the meeting—probably in advance of it—Mitchell prepared an executive order for Lincoln to sign that would have released $5,000 of federal colonization funds to the African Civilization Society. However, it does not appear that Lincoln ever signed the document.[16] A few months later, Cain sent the following letter to Lincoln. It was on African Civilization Society letterhead.

Washington D.C Jany 27 1864

To His Excellency. —President of the United States:

Sir the accumulating interests which are clustering arround our race amid the revolutions in this Country, prompts us to believe that we have a great work to perform in assisting in ellivating our people made free by your proclaimation. You well see, by the accompanying circular[17] the motives which prompt us in making a so reasonable request. *For permission and Authority, to establish Schools for the instruction of the Freedmen. Within the lines of our Armies*, that we may qualify them for citizenship, and the high duties of Moral, and social, as well as spiritual life by leading them to comprehend their high destiny in the future. We seek a General permit from the Government to enter and establish Schools and Churches among our Brethren throughout the Southern states. Always subject to the regulations proscribed by the laws, and in harmony with the interests of the People, and the Maintainence of the Authority of the General Government. The

Society and the friends of humanity, will highly appreciate such consideration from you, as will be, favourable to the objects contemplated by the Society for which we will ever pray.

R. H. Cain, in behalf of the Society. An early answer will greatly assist us in our good work.

I have the Honor to be Sir, your Servent with great respect
Richard H Cain[18]

Several members of the African Civilization Society went on to achieve significant things on behalf of the Union and southern freedpeople. In 1864 the society's president, George W. Le Vere, was appointed chaplain of the Twentieth USCT and after the war served as a missionary to freedpeople in East Tennessee. And Richard H. Cain, after serving as an AME minister in Brooklyn, would eventually move to South Carolina where he would serve as pastor of Emanuel AME Church and be elected to Congress.[19]

Black Pennsylvanians Support a White Minister for Work with Black Refugees

In the spring of 1863, a number of African Americans in Washington, D.C., asked Lincoln to appoint chaplain James D. Turner of the Fourth Pennsylvania Cavalry colonel of a black regiment (see chapter 3). Turner had long been a friend of the African American community. "I have always, since my earliest recollection, sympathized with the oppressed colored race," he told Lincoln in April 1863, "and have earnestly labored for their elevation not unfrequently at considerable personal sacrifice." But Turner's health was weak, and he was unable to assume command of the regiment.[20]

In the autumn of 1863, African Americans in Pennsylvania wrote to Lincoln in support of Turner's appointment to be superintendent of a contraband camp in the South. Turner had been a Methodist minister in western Pennsylvania since 1851 and was highly popular in that part of the state. The letter is dated 1864, but the docketing on the back reveals it was sent in 1863.

Washington County, Penna
Oct 14th 1864. [1863]

His Excelancy Abraham Lincoln   President of the US —
Sir

The undersigned Colerd citizens of Washington county & Westrn Penna. having Learned that Rev J D Turner has made application to yeour Excelancy for the superintendency of one of the Counteraband

Distrcts in the south having great confidence [in] Mr. Turner as a true friend of the Colord race and feeling desirous if possible to contribute something to his success in this matter believeing that it will be greatly to the interest of the Colord people that he should have some field of labour among them

We therefore earnestly pray your Excellancy to Grant Mr. Turners application

Very Respectfully,

your. obt. servants

[59 signatures beginning on a separate page]

Lincoln supported placing Turner in a position working with contrabands, writing, "I shall be glad, if a place can be found for Mr. Turner, in the connection indicated within." But Turner died in 1864 "after a painful and protracted illness" that dated to his time on the Virginia peninsula in 1862 with the Fourth Pennsylvania Cavalry. One newspaper reported that he died "in christian fortitude and hope."[21]

A Black Minister Wishes to Serve as a Hospital Chaplain

On November 1, 1862, Lincoln met with black Baptist minister Chauncey Leonard to discuss Leonard taking a trip to Liberia to explore possibilities for future colonization trips. Lincoln agreed and Leonard set sail in February 1863, but his trip was cut short due to illness. After returning to the United States and recovering his strength, Leonard sent the following note to Lincoln:

Abraham Lincoln. President of the United States.

Honorable Sir.

Being anxious to accomplish the greatest amount of good to the Colored Soldiers, of the United States Army; I most respectfully ask to be appointed, Hospital Chaplain, at the Hospital for Colored Troops in this place.

Alexandria, Va.

July 9th 1864.

Your Obt Serv't,

Chauncey Leonard.

Upon receiving Leonard's missive, Lincoln instructed his private secretary to send a letter to Secretary of War Stanton appointing Leonard to the position. Leonard accepted the position in early August, and for the next year

Group at L'Ouverture Hospital, Alexandria, Va., ca. December 1864–April 1865. From left to right: Tobias Trout (31st USCT), William DeGraff (22nd USCT), John H. Johnson (27th USCT), Jerry Lisle (28th USCT), Leander Brown (30th USCT), Samuel Bond (19th USCT), Robert Deyo (26th USCT), Adolphus Harp (19th USCT), Stephen Vance (30th USCT), George H. Smith (31st USCT), Adam Bentley (19th USCT), Rev. Chauncey Leonard. Courtesy of the Charles T. Joyce Collection.

and a half he served as the hospital chaplain at the L'Ouverture Hospital in Alexandria—a facility named after the Haitian revolutionary Toussaint L'Ouverture. There he cared for the physical and spiritual needs of sick and wounded black soldiers as well as black civilian refugees.[22]

A Black Religious Group Holds a Picnic on the White House Lawn

With Lincoln's express written permission, the black Roman Catholic community of Washington, D.C., held a grand picnic on the White House lawn on July 4, 1864, to raise money for the construction of a church building so that they would no longer have to meet in the basement of a white church. The success of the picnic—it raised $1,200—inspired other black religious leaders to follow suit.[23] On July 21, 1864, J. R. Pierre, the superintendent of the Third Baptist Sabbath School (Colored), sent the following note to Lincoln on stationery from the Navy Department's Bureau of Provisions and Clothing:

July 21st 1864.

His Excelency   President of the United States of America
Sir!

Your humble servant being impelled from a knowledge of the erepresible generosity, and of the meny demonstration that have been made by a decision of that great and wonderfull, as well, as benevolent mind that the great ruler of all nation, have endowed your noble personage with in behalf of the oppresed and down trodden of those who have to share the fate of the Affrican decent,

While feeling incapable of expressing the regret that prevade the right minded portion of the Community in regard as to ~~wh~~ not having made a demonstration of thir highly appreciated and much desired privelages that they are permited to enjoy since the freeing of the District of Columbia

Your humble petitioner being Superintendant of the "third Baptist Sabbath School" (Col^d) ~~to~~ desire the school to becom in posession of a banner which is to be known as the *Banner of Freedom*, the design are as thus   the banner are to have a life size stature of your noble personage with the emblem or motto of freedom extended to the oppresed, whilest they are on the way from there labour of the plantation to the Sabbath School or Church. Your petitioner humbly asks to be alloud the privalage of assembling the Sabbath School union, on the first Thursday of August, on the same grounds which were occupide by the Catholic friends on the fourth of July 1864, for the demonstration of ther great fullness to your honor ~~ho~~ and to the gentlemen that voted for the freeing of the slaves in the District of Columbia

I have the honor to be
Most respectfully
Your humble Servant
J. R. Pierre.

Again, Lincoln granted permission. On August 3, Pierre posted an advertisement in the Washington *Evening Star* calling on people to attend the picnic on August 4. Admission would be 25 cents for adults and 10 cents for children.[24]

Ironically, August 4 was a day Lincoln had set apart for "national humiliation and prayer." Nevertheless, the Third Baptist Sunday School assembled at the White House grounds at 10 A.M., with religious exercises commencing at noon. Throughout the day roughly five hundred picnickers ate fruits and cakes and drank lemonade as they listened to music and speeches. The celebration ended at dusk. Pierre raised enough money to make his "Banner of Freedom." It bore the words, "Whatever shall appear to be God's will, I will do," near Lincoln's signature. After the war, he loaned it out for African American celebrations in the District of Columbia.[25]

Attorney General Edward Bates took note of the irony of having a picnic on the White House lawn on a day set apart for humiliation and prayer. After reading an article in the *National Intelligencer* titled "The Negroes' Jubilee," he wrote in his diary:

> It seems by this that the *white* and the black understand the Proclamation differently, and use the day for different and opposite purposes.
>
> The Whites humble in fasting and prayer, as well they may, in view of their great and many sins, which have called down God's vengeance, and has brought upon us this desolating war, and still continues it.
>
> But the Blacks rejoice exceedingly, over the results of the war, already accomplished in their favor, and exult in the hope of the continuance of the war, in all its desolations. And this is reasonable *in them*; for they are taught by those at the North, who, ostentatiously claim to be their only friends, that the war is waged solely for their emancipation, and for wiping out the blot of negro slavery, from this continent. I do not believe that the negro[e]s desire that the Whites shall be reduced to slavery; but if, by the destructive processes of the war, their own personal freedom can be accomplished, we cannot expect them to reject that consummation, because, by the same processes, all the civil, social and political rights of white men may be destroyed.[26]

If Bates saw some hope in the expansion of social rights to African Americans, Democrats did not. The *Daily Milwaukee News* reported the following:

> Thursday, the day set apart by the proclamation of the president of the United States, as a day of fasting, humiliation and prayer, the negroes of the District of Columbia were permitted, by the express assent of Mr. Lincoln, to hold a pic-nic upon the grounds surrounding the

president's house. The first occurrence of this kind took place on the 4th of July last. Up to that time no body of citizens had been allowed to assemble there for purposes of diversion—not even white Sabbath School children. The negroes, emboldened by the success of their application on the 4th of July, repeated their request for a jolification on the same grounds on fast day. . . . The objects of the pic-nic were to praise the men who have elevated the negro to social equality with the white man, and also to purchase a banner ornamented with a life-size portrait of Abraham Lincoln.

After giving its own view of the matter, the *Daily Milwaukee News* reprinted two derisive paragraphs from the *Washington Constitutional Union*:

A vast crowd of negroes was present. The grand old trees in the grounds, that had been planted in the noble days of the republic, not more for the beauty of the park than for the dignity of the residence of the nation's President, were polluted by having swings attached to them whereby negro men could swing negro women. The grounds, held by all patriots as something set apart and sacred because invested with a national character, were prostituted and disgraced by the erection of stands for negro merchants to vend fruits and cakes and drinks to negro customers. Negro speeches were made eulogistic of the senseless and infamous fanaticism that to do what was done there on Thursday has ploughed horror and desolation through the whole country, as if there were crops to be harvested and garnered. Negro flattery tickled the ears of the imperial jester with perhaps a more grateful music than even the uncouth melody of "Picayune Butler," who bawled for his especial gratification over the corpse-be-strewn field of Antietam. And to crown all, negro revelries went on with the high approval of our rulers till the sun went down, and the stars began to gaze blushingly upon the disgraceful scene!

Now, mark you, these negroes who did these things, did it with the high approval and warm commendation of our president. But the permission has been asked for the use of the public grounds around the White House for pic-nic purposes by Sabbath schools of white men and ladies, and permission was refused! The public grounds were too sacred—of too high a character—in too close proximity to the residence of the august Abraham Lincoln for white men to use—their color would remind him too forcibly of the despotism he has erected on the ruins of the republic—perhaps, awake unpleasant reflections in the minds of soldiers, who, enlisting to fight the battles of their country, have been compelled to stand guard around his person as the white-turbaned Hindoos range close beside the throne of their sacred Rajas. But the negro is wooed to accept the gracious permission—nay, it may be, the urgent request—and the aghast country beholds the terrible spectacle of white men rudely spurned in requesting a privilege most eagerly and anxiously thrust forward to the blacks.[27]

These reactions to the black Baptist picnic on the White House lawn reveal how the Civil War meant vastly different things to different people. For many African Americans, this was a period of hope that the war would bring about freedom and equality. Many northern whites, by contrast, feared that social equality for African Americans would mean diminished rights for white people—and they blamed Lincoln for being the prime mover in that process. A few months after the picnic, a Pennsylvania newspaper sneered that Lincoln had done nothing "that has been beneficial to the country, or to the white man." From its perspective, "Mr. Lincoln is emphatically the black man's President and the white man's curse." Ironically, Frederick Douglass would approvingly call Lincoln "emphatically the black man's president" just six month later in a eulogy delivered in New York in June 1865.[28]

A Black Chaplain Asks for Improved Uniforms

Benjamin Franklin Randolph was twenty-seven years old when he was appointed chaplain of the Twenty-Sixth USCT in December 1863. Born free in Kentucky, he had studied at Oberlin College between 1857 and 1862 and was a licensed and ordained Presbyterian minister. From South Carolina, he sent a letter to Lincoln requesting an alteration in the uniforms for army chaplains.[29]

> Camp 26th U.S. Colored Troops.
> Near Beaufort S.C. Aug 23[d]. 1864.
>
> His High Honor, Abraham Lincoln. President U.S.
>
> Sir, I have the honor to request that some addition to Chaplain's uniform be made, if it may be your pleasure; for this reason—the present uniform has nothing to distinguish it from the ordinary clergyman's dress, and the consequence is, Chaplains frequently suffer indignities because they are not recognized as Chaplains, I know this by sad experience, and while I do this upon myown responsibility, I do it in behalf of many Chaplains whose modesty does not allow them to

Chaplain Benjamin Franklin Randolph. From *Harper's Weekly*, November 21, 1868.

make such a request, and hoping that it may be your pleasure to grant it, I am,

    Yours most respectfully

    B. F. Randolph,

    Chaplain 26th U.S.C.T.

A. Lincoln,

Pres. U.S.A.[30]

Following the war, Randolph remained in South Carolina, where he became active in Republican Party politics and the fight for equal rights. In 1868, while serving as a state senator and chairman of the Republican State Central Committee, he was brutally murdered in broad daylight by three white men. One newspaper lamented that he was the "victim of rebel hate."[31]

CHAPTER NINE

Seeking Economic Rights and Opportunities

Many ex-slaves hoped that freedom would bring new economic opportunities that had been denied to them in bondage. Unfortunately, newly freed men and women often found that former enslavers, northern investors, and government officials were not always willing to concede economic rights to them. In the letters that follow, African Americans petitioned Lincoln for the protection of their newfound economic rights, including the right to own and dispose of property and the right to pursue a lawful vocation of one's own choosing. They hoped that the creation of a new social order that protected these rights would help secure permanent and meaningful freedom within American society.

A Former Slave Asks for a Diplomatic Appointment

Aaron A. Bradley (ca. 1815–82) fled slavery in Georgia around 1834 and settled in Boston, where he worked as a shoemaker and lawyer until 1856, when he was disbarred after being convicted of seduction. At the very beginning of Lincoln's first term, he sent a letter to the president asking to be appointed to a diplomatic post in the Caribbean. He appended a postscript claiming to have support from some of the most powerful politicians in New England.

> To His Excellency (A Lincoln) The President of the United States:—
> Your humble Petitioner pray that he be appointed & sent a Commissioner to *St.* Domingo & Hayti (or W[endell] Phillips) to watch the interest & Commers [Commerce] of the United States.
> Aaron A Bradley
>
> Boston April 1st A D 1861:
> His Excellency John A Andrew this day informed me that he would be pleased to recommend & give the President any information of the Petitioner; & the Hon John P Hale[1] Charles Sumner & A Burlingame[2] are personally acquainted with your Petitioner & he thinks they will with Govenor Andrew favour the pray[er] of your Petitioner.
> A A Bradley

No other papers appear in Bradley's State Department file, suggesting that these others may not have supported his candidacy, as he claimed. In fact, a week earlier, Governor Andrew had sent a letter to Lincoln recommending someone else to be commercial agent to Haiti.[3]

Following the war, Bradley led a tumultuous life. He worked as a labor leader for African Americans and held elective office in Georgia several times, but he also faced stiff (and sometimes violent) opposition from white ex-Confederates and some African Americans, who believed that Bradley took advantage of them.[4]

A Black Pennsylvanian Seeks Legal Assistance

The following letter captures some of the unusual ways that northerners looked to Lincoln for help. Little is known about Emery Watson. The 1860 census lists him as a forty-year-old day laborer in Delaware City, Delaware, with a wife and seven children (the oldest being only eleven years old). His total property in the census was valued at twenty dollars, and his wife, Elizabeth, was listed as illiterate. A search of military records suggests that he never joined the service. In the midpoint of the war, he sent the following letter to Lincoln. The salutation almost makes it appear that he is seeking legal advice from a lawyer.

Chester Jan 23 1863

Mr A Lincon &, Company

I take this opportunity to inform you how me & my family have bin abused   15 years ago I purched a piece of property from John Mac Intine & have paid forit, and have the deed & it recorded at Newcastle, and I purched again from the same Gentleman & give him bond & Morgage for to make him safe   the whole amount of the two purches was $,700   four years ago the city orthurities valued the pro[p]erty of the city and mine was valued at one thousand dollars. and since that time I was offered $,15,00, forit, and me being a colored man and living in the hart of the city thare has been a dispositon for years to deprive me of the place that I occupied so thay sought every opportunity to take the advantage of me, and on the 21 of desember 1862 the Sheriff come to my house saying that he had power to put me and my family out of doors, and went on so to do   I have papers to show up to date that all the Money I owed him was $1,50 one hundred and fifty dollars, thay give me only nine days notice and on the day of sale thay shut themselves up in the barroom and would not allow me nor my friends to come in. I have no knowledge of any disaster ever happened in my family to my knowledge to cause them to serve me as thay did, and them that would of assisted me was afraid on the account of those who are apposed to the people of color, all of this happened with me while I was in Delaware State, and in Delaware City. I was brought up in this state and can get my recomendation from Miss Ann Green who advised me to hold on to the property with many others. I went to Judge [Edward W.] Gilpin on newyears day 1863 and he told me that the sale of my property was presented to him in such manner that he could not understand it to be of as much value as it realy was   and now I ask you in the name of God what are we poor people to do in cases like this   please answer me as soon as posible   please direct your ans to old Chester Pa, Delaware County   I have a family of seven children and the oldest one is going in fourteen years of age

I remain your humble Servent

Emery Watson[5]

The Lincoln administration does not appear to have replied to Watson's letter. Nor would the president have had any authority in such a dispute.

A Former Slave Asks for Permission to Cultivate Government Farms

Edward T. Laburzan was born into bondage in Virginia in 1824 and sold through the domestic slave trade to Louisiana in 1847. He became free in May 1863, when the Union army gained control of his part of Louisiana. On August 22, 1863, he enlisted in the Seventeenth Corps d'Afrique (later designated the Eighty-Eighth USCT), and three days later was appointed first sergeant of Co. K. In his letter to Lincoln, Laburzan described the work he had done recruiting black soldiers for the Union army and then asked for permission to hire black refugees to raise cotton on abandoned plantations.

March 15 1864

Goveerment   Congress & Presadent of the USA

I E T Labuzan am orderly Sargent of the 17 Regment Co K cda [Corps d'Afrique]

I with pleasuer and gratitude this mornning state to the constitutian my wishes with Lawal [loyal?] promision   I has bin of former a slave born in the state of va in eight teen twenty four and came out in the south in eight teen forty seven and heare Remaned under Bonnage untell Delivered By the yankys on the 27 of may 1863   I came to Port Hudson and ware sent contraband to the goveerment farm   thare I Remaned untell I larnt thet Black solders ware offered for   then I volenteared my self and others that I could get to jion and made out a list of them   then after I had in listed forty on the place I went to the next place I got forty six   I placead one of my volentears on the Road to watch for an incruteing [recruiting?] officeer as I ware not alouded to take my troop out of the plantation   on the 23 of August 1863 [Second] Lt [Charles A.] Loud of co G pased the Road and this man of mine told him of me and my troop of volenteers   he then amedently came in to see me   I then called all of my men togeather and left the same day   Lt Loud told me that I should have a large sum [three words erased] But not thet I care for the sum I only wished to bee in goverment sirveces   the hold [whole] number of my volenteers ware 86   I have also got [stray character]⁶ two or three Recrautes to my company since I have bin heare in Port Hudson and now my company are small and has [stray character] But 36 men in it   I Do solamly ask Promision of [stray character] the constitutian to grant me leaf to go out and fill my company of men thet are not solders   I Do not want conscripted men But willfully volenteered with thare own consent becaus thay make the best solder   they scearce ever trys to Desert   thare in the 17 Rgt thare scearce eny Desertion hard [heard] of But Because they are volenteers and in the 18 Regment thay are all ways some one going off   I am quite new to this work But I in tend with Gods accistence to Devout my life in the pertuttion of Ellegence   the farm thet I left when I came out of slavery was Mrs L L Taylors an exstencive large farm   I have knoon 500 to 575 Bales of cotton to bin made on that place an year be sides corn and other Provision to Do the place   I Do ask of the congress senate govenment and presendent of the united State of Amearica ABraham Lincon for promision pleas promet me promision with Lawalty to make crops on this farm or some one this year and thence untill the war is over   the people most of them have come away   I can make a crop of cotton this year though it now late as I think cotton is wanting for the use of the govenment   not thet I wold not loose my time in the sirvece But I could put a man on the place to see Right and jestece [justice] with the people with legal promision leting me have enugh of the contraban folk such as women old men afflicted men and Boys with Legal Leaf to get provision heare at port Hudson of the govenment stores and at New orleans   the are enugh tools on the place mouels [mules?] probly may be wanting of the govenment

the wages and hire of the hands with all promision can be payed out of the crop   I would like to git that place of the goverment   I know it for a number of years   another large cotton farm joining formly belonging to j p pringle   with Leaf of Ellegence I would take By being Replenisheed By the goverment and all Dets payed out of the crops   theas Plantatians is nine miles belooe [below] the mouth of Red River one on the Latusache Bayyou the other on old River   I am happy of the Goverment to let me know is soon as possible   I wish to show what a crop I can Rais for the goverment   I hope thet my Rugh bad hand write may be excuseed knonwing thet my hands are heavy and stiff By the Rugh usegg of a slaves life   pleas excuse all mis stakes and bad letters   E T Labuzans pertision to the goverment and congress and Presadent of the united State ABraham Lincon

A government clerk misread the salutation of this letter, believing it was from someone named "I. E. T. Labayan." It is unclear whether Laburzan ever received a reply. In August 1864 he was transferred to the Ninety-Seventh USCT, and the following month he was reduced to the rank of private. He was discharged for disability in February 1865.[7]

South Carolina Freedmen Protest Being Gouged by a Northern Investor

The Union military gained control of the Sea Islands in South Carolina in November 1861, and former slaves grew cotton on abandoned plantations there in a federal program known as the Port Royal Experiment. Slaves in this region had been used to working with less supervision by whites. In addition, they had been able to earn money by producing extra crops and raising animals after they had finished their work for their enslavers. By some estimates, some Sea Island slaves owned hundreds — even thousands — of dollars of property by the time the Civil War began.

As soon as Union troops gained a foothold in South Carolina, white planters fled the area, abandoning their houses and other property. Military authorities began putting the "hordes of negroes" to work in "contraband camps." African Americans from the Sea Islands and mainland South Carolina performed labor in exchange for clothing and modest pay ($3–$5 per month for common laborers and $8 for carpenters). Meanwhile, former slaves claimed property on nearly two hundred plantations and in 1862 began planting their own crops on land that had previously been used for cotton.

Abolitionists and other antislavery activists began flocking to South Carolina as teachers, missionaries, and medical professionals to care for the needs of the freedpeople. For a period, the Treasury Department oversaw a program in which former slaves labored on plantations under the supervision of benevolent white northerners, but the program was underfunded and the African American workers never received the full compensation they had expected. One former supporter of this plan, Edward S. Philbrick, came to believe that the plantations could be run more efficiently and profitably by private enterprise than by government bureaucrats. Under government leadership, he said, the former slaves "are all shivering in their cabins & churches for want of sufficient clothing." On some occasions, when the government was delinquent in paying former slaves, Philbrick fronted the money at his own expense.

In June 1862, Congress enacted a direct tax on property in the Confederacy. If landowners neglected to pay the tax, their land and buildings would become the property of the federal government, which could then lease or sell the property to private investors or former slaves. Philbrick gathered together a group of northern investors to invest in abandoned plantations in the Sea Islands. He knew this would be a risky venture—he allegedly invested between ten and twenty thousand dollars of his own money—and he warned the other subscribers "not to give more than they were willing to lose outright." Still, he saw his motivations as at least partly altruistic—*"on behalf of the interests of the U.S. Government, of the laboring population now resident upon said estates, and my own wishes."*

Some whites feared that the influx of northern investors would simply result in "a change of masters from slaveowners to capitalists." Their solution was that some land should be retained for the freedpeople. Heeding this advice, Congress amended the Direct Tax Act in February 1863 to provide for some land to be reserved for former slaves, and Lincoln instructed the military authorities in South Carolina to set aside land for them. In the end, some sixty thousand acres were reserved for possible use by freedpeople, while twenty thousand acres were made available for sale to private investors. (Unfortunately, some of the land reserved for freedpeople would be open to public bidding in February 1864.)

Philbrick's group raised capital and purchased eleven plantations, leasing two others from the federal government. The plantations were managed by superintendents who received pay in proportion to the profits of the plantation. According to one observer, "Mr. P. and his 'concern' are making money by the enterprise, and they deserve to if anybody ever did. He was one of the original and largest subscribers to the Educational Commission, and not content with that threw himself into the work personally. . . . The first year, while it was an experiment, he constantly advanced from his own purse to pay the workmen, as government was very dilatory in payments, and bought goods from the north which he sold to the negroes at less than cost." According to this observer, Philbrick's expenses in 1863 amounted to $50,000, but the sale of cotton would "cover this and leave a profit."

Former slaves, however, were upset by Philbrick's business approach to the land. They resisted his attempts to pay them a daily wage, instead forcing him to pay them "by the *piece* or *job*." (Ex-slaves preferred this approach because it gave them more autonomy in how they structured their daily lives.) Even still, the wages were significantly less than northern laborers would earn, and in light of wartime inflation, former slaves' purchasing power was at times insufficient to meet subsistence needs.

Philbrick hoped that following the war, "the more intelligent and Enterprising of the negroes . . . would eventually become proprietors of the soil" — and he promised to eventually relinquish his land holdings for that purpose. But according to the editors of the Freedmen and Southern Society Project, "Laborers on Philbrick's plantations took his vague promise as a binding commitment to sell them the land at his cost." They were thus sorely disappointed when he refused to sell at a dollar per acre.[8] At the same time, some of the freedpeople on Philbrick's plantations received encouragement from whites to protest what they perceived as unjust treatment. In mid-February 1864, a white minister told a group of freedmen, "If the time comes when you *have to give up* what God has just given you, let it cost the Government a *struggle* to turn you off! *Cling to your land!* Hang on! Dont give it up till you are driven off! Go on planting & sowing your patches. If you are finally driven off I shall weep with you. God is on your side. Changes may come but God can change it back."[9] Heeding this advice, a number of freedpeople sent the following petition to Lincoln:

St Helena Island S.C. Mar 1st 1864
    Sir Wee the undersigned. beleaveing wee are unfarely delt with, Are led to lay before you, these, our greaveiences first; then our petetion. And wee here beeg, though it may be long, You will beare kindly with; Reade & answere uss, And as now so, henceforth, our prayrs shall

asscende to the Throan of God, for your future success on Earth. & Tryumph in Heaven.

For what wee have receaved from God, through you, wee will attempt to thank you, wee can only bow our selves, and with silent lips feel our utter inability to say one word, the semblence of thanks. Trusting this our Peteticion in the hands of Allmighty God, and your kindness, wee now say, Let there be what success may in stor for you and your Armies, Wither our freedom is for ever or a day, wither as Slaves or Freemen, wee shall ever, carry you & your kindness to us in our hearts, may Heaven bless. you.

Our greaveincess

Mr Edward Philbrick. (A Northern Man) has bought up All our former Masters Lands under falls pretences;

To wit

He promis'd to buey in, at public sale, with our consent all the Lands on the following Plantations,

Mr Coffin's Place, Mr. Coffin's Cherrie Hill, Maulbuery Hill place. Big House place. Corner place. Dr Fuller's place, Pollawanney place, Mary Jinkins'es place. Hamelton Frip place, Morgan Island, & John Johntson's place, of Ladies Island.

Before bueying he promised to sell to us again any ammount of the Land at $1.00 one Dollar pr Acre wee wish'd to purchas,   Said sail was to be made when ever the Government sold the balance of its Land to the People resideing thereon,

On the 18th day of last month sailes of Publick Lands began in Beaufort, & what doo wee see to day, on all the Plantations our Breathern are bueying thr Land. getting redy to plant ther cropps and build ther Houses, which they will owne for ever

Wee hav gon to Mr Philbrick & Ask'd him to sell us our Land, and get for an answere he will not sell us one foot, & if he does sell to any one he will charge $10.00 Ten Dollars pr Acre. Wee have work'd for Mr Philbrick the whole year faithfully, and hav received nothing comparatively, not enough to sustaine life if wee depended entirely uppon our wages,   he has Stors here chargeing feerefull prices for every nessary of life, and at last the People have become discouraged, all most heart broken.

He will not sell us our Land neither pay us to work for him; And if wee wish to work for others where wee might make something, he turns us out of our Houses, he says wee shall not live-on his plantation unless wee work for him, If wee go to Genl Saxton he tells us if Mr Phlbrick sees fit he will sell us the Land according to agreement   If not then wee must go on Government Land where wee can buey as much as wee please, But, the Tax Commissioners say they cannot sell to us unless wee are living on the Plantations now selling, Wee go to the Sup^t Genl of the Island; Mr [Reuben] Tomlinson, he says work For Mr Phibrick for what ever wages he sees fit to pay   if wee do not Mr Philbrick may drive us off the Land and wee shall not taks our Houes with us,   He says, 'Mr Philbrick bought everything Houses Lands & all.[']

Why did Goverment sell all our Masters Land's to Mr Philbrick for so trifling a sume; we are all redy & willing of truth anxious to buey all our Masters Land, & every thing upon them; and pay far more than he did for them

Wee will not attempt to lay all our greaveinces before you as t'will take much to long   we will only mention one cas which exceedes anything done in our Masters time   Charl's Ware an agent of Mr Philbrick's turn'd the cloths of a Colard Girl over her head turned her over a Barrel, & whipd her with a Leathern Strap   She had been confined but two days before & allthough the case was reported to Mr Tomlinson Sup^t. Genl the Agent still retains his place,   Thiss is shamefull, wee blush [to] write or send it you but the truth must be told,   But you may ask what wee would have done,

If possible wee Pray for either one of theese two things.

Petetion

1st Either let Mr Philbrick be compeeld to live up to his promises with us, and sell us as much Land as wee want for our owne Homes at a reasonabele price, giving us cleare deeds for the same.

2nd Otherwise wee pray Goverment to repurchas the Land of Mr Philbrick and then let us farm it giveing one half of all that is rais'd to the Goverment   wee would much rather this and will furnish everything ourselves and will warrent there will be but few feet of Ground Idle. As Mr Philbrick has broken his part of the contract is Government bound to keep thers?

And wee will her mention, that many of us told Mr Philbrick not to buey the Land as wee wanted it our selves.

3rd And wee furthermore beeg that an Agent may be sent us, who will see not wrong; but right done us one who will deal justly by us.

Wee doo not want a Master or owner Neither a driver with his Whip wee want a Friend

Trusting this may be lookd upon kindly beeging a immediate answer that wee may know what to doo Wee are with very great respect your most Humble & Obdt Srvt's

[19 signatures]

Please answer to care of John S Smallwood   Beaufort SC

The writer of this would meerely say in conclusion, that were the Grounds Farmed by the Cold people [the] Government would make more in one Year than would pay for two plantations at $1.25 pr Acre. It does not require then an agent on every Plantation   one man could attende at leas six or eight   Very Respec^t Submitted by

John S. Smallwood

The Lincoln administration tasked Treasury official Austin Smith with investigating the complaints. Smith reported that Philbrick saw himself "as the friend of the negro, an Abolitionist, & Philanthropist," but that he had used his knowledge of the area to purchase the best plantations on the Sea Islands for himself. Nevertheless, Smith reported "that Mr. Philbrick promised to let the negroes have lands for homes, *when the war should close.*" As for the whipping incident, Smith stated that the girl punished was "a very immoral & bad girl . . . but not under the circumstances, nor with the severity stated." And Smith was convinced that such a punishment would not take place again.

Smith believed that Philbrick and his investors "mean to do right in the end," and he hoped that Philbrick would sell the land to the freedpeople sooner than the end of the war. "In view of the large profits realized upon the investment, these gentlemen can well afford to grant homesteads to these people at a nominal price. Justice & equity demand that the freedmen should be provided with homes. They are loyal citizens." Unfortunately, from the freedpeople's perspective, Philbrick did not sell any land to them until January 1866, and then at $5 per acre.[10]

A South Carolina Freedman Seeks Protection of His Property

Laura Towne (1825–1901), a native of Pennsylvania, traveled to the Sea Islands of South Carolina in April 1862 to work with former slaves. In June 1862 she opened a school for freedpeople, which became known as the Penn School. Initially operated out of the back room of a plantation house with

Laura M. Towne's School, St. Helena Island, South Carolina.
Courtesy of the Library of Congress.

only nine students, Towne ran the Penn School until her death in 1901. The freedpeople knew her as one of the "bukra [white] ladies at church."[11]

In 1864, Towne wrote the following letter to Lincoln on behalf of a freedman in South Carolina. Don Carlos had originally lived in Virginia, before being enslaved by William Henry Brisbane in South Carolina. Around 1833, Brisbane sold his slaves and moved to Cincinnati, where he converted to antislavery. Feeling guilty, he returned to South Carolina to repurchase his slaves so that he could set them free. Brisbane was able to free all his slaves but one—Carlos. Carlos thus did not achieve freedom until the arrival of

Union soldiers nearly thirty years later. Nevertheless, Carlos had learned to read before the war, and teacher Charlotte Forten called him "a man of considerable intelligence."[12] The entire letter is in Towne's hand except for the signature, which appears to be in Carlos's.

St. Helena Is. S.C.
Frogmoor May 29th 1864

To the President of the United States, Abraham Lincoln,

My name is Don Carlos, and I hope my letter will find you and your family in perfect health. Will you please to be so kind Sir, as to tell me about my little bit of land. I am afraid to put on it a stable, or corn-house, and such like, for fear it will be taken away from me again. Will you please to be so kind as to tell me whether the land will be sold from under us or no, or whether it will be sold to us at all. I should like to buy the very spot where I live. It aint but six acres, and I have got cotton planted on it, and very fine cotton too; and potatoes and corn coming on very pretty. If we colored people have land I know we shall do very well—there is no fear of that. Some of us have as much as three acres of corn, besides ground-nuts, potatoes, peas, and I don't know what else myself. If the land can only be sold, we can buy it all, for every house has its cotton planted, and doing well, and planted only for ourselves. We should like to know how much we shall have to pay for it—if it is sold.

I am pretty well struck in age Sir, for I waited upon Mrs. Alston that was Theodosia Burr, daughter of Aaron Burr, and I remember well when she was taken by pirates, —but I can maintain myself and my family well on this land.[13] My son got sick on the Wabash (Flagship at Hilton Head) and he will never get well, for he has a cough that will kill him at last. He cannot do much work, but I can maintain him. I had rather work for myself and raise my own cotton than work for a gentleman for wages, for if I could sell my cotton for only .50 cts a pound it would pay me.

What ever *you* say I am willing to do and I will attend to whatever you tell me.

Your most obedient servant,

    don carlous [illegible word][14]

P.S. After the Government Superintendent gave me leave to pick one of the new houses I pitch upon the one I live in. Then I fill up the holes in the garden, and in the house, I lath it & fill in with moss till it is comfortable in the winter. I did a heap of work on it, and now it would hurt my heart too much to see another man have it. I should not like it at all.

The letter above was dictated to me by a Freedman on St. Helena Island who is a refugee from Edisto and who was formerly confidential servant in the Alston family. He can read & write but is too old to do it with ease. He, with others of the Freedmen, often expresses a wish to be able to speak to Massa Linkum, feeling sure that *he* will listen to their plea for land & do what is best for them. At Carlos desire, I took down from his own lips the words he was restless to speak to the President, intending to hand the letter to him at the Sanitary Fair, but I refrained from so doing that business might not be thrust in upon pleasure.

I have given my promise to Carlos that I will do my best to let his "own word" reach the ear in which he has unbounded trust & hope, and therefore I forward this letter to Washington, begging no one to prevent its reaching its destination.

Very respectfully

Laura Towne

Teacher of Freedmen on St. Helena Is.[15]

Little is known about what happened to Carlos after the war. However, in 1879, Towne received a letter from Carlos's grandson, Andrew Seabrook, asking for a letter of recommendation for admission to the New York Academy of Design so that he could train to become a landscape painter. Seabrook had been a student of hers at the Penn School. She wrote, "The curious part of it is that he is nearly white, and belonged to the Allston family, of which family Washington Allston came. Is it *heredity*? He has been making a living as a waiter, and is just twenty-one. I shall write what I know of him to Mr. [D. H.] Huntingdon, and send him a letter for the Academy—but I don't suppose I can do anything for him worth speaking of."[16]

Southern Freedmen Petition Lincoln for Reimbursement for Seized Cotton

On March 12, 1863, Congress enacted a law that authorized the secretary of the Treasury to oversee the collection and sale of captured and abandoned property in the South, such as land, houses, and especially cotton. According to the law, such property could be "appropriated to public use" or sold at public auction, with the proceeds going to the Treasury of the United States. Any person who claimed to have been the owner of captured or abandoned property could file a claim in the U.S. Court of Claims.[17]

Secretary of the Treasury Salmon P. Chase designated several clerks in his office to handle these new responsibilities. (In 1869 this group became officially known as the Division of Captured and Abandoned Property.) The following petitions from black Georgians reveal the amount of property some of these men had owned prior to the arrival of Union soldiers under General William Tecumseh Sherman in the fall of 1864.

United States of America
State of Georgia
City of Savannah

To His Excellency Abraham Lincoln   President of the United States

The petitioner John Habersham, a Freedman, would respectfully state that he is a native of the City of Savannah and State of Georgia that he is 26 years of age and has been employed for the past five years as a Sampler and storer of Cotton by his then master, Robert Erwin of Savannah, who has always given him from year to year during that time the loose cotton and samples.

Your petitioner states that upon the occupation of this City by the national forces he was the lawful owner of Fourteen Bales (14) of Upland Cotton and (155) one hundred and fifty five lbs of loose cotton in bulk that the same was stored as follows (viz) Ten Bales marked {JH} in Jones building north side Bay street and east of Drayton Street—One Hundred & fifty five (155) pounds of loose cotton, stored in the same place as above described ten 10 Bales, and Four Bales stored in a building three doors west of Wetters Flour and Grist mill. And—

Your petitioner further states that in obedience to and in pursuance of a General order from the Military Authorities at this place he returned and reported to Col [H. C.] Ransom U.S.A and Government Agt. all of the above described Cotton, and that since said return was made, a portion, of said Cotton has been removed by said Col Ransom, and, petitioner has good reasons to believe that the remained [remainder?] of his Cotton will in like manner be taken and removed beyond his controll without reference to petitioners civil or repolitical [political] status, and without furnishing him with any receipt or other evidence of ownership of said Cotton.

The petitioner in view of the facts stated, and in consideration of the additional fact, that he has never at any time violated any law or laws of the United States, Prays, that your Excellency will be pleased to order his rights in property described, and obtained as stated in this petition, to be respected, and that the said property be returned to him, or if the same be converted into money, he prays that the ~~same~~ proceeds of same be in like manner be paid over to him after deducting such costs and charges as the Government shall deem proper

{as Your petitioner will ever pray}

Jno Habersham

Signed in the presence of

   H C Freeman

   A Wilber

Savannah Feb 23ᵈ 1865.

We the undersigned citizens of Savannah do hereby certify that we have known the petitioner, John Habersham, for many years. That he is an honest and truthful negro, and that he is the lawful owner of property described in this petition—   *H C Freeman*

Test   A. Wilbur[18]

United States of America
State of Georgia
City of Savannah

To His Excellency Abraham Lincoln President of the United States

The petitioner Henry Fields, a Freedman would respectfully state that he is a native of the City of Savannah and State of Georgia, that he is (32) thirty two years of age and a butcher by trade.

Your petitioner further states that, when this city was occupied by the National forces on the 21ˢᵗ day of December last, he was the lawful owner, in his own right and title and for his own exclusive use, benefit and behoof, of (5) Five Bales of Upland Cotton marked "H. Fields" and also marked "M," which was stored on Arnold Street in said City of Savannah (4) four doors from Wetters Mills. This Cotton was purchased by petitioner with his own funds the proceeds of his personal labor, was as above stated his exclusive property, and held by him as an investment preferable to Securities in which he had no confidence.

Your petitioner further States that in obedience to and in pursuance of a General order from the Military Authorities of the United States dated January 6th 1865, City of Savannah, he returned and reported to Col Ransom U.S.A and Government Agt, all of the above described Cotton and that since said return was made, all of said cotton has been taken possession of and will be removed by said Col Ransom, beyond petitioners control without reference to his civil or political Status, and without furnishing him with any receipt or other evidence of ownership of said cotton.

The petitioner in view of the facts stated, and in consideration of the additional fact, that he has never at any time violated any law or laws of the United States, *Prays*, that your Excellency will be pleased to order his rights in the property described and obtained as stated in this petition, to be respected, and that the said property be returned to him, or if the same be converted into money, he prays the proceeds of the same be in like manner paid over to him after deducting such costs and charges as the Government shall deem proper. And your petitioner will ever pray &c.

Henry Fields
Signed in the presence of
   Peter Duncan
   John H. Habersham
   M Benedict
   Provost Judge
   City of Savannah
We the undersigned Citizens of Savannah do hereby certify that we have known the petitioner Henry Fields for many years, That he is an honest truthful man, and that he is the lawful owner of the property described in the petition.
Test   Peter Donelan
         J. R. Martin[19]

The following correspondent, Charles Bradwell, was forty years old in 1865. He had been a slave in Liberty County, Georgia, until freed by the will of his master, J. L. Bradwell, in 1861. At the time he wrote this petition, he had been a minister in the Methodist Episcopal Church for about a decade. On January 12, 1865, Bradwell was one of only twenty Savannah-area African American pastors chosen to meet with Secretary of War Edwin M. Stanton and General William T. Sherman to discuss the needs of former slaves.[20]

United States of America
State of Georgia
City of Savannah

To His Excellency Abraham Lincoln   President of the United States

The petitioner Charles L Bradwell a free man of Color, would respectfully state that he is a native of Savannah, and a citizen of same, Aged forty years and by occupation a Blacksmith and minister of the Gospel. The petitioner states that upon the occupation of the City of Savannah by the National forces, he was the lawful owner of Four (4) Bales of Cotton three of which were Sea Islands, and one uplands, all marked "C L Bradwell" and stored on his premises in Currytown Berrian Street near the City Commons, said four Bales weighing in the aggregate [blank space] Lbs.

In persuance of a general order from the Military authorities at this place the petitioner ~~repeat~~ reported to Col Ransom U.S.A., and Government Agent the above described Cotton giving in said return the marks and specifications as above; and whereas, the bulk of the Cotton in this City returned as above stated, has been removed, and the balance is now being removed, as rapidly as possible by said Col Ransome's order's;—the petitioner has therefore good reasons to know that his four bales will in like manner be taken from him, and no receipt or other evidence of ownership given petitioner for same.

The petitioner further states that he is and ever has been a true and lawful citizen of the United States; that he has never at any time or in any manner engaged in, aided or abetted in the rebellion against the Government of the United States, nor has he at any time ever committed any Act which would in anywise jeopardize his rights as a citizen of the U.S.

The petitioner in view of the facts stated and premises considered Prays, that your Excellency will be pleased to order the payment to him or his duly constituted agt the value of his four bales of Cotton, after deducting such costs and charges as the Government shall deem meet and proper, and your petitioner will ever pray.

Charles Bradwell

Subscribed & Sworn to before me this 1st Day of March 1865

M. Benedict
Provost Judge
City of Savannah

Henry Bates and John Johnson state upon oath that they have known Charles L Bardwell [Bradwell] for twelve years, that they know him to be a correct hardworking industrious man, a black smith by trade, and also Minister of "Andrews Chapell" a place of public worship in the City of Savannah. That he is the owner of the four Bales of Cotton stored under his residence on Berrian Street between Montgomery and West Broad Curry town near City Commons, and that said four Bales of Cotton was purchased by said Charles L Bradwell with money saved by his earnings at his trade.

   Henry Bates

   John Johnson

Sworn & Subscribed before me this 1st Day of March 1865

   M Benedict

   Provost Judge

   City of Savannah[21]

United States of America

State of Georgia

City of Savannah

To His Excellency Abraham Lincoln   President Of the United States

   The Petitioner Delancey Jenks a free man of color, Citizen of Savannah, State of Georgia, United States of America, would respectfully state, that he is a blacksmith by trade and aged 30 years.

   That, upon the occupation of the City of Savannah by Genl Shermans army, he was the Lawful owner of three (3) Bales of Cotton stored on his premises, on Mill street, and marked "D Jenks" and,

   Petitioner further states, that in persuance of a general order from the Military Authorities at this place, he reported and returned to Col Ransom U.S.A and government agent the above described ~~four 4~~ three (3) Bales of Cotton giving in said return the marks and specifications as above, and

   Petitioner states that after return was made as above stated the above described three Bales of Cotton was seized and removed by order of Col Ransom, and no receipt or other evidence of ownership given petitioner for said three bales Cotton.

   The petitioner states, that he is and ever have been a true and lawyal citizen of the United States; that he has never at any time engaged in, aided or abetted, in the rebellion against the United States Government, nor has he at any time committed any act which would in any manner jeopardy[ize] his rights as a true and laway [loyal] citizen of the United States.

The petitioner in view of the facts stated and premices considered, "Prays," that your Excellency will be pleased to order that his rights in the property described be respected; and, that you will be pleased to order the return of said three bales of Cotton to him; or, the payment to him or his duly constituted attorney or agent, of the value thereof, after deducting such costs and charges as the Government shall deem meet and proper, as your petitioner will ever pray.

Delancy Jencks[22]

Subscribed and Sworn to Before this First Day of March 1865.

M. Benedict

Provost Judge

City of Savannah[23]

Regardless of the race of the person involved, cases like these could take years—even decades—to resolve. In 1870, for example, the Court of Claims awarded Delancy Jenks $496.71 and John Habersham $1,655.70. Five years later, the court awarded Jenks another $29.28 and Habersham $97.60. The following year the court awarded Jenks an additional $525.99 of his $1,350 claim; by 1876, however, Habersham had died, so his executor received $1,753.30 of his original $6,439.50 claim. Some cases took even longer. In 1888, Charles L. Bradwell was finally paid $1,532 in accordance with an act of Congress.[24]

Suffering Freedpeople in North Carolina Ask for Assistance

After Union forces captured Roanoke Island, North Carolina, in February 1862, hundreds of enslaved people began flocking there. In May 1863, the military established a freedmen's colony on the island, and by 1865 some 3,500 ex-slaves lived there. Each family was given a one-acre plot of land for subsistence farming, but most of the adult men were off fighting for the Union. As one army chaplain wrote, "The able bodied males with few exceptions are in the army, and there are not many families on the Island that have not furnished a father, husband or son, and in numerous instances, two and three members to swell the ranks of our army." Those left behind, he continued, were "Aged and Infirm, Orphan children and soldiers wives and families" who were reliant on army rations. According to the chaplain, the soldiers had enlisted "with the assurance from the Government that their families should be cared for, and supported in their absence," but army rations had recently been reduced and now "hundreds [are] suddenly face to face with starvation." He continued, "It is a daily occurrence to see scores of women and children crying for bread, whose husbands, Sons and fathers are in the army today."[25]

In the midst of this emergency, Richard Boyle, a black schoolteacher on the island, traveled to Washington, D.C., and presented the following petitions to the War Department on April 6, 1865:

Roanoke Island N.C. march 9th 1865.

M[r] President Dear Sir   We Colored men of this Island held a meeting to consult over the affairs of our present conditions and our rights and we find that our arms are so Short that we cant doe any thing with in our Selves So we Concluded the best thing we could do was to apply to you or Some of your cabinets   we are told and also we have read that you have declared all the Colored people free bothe men and woman that is in the Union lines and if that be so we want to know where our wrights is or are we to be Stamp down or troden under feet by our Superintendent which he is the very man that we look to for assistents,   in the first place his Proclamation was that no able boded man was to draw any rations except he was at work for the Government   we all agreed to that and was willing to doe as we had done for $10,00 per month and our rations though we Seldom ever get the mony

the next thing he said that he wanted us to work and get our living as White men and not apply to the Government and that is vry thing we want to doe, but after we do this we cant satisfie him   Soon as he Sees we are trying to Support our Selves without the aid of the Government he comes and make a Call for the men, that is not working for the Government to Goe away and if we are not willing to Goe he orders the Guards to take us by the point of the bayonet, and we have no power to help it   we know it is wright and are willing to doe any thing that the President or our head Commanders want us to doe but we are not willing to be pull and haul a bout so much by those head men as we have been for the last two years and we may say Get nothing for it, last fall a large number of we men was Conscript and sent up to the front and all of them has never return   Some Got Kill Some died and When they taken them they treated us mean and our owners ever did they taken us just like we had been dum beast

We Colored people on Roanok Island are willing to Submit to any thing that we know the President or his cabinet Say because we have Got since [sense] enough to believe it is our duty to doe every thing we Can doe to aid Mr Lyncoln and the Government but we are not willing to work as we have done for Chaplain [Horace] James and be Troden under foot and Get nothing for it we have work faithful Since we have been on the Island we have built our log houses we have Cultivate our acre of Ground and have Tried to be less exspence to the Government as we Possible Could be and we are yet Trying to help the Government all we Can for our lives those head men have done every thing to us that our masters have done except by and Sell us and now they are Trying to Starve the woman & children to death cutting off they ration they have Got so now that they wont Give them no meat to eat, every ration day beef & a little fish and befor the Ten days is out they are going from one to another Trying to borrow a little meal to last until ration day M^r [Holland] Streeter will just order one barrell of meet for his fish men and the others he Gives nothing but beaf but we thank the Lord for that if we no it is the President or the Secretarys orders this is what want to know whoes orders it is, one of our minister children was fool to ration house and Sent off and his father working three days in every week for his ration

Roanoke Island N.C march 9th 1865
we have appeal to General Butler and Genl Butler wrote to Capt James to do Better and Capt James has promies to do Better and instead of doing better he has done worst and now we appeal to you which is the last resort and only help we have got, feeling that we are entily friendless, on the Island there numrous of Soldiers wives and they Can hardly get any rations and some of them are almost starving

we dont exspect to have the same wrights as white men doe we know that [we] are in a millitary country and we exspect to obey the rules and orders of our authories and doe as they say doe, any thing in reason we thank God and thank our President all of his aids for what has been done for us but we are not satisfide with our Supertendent nor the treatement we receives now we want you to send us answer

what to depen upon   let it be good or bad and we will be
Satisfide   Respectifully yours
      Roanoke Island   N.C.

                                    Roanoke Island   N.C   march 9th 1865
      we want to know from the Secretary of War has the Rev Chaplain
James which is our Superintendent of negros affairs has any wright to
take our boy Children from us and from the School and Send them to
newbern to work to pay for they ration without they parent Consint   if
he has we thinks it very hard indeed   he essued a Proclamation that
no boys Should have any rations at 14 years old   well we thought was
very hard that we had to find our boy Children to Goe to School hard
as times are, but rather then they Should Goe without learning we
thought we would try and doe it and say no more a bout it and the first
thing we knowed Mr Stereeter the Gentlemen that ration the Contrabands had Gone a round to all the White School-Teachers and told
them to Give the boys orders to goe and get they ration on a Cirtain
day   so the negros as we are Call are use to the Cesesh [secessionist]
plots Suspicion the Game they was Going to play and a Greate many
never Sent they Children. So Some twenty or twenty-five went and M^r
Streeter Give them they rations and the Guard march them down to
the head quarters and put them on board the boat and carried them to
newbern   here is woman here on the Island which their husbands are
in the army just had one little boy to help them to cut & lug wood & to
Goe arrand for them   Chaplain James has taken them and sent them
away   Some of these little ones he sent off wasen oer 12 years olds. the
mothers of Some went to Chaplain and Grieved and beg for the little boys
but he would not let them have them   we want to know if the Prisident
done essued any ration for School boys   if he dont then we are
satisfide   we have men on the Island that Can Support the boys to Goe
to School but here are Poor woman are not able to do it So the orphans
must Goe without they learning   that all we can say a bout the matter
      the next is Concerning of our White Soldiers   they Come to our
Church and we treat them with all the Politeness that we can and
Some of them treats us as though we were beast and we cant help our
Selves   Some of them brings Pop Crackers and Christmas devils and
throws a mong the woman and if we Say any thing to them they will
talk about mobin us. we report them to the Capt   he will Say you must
find out Which ones it was and that we cant do but we think very

hard it   they put the pistols to our ministers breast because he Spoke to them about they behavour in the Church,   the next is Capt James told us When he got the mill built he would let us have plank to buil our houses   we negroes went to work and cut and hewd the timber and built the mill under the northern men derection and now he Charges us 3 and 4 dollars a hundred for plank and if we Carry 3 logs to the mill he takes 2 and Gives us one. that is he has the logs haul and takes one for hauling and one for Sawing and we thinks that is to much Without he paid us better then he does. and the next thing is he wont allow a man any ration While he is trying to buil him Self a house. to live in and how are negroes to live at that rate   we Cant See no way to live under Such laws, Without Some Altiration

Roanoke Island N.C. March 9th 1865

here is men here that has been working for the last three year and has not been paid for it. they, work on the forts and Cut spiles and drove them and done any thing that they was told to do   Capt James Came on the Island Jan. 1864 and told they men that he had made all the matters wright a bout they back pay and now says he I want all of you men that has due bills to carry them to Mr Bonnell at head quar-ters and all them has not got no paper to show for they work I will make them Swear and kiss the Bibel   and the men done just as he told them and he told us that he had made out the rolls and sent them up to Washington City and now he says that money is all dead   So we are very well Satisfide just So we know that he has never received it for our head men has fool us so much just because they think that we are igorant we have lost all Confidince in them. so all we wants is a Chance and we can Get a living like White men   we are praying to God every day for the war to Stop So we wont be beholding to the Government for Something to Eat   Yours Respectfully

Roanoke Island.^{26}

These petitions wended their way through the federal bureaucracy until they wound up in the hands of the very man who had precipitated the freed-people's grievances — Horace James, the Freedmen's Bureau superintendent in eastern North Carolina. On July 10, 1865, James reported indignantly: "The col-ored people who have been within our lines three years or more have been so long receiving aid from the government, as to count it their *right* to receive it, even when in many cases they might support themselves." He noted that the bureau had required boys fourteen years old and older to work instead of receiving rations, but this led to "a howl of dissatisfaction . . . by the colored people." Moreover, he claimed, that "when beef and fish are given them instead of *bacon* they complain of having 'no meat,' and speak of starvation," but that there were really no instances of starvation in the colony. He concluded that the statements in the petitions were "gross exaggerations."[27]

The assistant superintendent of Negro affairs at Roanoke Island and several missionary teachers offered a very different perspective, reporting to Union general Oliver Otis Howard, "Those who are able to work have proved themselves industrious and would support themselves, had they the opportunity to do so, under favorable conditions." However, the realities on the ground required "such assistance as humanity shall dictate to the infirm and helpless, and such support as may be justly claimed for the families of soldiers whose wants the Government is bound to supply until they can be placed in a position to be able to Sustain themselves." Accordingly, they concluded, "We [make this appeal] with a feeling that the emergency demands immediate action to prevent suffering which justice, humanity, and every principle of christianity forbids." Upon reading this appeal, as well as other complaints from soldiers whose families were suffering, General Howard ordered that army rations continue to be provided to soldiers' families until further orders were issued.[28]

Over the next few years, most of the freedpeople left Roanoke Island, and in 1867 the colony was decommissioned.

A Government Mill Worker Asks for Equal Pay

Black soldiers were not the only people who protested unequal pay. Freedmen who worked for the government also wrote to Lincoln to demand equal pay for equal work. The following letter came from an African American man who was working at a government lumber mill in Virginia. In 1865, the mill employed about one hundred black men, many of whom had their families there with them. Like other letters sent to the president, this one was written by a freedmen's teacher.

Government Mills, Via. April 4th/65

Pres. Abraham Lincoln Washington, D.C.

Dear Sir,

I think that if those who have things in charge were faithful we should have our wages oftener than once or twice a year. We were partly paid off two months ago and then we had been five months without pay. I want to ask if a colored man is not entitled to the same wages as a white man if he does the same work? I have been engineer of the Richmond mill here, one year and five months. The first year my wages were $25,00, twenty-five dollars a month, since then $26,00, twenty six dollars. The white man who runs the Page mill receives seventy-five dollars a month, and his work is precisely the same as mine. Now I can not see any reason why he should have so much more than I. I believe you are a good friend to the colored people and wish to have them treated as they should be, but I suppose you have many cares and cannot attend to every thing, but if you can, let us shere equally with the white laborers.

Very Respectfully your servant

James Wilson.[29]

Immediately following Wilson's letter is the following note written in the same hand. The author, Miss Esther W. Douglass, had been born in Grafton, New Hampshire, in 1824, and by 1860 was working as a schoolteacher in Decorah, Iowa. In January 1865 she began work as a missionary and teacher for freedmen and women in Virginia through the American Missionary Association.

Much esteemed President,

At the earnest request of one of my pupils I have written the above, yet I have felt that owing to your many cares, it will probably avail nothing. There is a bad state of things here. The white men employed as overseers, are none of them Christian men, and few feel any interest in the colored people. On the contrary most of them would rather that they should be kept down than otherwise. The wagon master is *dreadfully* profane and vents his curses on those whom he sees trying to learn to read. He says provoking things to those under him, and then curses them if they get angry and reply. It has seemed to me unjust that there should be difference in pay between two individuals doing precisely the same work, as is the case I believe in other instances besides the one referred to. I have talked to the white men about it, but have never said anything to the colored men because I did not wish to make them dissatisfied. I did not know until urged to write this letter, that they were aware of the difference. Hoping that the time will come when wicked men will no longer tyranize over the unfortunate and praying that He with whom are the treasures of wisdom may guide and sustain you in all your responsible duties

I remain Very Respectfully,

E. W. Douglass, Freedmen's teacher, Government Mills, Via.[30]

Lincoln was assassinated ten days after this letter was written, and he likely never saw it or had an opportunity to act on Wilson's request. Miss Douglass continued to teach the freedmen at her school in Hampton Roads. When she first arrived in the area in January 1865, she was wary of her black students, who worked by day and came to school in the evening, but she very quickly came to have a great deal of affection for them. "I love them and I think they love me," she wrote on March 4, 1865. She found that a "cause of sadness" for her came when local whites complained "about the 'niggers' and as I am compelled, if I speak, to differ with them, it is unpleasant." She added, "I wish some of the Christian men of the North were here to control affairs instead of men who care only to make money."[31]

CHAPTER TEN
Mementos

Lincoln received gifts from several African Americans during the war. In the spring of 1864, a woman from Philadelphia created a beautiful wax fruit display that she presented to him in the White House library. In September of that year, a delegation of Baltimore ministers gave him an expensive pulpit edition of the Bible to express their gratitude for all he had done for their race. The Bible bore a gold plate with an inscription that thanked Lincoln as "The Friend of Universal Freedom / From / the Loyal Coloured People of Baltimore / as a token of respect and Gratitude." A few months later, in November, a "self emancipated woman" from Natchez, Mississippi, sent him "a nice *Liberty Cake*" to express her thanks for what he had accomplished for slaves in the Confederacy. Whatever a "Liberty Cake" was, it and the wax fruit display are long since gone, but the Bible presently sits on display in a glass case on the second floor of the John Hope and Aurelia E. Franklin Library at Fisk University in Nashville, Tennessee, where it has been since Robert T. Lincoln donated it to the historically black university in 1916.[1]

A few other mementos survive in Lincoln's personal collection of papers at the Manuscript Division of the Library of Congress. Lincoln received the following four letters from formerly enslaved men who either joined the Union army or found refuge in contraband camps. The president was apparently so touched by these missives that he kept them in his personal papers.

South Carolina Freedmen Give Thanks
for the Emancipation Proclamation

January 1, 1863, was a momentous day. African Americans throughout the North and South celebrated Lincoln's signing of the Emancipation Proclamation. In Beaufort, South Carolina, the former slaves attending Tabernacle Baptist Church adopted resolutions thanking Lincoln for what he had done. Their pastor, Solomon Peck, a white missionary and teacher from Boston, sent the resolutions to Lincoln, explaining that they had been "adopted by them unanimously at a special meeting held in their 'Tabernacle' this first day of January, 1863." He continued, "The sentiments & the words of the

Resolutions were dictated by a Committee of themselves, chosen for the purpose; & having been taken in writing *while* & *as* they were spoken, are their own. The Committee have also, by direction of the Church, subscribed severally their names, or marks. It seems proper to add, that the members of this Church, *now* resident on Port Royal & islands adjacent, are, with one exception, *people of color proclaimed free this day*, & numbering more than eleven hundred." He concluded, "Accept, Sir, the assurance of my highest consideration, & of my own most hearty participation in the spirit & scope of the Resolutions."[2] The following is in Peck's hand:

*Extract from the Minutes of the Baptist Church
of Christ in Beaufort, S.C. —*

"Beaufort, Jany 1. 1863.

"1. *Resolved*, That we all unite, with our hearts & minds & souls, to give thanks to God for this great thing that He has done for us; that He has put it into his (Mr. Lincoln's) mind—that all should come to this very stand, according to the will of God, in freeing all the colored people. We believe that Jesus Christ will now see of the travail of his soul, in what he has done for us.

"2. *Resolved*, That we all unite together to give Mr. President Lincoln our hearty thanks for the Proclamation. We are more than thankful to him & to God, & pray for him & for ourselves. May the blessing of God rest upon you. May grace, mercy & peace sustain you. May you go on conquering & to conquer this rebellion. We have gathered together two or three times a week for the last five months, to pray that the Lord might help you & all your soldiers, hoping that the Almighty would bless you in all your goings, & crown you with a crown of glory & a palm of victory. We never expect to meet your face on earth; but may we meet in a better world than this;—this is our humble prayer.

"*Voted*, That the Committee sign the Resolutions for us, —& that we request our Pastor Dr. Peck to send them to Mr. Lincoln."

Jacob Robinson	(by his mark)			X
Daniel Mifflin	"	"	"	X
Joseph Jenkins	"	"	"	X
June Harrison	"	"	"	X
January	"	"	"	X
Harry Simmons	"	"	"	X
Caesar Singleton	"	"	"	X

Thomas Ford	"	"	"	X
Kit Green				Kit Green
Charles Pringle	"	"	"	X
Peter White	"	"	"	X
Elias Gardner	"	"	"	X
Moses Simmons	"	"	"	

A South Carolina Freedman Expresses
His Enthusiasm for the War

John Proctor was either twenty-six or twenty-eight years old (the records disagree) when he enlisted in the Second South Carolina Volunteers (Thirty-Fourth USCT) at Beaufort, South Carolina, on March 20, 1863. His enlistment record listed him as a servant or waiter who had been born in Charleston. Having *stolen* a bit of education, as he explains in the letter that follows, he was appointed a sergeant in his regiment.

In the spring of 1863, Lincoln sent his private secretary John Hay on a mission to South Carolina. There, Hay met Sergeant Proctor and promised to take a letter from him to "Mass Lincum." But Hay departed before returning to see Proctor, so Capt. Edward W. Hooper, an officer on Gen. Rufus Saxton's staff, sent it to Hay in late May, who then delivered it to Lincoln.

Beaufor So Ca April 18 1863
To the Excelency the President of the united States

Deare Sir I have had the onner of righting to you these fue lines hoping that tha may find you in A most Perfic state of helte as it left me the saim. Deare Sir I have had the oner of righting to you By the request of capt. hoopper of genrel Saxten staff and I then think that it was the Greatist oner that I cold have had. sir I wold that I only cold have right Better so that I cold Exspriss my word Better—tho wat little I have got I Stold it when I wEr with my rebble master so that I hav never had the right schooling—

But I hope that you ma under stand wat little I have Sed. sir sence I have got a way from the rebbles I hav throne my Self in to the collard regemint So that I may have the Pleger of capttor my master Bueregaurd   as I have Binn Sirvin under him so long I think no know is the time for me to let him Spinte [spend?] sum of his time under me and my hot shot.

I only wish that I only cold have the Pleger of coming to Be hold
you. with mine eyes   I am verry much longing to see you   remember
me to all of my Brothers felow cittysons of the united States
> I am now your humble
> Sirvant. John. Proctor.
> of the 2 So Ca. V. .C.o. C³

Proctor's desire to meet Lincoln in person was shared by many enslaved
men and women. As we saw in the foregoing chapters, some former slaves
were able to meet him at the White House and to present him with petitions
for their rights. Curiously, in the 1930s approximately twenty-five of the ex-
slaves interviewed by the WPA claimed that they had met Lincoln in the Deep
South during the war (some believed he wore a disguise).[4] Proctor likely
never saw his commander in chief, but the "oner" he took in "righting" to
Lincoln and of speaking of his "felow cittysons of the united States" clearly
had an effect on both him and the president, who retained the letter in his
personal papers.

Lincoln Receives a Poem from an Ex-Slave

A surgeon in the Twenty-Second Illinois Volunteers sent the following letter to Lincoln, enclosing a poem that an ex-slave had written for the president. The poem appears to have been partly original and partly copied out
of the February 20, 1864, edition of *Harper's Weekly*. For Lincoln, it likely
stood as a testimonial of what a former slave could learn once he began to
receive an education in the Union army.

> Div No 2 Genl Hospital Murfreesboro Tenn
> Abril 11, 1864

Hon Abm Lincoln President of the United States
Sir
    Permit me respectfully to enclose to you a letter received by me a
few days since. The writer was a Slave held in bondage by a man
named "Green" in Lincoln Co Tenn. In August last he escaped and
came to me at the U S Gen Hospital at Tullahoma Tenn. While there
the Soldiers taught him to read and write, for prior to that time he
could do neither. Early this spring he enlisted as a Soldier. This Mr
Lincoln is but a sample of the glorious fruits of your "Proclamation" of
Liberty. When at Springfield Ill as you were leaving for Washington

you said "Pray for me" a thousand hearts responded, and we now thank God who has so "led you into all truth" and thousands in the army rejoice in your work and pray for you that you may be sustained till the great work which God has called you to is fully accomplished.[5]

I am Sir

Your Obt Servant

Benjn Woodward

Surgeon 22nd Ill Vols

[On a new page and in a different hand:]

From a man of no Education. And have been Doomed to Slavery—
During life, And was born In Powhatan C^o And was raised In—
Richmond Virginia. And I am now a Soldier In U.S. Army.—
And I will Speak these few words In Answer to all whom it—
May Concern. Where Ever it may roam.

I. have left my wife And Children but—
Tho. I. have not yet for Saken them and made one grasp—
at the Flag of the union and Declared it shall neaver fall—
For we Love it like the Sunshine and the Stars and azure air.—
Ho for the flag of the union. the Stripes and the Stars of light.—
A million arms. Shall guard it. and may god defend the right.—
Ay, brothers let us love it, and let Every heart be true.—
And let Every arm be ready, for we have glorious work to do.—
Ho. for the Flag of the union, the Stripes and the Stars of Light.—
a million arms shall guard it. and may god defend the right.—
I. Hope we may meet again In the bonds of love to greet
fare well I. hope History may tell

Hannibal Cox

Co. B. 14th U. S. Col^d Troops

Chattanooga Tenn

march 30th 1864

I. Sends this for you to look at
you must not laugh at it.

Cox's closing sentiment—that he hoped Lincoln would not laugh at his handiwork—underscores the personal connection that developed between Lincoln and enslaved Americans. Cox believed that Lincoln would see and hold this letter, which he almost certainly did. He understood Lincoln in human terms, not as a distant figure who was larger than life but as a man who might react to his words in an emotional way. Cox was honorably discharged from the service in 1866 and settled with his wife, Anna, in Ohio. He died in 1890.[6]

An Enslaved Man Dreams of Lincoln

Many Americans likely dreamed about Lincoln during the Civil War. A few recorded their dreams in letters and diaries. Some Confederates dreamed that Lincoln went to hell, while Union soldiers dreamed of meeting with him and receiving a promotion. Prisoners of war had dreams about Lincoln working to secure their release from captivity, while a few northerners dreamed that he would bring freedom for the slaves. Slaves also had dreams about Lincoln. In 1864, one Georgia slave "had a dream last night . . . that Massy Lincoln's soldiers had set us free."[7]

One ex-slave was so moved by his dreams about Lincoln that he insisted on sending a dream report to the president. The former bondsman, George Washington, dictated the following letter to his teacher, Mrs. Luther Fowler. He was so earnest that the president should receive this letter that he wept as he told Mrs. Fowler what to write.

Stono plantation.   March 19th/65

Most respected friend

I take this opportunity this holy Sabbath day to try to express my gratitude and love to you. With many tears I send you this note through prayer and I desire to render you a thousand thanks that you have brought us from the yoke of bondage. And I love you freely. I am now 53 years old. Inauguration day was also my Birth-day. I have come 278 miles from Savannah and from there to Hilton Head. I have lain awake four nights and my mind so bore upon you that I could not rest till I sent you a letter. I lived in Butts Co. Ga. I am obliged to send you this to satisfy my mind   I wish you all the blessings that can be restored by the Almighty.

I would be glad to go back to see my family. I do love my wife and children. I have been a Baptist member for 25 years and I have been praying for this for 17 years. At that time I had a vision and you was made known to me in a dream. I saw a comet come from the North to the South and I said good Lord what is that? I heard a voice "There shall be wars & rumors of wars"   I saw many signs and wonders. My soul is filled with joy at the pleasure of letting you know. I have had a heap of high mountains and deep waters to cross. My master threatened my life if I should talk about this. But I just put all my trust in the Lord and I believe he has brought me conqueror through. I give my mind to pray for you the balance of my days. It would satisfy me if you would condescend to send me an answer to this on account of my fellow servants. If you should answer please direct to Mrs Luther Fowler. Stono plan[tation] Hilton. Head, S.C.

Yours with the greatest esteem

George Washington.

P.S. I have written the above precisely as dictated by a poor colored man who came to me in a flood of tears and begged me to write to the President for him. It is so entirely expressive of the feelings of all "Freedmen" that I send it. We have a large mission school in our house attended by nearly 800 people. A large number of them are adults and if it would not be too great an intrusion on your time I would be happy to receive a note from you for the "Freedmen" of the island.

Yours with respect

Mrs L Fowler

President Lincoln[8]

Dreams carried great spiritual meaning for African Americans in the midnineteenth century. Often they were used as evidence of conversion to Christianity or of a call to the ministry. Many slaves believed their dreams could predict the future. For some, dreams at night were a form of freedom from the awful circumstances of their waking lives. Dreams and dream reporting thus gave enslaved men and women a sense of autonomy that they lacked in daylight.[9] Lincoln was also something of a believer in dreams. It is little wonder that he was so moved by the words and message of this letter that he kept it in his personal collection of papers.

Epilogue
"I Have Lost a Friend"

During the Civil War, many African Americans came to equate Abraham Lincoln with the federal government, and they thought of the Union army as "Massa Linkum's Sojers." One New York infantryman remembered, "They wanted to know when 'Massa Linkum' was coming; they seemed to think he was near by, and were anxious to see the man they had been taught to fear, but whom they now discovered to be their friend."[1] For many former slaves, "Lincoln" replaced the only form of authority they had ever really known. When asked whom she belonged to in 1863, one former slave in Norfolk, Virginia, replied, "I don't know, I reckon I'm Massa Lincoln's slave now."[2] Mary Lincoln's seamstress, Elizabeth Keckly, captured this in an encounter she had with a black refugee who had come to Washington during the war. As Keckly explained, "She thought, as many others thought, that Mr. and Mrs. Lincoln were the government, and that the President and his wife had nothing to do but to supply the extravagant wants of every one that applied to them." This elderly ex-slave had been used to receiving two new shifts every year from her mistress, and she did not understand why, after eight months of her living in Washington, "Mister and Missus Government," by which she meant Abraham and Mary Lincoln, had not yet given her new clothing.[3] For the New York Presbyterian minister J. W. C. Pennington, "a kind and wise Providence" had brought "Mr. Lincoln into the Presidential chair." Lincoln was "OUR President," Pennington insisted, "because he is the only American President who has ever given any attention to colored men as citizens." Accordingly, Pennington called on "colored men [to] do their duty at the ballot box" in the presidential election of 1864 so that "[we] keep our present Chief Magistrate where he is."[4]

This deep identification of Lincoln with federal authority meant that when "the Great Emancipator" died in April 1865, many African Americans felt as though the government itself had died. One grieving woman in Charleston wailed over and over again, "O Lord! Massa Sam's dead!" When asked, "Who's Massa Sam?" she wrung her hands in utter hopelessness and replied, "Uncle Sam! . . . Mr. Lincum!" On the Sea Islands, teacher Laura M. Towne met a freedman who remarked, "I have lost a friend." When she asked who it was, he replied, "They call him Sam. Uncle Sam, the best friend ever I had."

Another whispered to Towne in disbelief that "Government was dead." African Americans in the Upper South used the same language to describe the martyred president. "The colored people feel it so deeply," wrote abolitionist Julia Wilbur in her diary on April 16, 1865. "Every face is sad. They realize that they have lost a friend. They are in the habit of calling him *Uncle Sam*, & they now speak of '*Uncle Sam's* being killed,' of *Uncle Sam's* being shot by secesh."[5] On the Sea Islands of South Carolina, the freedmen and women responded with "blank stares" when they were told that they would have to obey the government. "What was a government?" wrote historian Eugene Genovese when explaining the situation. "The assassination of Lincoln stunned the freedmen not only because they had come to love him as a deliverer but because they had great difficulty in imagining that the government, which was protecting them, could survive or indeed had ever existed apart from his person."[6] In fact, some former slaves feared that they would be reenslaved now that Lincoln was gone.[7]

What was a government? What would their relationship to it be? And what would it be like without Lincoln? These were important questions that African Americans would have to answer during the Civil War era—a period that saw an expansion of executive power that had been previously unknown in American history.

In the antebellum period, African Americans had limited encounters with the three branches of the federal government, and the results of these experiences were decidedly mixed. Prior to the *Dred Scott* decision in 1857, black men and women—including the enslaved—had routinely sued and been sued in state and federal courts, sometimes seeking relief from state and federal authorities when they were wrongly enslaved.[8] As historian Kimberly M. Welch has shown, free and enslaved African Americans in the South were able to win cases against whites by utilizing "the language of property" to exploit "the tension between whites' interests in controlling people of African descent and their dedication to private property."[9] But Chief Justice Roger B. Taney's ruling in *Dred Scott* held that African Americans were not U.S. citizens and could not bring suit in the federal courts. For decades, free blacks and their abolitionist allies in the North had occasionally petitioned Congress, but these had met with limited success.[10] Finally, black Americans had very limited interactions with the executive branch of the federal government (these included mail delivery, service in the navy, and pursuit of fugitive slaves by U.S. marshals). In President Lincoln they believed they had finally found, for the first time, an advocate and friend in the federal executive. And Lincoln came to symbolize the entirety of the government in many of their eyes.

For African Americans of the Civil War generation, politics was highly personal, and Lincoln personified their politics. This is why they called him "friend" and were so eager to write to him during the war. At long last they felt entitled to ask a sitting president for assistance, just as Lincoln's white constituents did. Writing in 1962, historian Benjamin Quarles beautifully captured this aspect of black politics of the mid-nineteenth century in his classic work, *Lincoln and the Negro*. "The Negroes of the war years viewed history not in terms of forces or movements, but in terms of a personal hero," wrote Quarles. "To them, Lincoln admirably fitted into this role." The "high opinion" that they had of Lincoln gave each African American "one inestimable boon—the feeling that he had a stake in America. And as the war moved toward its close, the Negro's sense of identity with the land of his birth grew deeper, nourished anew by its source—Abraham Lincoln." Even in the momentous presidential election of 1864, writes Quarles, African Americans were not preoccupied with "power politics" but with "a personality: Lincoln."[11]

Upon entering freedom, former slaves sought to develop new relationships with the federal government. Yet these were uncharted waters, and the freedpeople did not yet fully grasp how the government would function in their lives. In the postwar period, African Americans continued to expand their role in politics and their participation in government. Rather than simply petition Congress, they now organized politically and ran for and won seats in the House and Senate, as well as state and local offices throughout the states of the former Confederacy.[12] Several of Lincoln's African American correspondents—including Aaron A. Bradley, Richard H. Cain, J. Sella Martin, John Willis Menard, Benjamin Franklin Randolph, and James T. S. Taylor—were among those who held elective office during Reconstruction. Others, like Abraham Galloway, Frederick Douglass, and Paschal B. Randolph, stood at the forefront of the fight to expand the right to vote to black men. During the war and postwar years, African Americans also gained new rights in the judiciary—serving as jurors, witnesses, and litigants.[13] But their interactions with the presidency became less frequent and positive. To be sure, African Americans continued to correspond with postwar presidents, just as they had with Lincoln. In October 1864, Andrew Johnson had publicly declared that he would be "the Moses of the colored men." At first, African Americans believed him. In June 1865, a delegation of black men from Richmond traveled to the White House and presented a petition to Johnson, addressing him "as our best friend." Johnson appears to have shown sympathy when he met with this group, but when he received other black leaders like Edmund Kelly and Frederick Douglass, he treated them with contempt and condescension. (After Douglass and his companions departed, Johnson called them "those d—d sons of b—s" and said that Douglass was "just like any nigger" and "would sooner cut a white man's throat than not.") Soon African Americans no longer felt welcome at White House social functions, as Alexander T. Augusta had been in 1864.[14]

The memory of Lincoln's kind reception of African Americans like Abraham Galloway and the other North Carolina slaves quickly faded. When Teddy Roosevelt invited Booker T. Washington to dine with him at the White House in 1901, white southerners reacted with outrage, castigating Roosevelt for his "unprecedented . . . mistake."[15] Of course, Roosevelt's invitation to Washington was not entirely unprecedented. Lincoln and the black community had begun to forge a new relationship between African Americans and the federal government. Sadly, that experiment in self-government proved short lived. It would take another civil rights movement one hundred years after the Civil War for equality and political rights to again seem within reach.

Acknowledgments

In collecting the letters in this book, I am standing on the shoulders of some of the greatest research projects on Abraham Lincoln and the Civil War. Past and present editors of the Papers of Abraham Lincoln (PAL)—including Ed Bradley, David Gerleman, Chandler Lighty, Stacy Pratt McDermott, Christian McWhirter, Sean A. Scott, Daniel W. Stowell, and Daniel Worthington—were all tremendously helpful and generous, often alerting me to letters that might be of use or answering questions about things I'd found.

The many volumes produced by the Freedmen and Southern Society Project at the University of Maryland at College Park were also essential to this research and pointed me to several of the letters in this book. The work of Ira Berlin, Leslie Rowland, and their colleagues there has transformed the way we think about the Civil War today. My teachers at the University of Maryland—especially Herman Belz, Ira Berlin, Mark Graber, David Grimsted, James Henretta, Al Moss, Keith Olson, Whit Ridgway, and Leslie Rowland—all pushed me to become a better historian. I have the deepest admiration for them and the utmost gratitude for all they have done for me. Working as Ira's research assistant for two years was one of my best experiences in graduate school. I only wish that he could be here today to see this book.

As always, Mark Simpson-Vos and the team at the University of North Carolina Press are a pleasure to work with. Edna Greene Medford, Sylvia Frank Rodrigue, John David Smith, and the peer reviewers for the press read the entire manuscript and gave me generous and helpful comments for improving it. Robert Colby read the introduction and epilogue and helped me think through the framing of the book.

I thank my students at Christopher Newport University (CNU)—Daniel Glenn, Xenia Kerstanski, Sarah Hopkins, Courtney Leistensnider, Lizzy Wall, Will M. Palmer, Katie Brown, Hannah Broughton, Taylor Bagwell, Maggie Byers, Michael Sparks, and Lydia Davis—for their assistance with various parts of this project. Maggie Byers and Michael Sparks also helped me proofread each transcription—a major undertaking. CNU's interlibrary loan specialist, Jesse Spencer, tracked down many books, articles, rare newspapers, and microfilm reels. Will Kurtz of the University of Virginia sent me the letters of James T. S. Taylor that appeared in the *Anglo-African*. Ron Coddington, editor and publisher of *Military Images* magazine, generously provided me with high-resolution scans of several of the images in this book. Trevor Plante and Haley Maynard of the National Archives and Michelle Krowl of the Library of Congress are always a pleasure to work with. Finally, the Provost's Office, the College of Social Sciences, the Department of Leadership and American Studies, the Center for American Studies, and the Office of Undergraduate Research and Creative Activity at Christopher Newport University all provided generous financial support for this project.

Notes

Abbreviations in Notes

BAP   C. Peter Ripley, ed., *The Black Abolitionist Papers*, 5 vols. (Chapel Hill: University of North Carolina Press, 1985–92).

CMSR Compiled Military Service Record, RG 94, Entry 519 (Records of the Record and Pension Office, Carded Military Service Records, 1784–1903, Civil War, 1861–1865, Carded Records, Volunteer Organizations, Civil War), NARA.

Court-Martial Case File
      General Court-Martial Case Files, RG 153, Records of the Office of the Judge Advocate General (Army), NARA. (Each case file includes an alphanumeric case number.)

CWL   Abraham Lincoln, *The Collected Works of Abraham Lincoln*, ed. Roy P. Basler et al., 9 vols. (New Brunswick, N.J.: Rutgers University Press, 1953–55).

Lincoln Papers
      Abraham Lincoln Papers, Manuscript Division, Library of Congress, Washington, D.C.

O.R. *War of the Rebellion: A Compilation of the Official Records of the Union and Confederate Armies*, 128 vols. (Washington, D.C.: Government Printing Office, 1880–1901).

PAL   Papers of Abraham Lincoln.

Pardon File
      RG 204 (Records of the Office of the Pardon Attorney), Entry 1a (Pardon Case Files, 1853–1946). (Each case file includes an alphanumeric case number.)

Stat. *United States Statutes at Large*. (Each citation is preceded by a volume number and followed by page numbers.)

Prologue

1. Washington, *They Knew Lincoln*, 190–93; Lincoln to C. R. Welles, September 27, 1852, in Lincoln, *Collected Works of Abraham Lincoln*, 2:159 (hereafter cited as *CWL*); Lincoln to Major W. Packard, February 10, 1860, in *CWL*, 3:518; Dirck, *Lincoln the Lawyer*, 149, 207.

2. Keckley, *Behind the Scenes*, 102–5.

3. William Florville to Lincoln, December 27, 1863, Abraham Lincoln Papers (Lincoln Papers), Manuscript Division, Library of Congress (hereafter cited as Lincoln Papers).

4. Lucian Tilton's family rented the Lincoln home at Eighth and Jackson Streets in Springfield, Illinois, from 1861 to 1869.

5. Washington, *They Knew Lincoln*, 199–201; Burlingame, *Abraham Lincoln*, 2:351.

Note on Method

1. This description of the formal and informal roles of the president is derived from the Pearson learning company.

2. Rollin, *Life and Public Services*, 170.

3. Berry, "Civil War Letters."

4. On this point, see Gordon, "Getting History's Words Right," 197–216.

Introduction

1. See Table A.5 in Keyssar, *Right to Vote*, 342.

2. *Cincinnati Commercial Tribune*, November 12, 1860; *Daily Illinois State Register* (Springfield), October 13, 1860; *Gettysburg Compiler*, October 22, 1860; *Public Ledger* (Philadelphia), October 6, 1860; *Buffalo Daily Republic*, October 8, 1860.

3. W. T. Boyd and J. T. Alston to Simon Cameron, November 15, 1861, in Aptheker, *Documentary History*, 460–61.

4. Richard Hackley to John A. Broadus, November 5, 1860, in Woodson, *Mind of the Negro*, 536–37.

5. Chandler, "Reminiscences of the Sunny South," 382; Higginson, *Army Life*, 46, 55; Jackson, "Story of Mattie J. Jackson," 253; Colby, "Continuance of an Unholy Traffic," 281; Robinson, *Bitter Fruits of Bondage*, 41–43; Clavin, *Aiming for Pensacola*, 149–50, 160.

6. Egerton, "Slaves' Election," 35–63; Washington, *Up from Slavery*, 8–9.

7. On black activism in the nation's capital, see Masur, *Example for All the Land*.

8. Andrews, *Oxford Frederick Douglass Reader*, 225.

9. White, Fisher, and Wall, "Civil War Letters of Tillman Valentine," 178.

10. Adams, *On the Altar of Freedom*, 83.

11. Redkey, *Grand Army of Black Men*, 205, 219. See also Adams, *On the Altar of Freedom*, 21; Samito, *Becoming American under Fire*, 5–6, 22–23, 26–102, 134–71.

12. See, for example, Fannin, "Jacksonville Mutiny," 368–96; Samito, "Intersection between Military Justice," 170–202.

13. Berlin, Reidy, and Rowland, *Freedom's Soldiers*, 23–50.

14. Donald, *Lincoln*, 311.

15. Conroy, *Lincoln's White House*, 200.

16. See also Cole, *Freedom's Witness*; Blackett, *Thomas Morris Chester*; Smith, "Civil War Letters of John C. Brock."

17. Anderson, *Education of Blacks in the South*, 16–17; Butchart, *Schooling the Freed People*, 1–7, 193n18.

18. Redkey, *Grand Army of Black Men*, ix.

19. See, for example, White, Fisher, and Wall, "Civil War Letters of Tillman Valentine"; Brown, "Letters of Three Ohio Soldiers," 72–79. For an excellent analysis of black soldiers' pension records, see Regosin and Shaffer, *Voices of Emancipation*.

20. Slap, "Tintype That Proved a Pension Claim," 44–45.

21. See, for example, Silkenat and Barr, "Serving the Lord and Abe Lincoln's Spirit," 75–97. Hahn's essay "But What Did the Slaves Think of Lincoln?" contains very little

firsthand evidence of what slaves actually thought of Lincoln. One valuable exception is McPherson, *Negro's Civil War*, chap. 21, although this short chapter focuses only on the years 1864 and 1865.

22. On this point, see Smith, "Black Images of Lincoln," 2; Douglass, *Life and Times*, 595–96; Booker T. Washington, "Speech draft re: influence of Lincoln, Given at New York Republican Club of NYC," February 12, 1909 (GLC07232), Gilder-Lehrman Institute of American History.

23. Donald, *Lincoln*, 310; Wilson and Davis, *Herndon's Informants*, 331; Burlingame, *Abraham Lincoln*, 2:289.

Chapter One

1. For discussion of the courts in Washington, D.C., during the Civil War, see White, *Guide to Research*, 53–57; White, "Sweltering with Treason."

2. Doig, "Lincolniana Notes," 310.

3. L. A. Whiteley to Lincoln, October 30, 1863, Pardon File A-491 (PAL 204673); Lincoln pardon of Anderson, November 2, 1863, RG 59, Entry 897 (PAL 209170b).

4. United States v. Hamilton Anderson, RG 21, Entry 77, Case File #627; RG 21, Entry 74, vol. 1, p. 20. I thank Bob Ellis of the National Archives for tracking down these files for me.

5. B. F. Reimer and others to Lincoln, [September 1864], Pardon File A-548 (case of John N. Still).

6. Palmer, "Unpardoned by Lincoln," 4.

7. Henry Addison to Lincoln, April 17, 1861, RG 59, Entry 902 (PAL 236060); Charles Myers and Son to Lincoln, April 17, 1861, RG 59, Entry 902 (PAL 236061).

8. The word "in" appears to be written over the word "by."

9. Elizabeth Booth to Lincoln, April 18, 1861 (PAL 236062), RG 59, Entry 902.

10. Pardon file of John Booth (PAL 241769); pardon of John Booth, June 17, 1861, RG 59, Entry 897 (PAL 236702b); Stowell, "President Lincoln Pardons John Booth," 7.

11. U.S. v. Isaac Hamilton and 14 others of the Ship *Challenger*, RG 21, National Archives at New York City; *New York Commercial Advertiser*, May 7, 1861; *New York Evening Post*, May 23, 1861; *National Police Gazette*, May 25, 1862; *New York Sun*, May 24, 1861.

12. John Peterson et al. to Lincoln, n.d., enclosed in Frank Norman to Lincoln, August 6, 1861, RG 45, Entry 36 (PAL 291627 and 291628). Several of the names appear to be spelled differently at the beginning and end of this petition. The signature portion of the document appears to be written in a different hand.

13. Foote, *Gentlemen and the Roughs*, 30.

14. An Act to amend An Act to prohibit the sale of Spirituous Liquors and Intoxicating Drinks in the District of Columbia, in certain Cases, August 3, 1863, 12 Stat. 286; An Act to prohibit the sale of Spirituous Liquors and Intoxicating Drinks in the District of Columbia, in certain Cases, August 5, 1861, 12 Stat. 291–92.

15. John Ames to Lincoln, ca. September 1861, RG 204, Entry 1a (PAL 242142). I thank Bob Ellis of the National Archives for checking RG 21, Entry 108, vol. of John D.

Clark, 1861–64, and RG 351, Entry 125, for materials related to Ames's case. None appear to exist.

16. Pardon File of Jackson Shepherd, alias John Fisher (PAL 242031); Hiram I. King and others to Lincoln, October 23, 1861, RG 59, Entry 902 (PAL 236122); pardon of Jackson Shepherd, alias John Fisher, RG 59, Entry 897 (PAL 239067).

17. Pardon File of John F. West (PAL 242318).

18. John F. West and others to Lincoln, ca. November 1862, Pardon File of John F. West (PAL 242319); pardon of John F. West, RG 59, Entry 897 (PAL 239131).

19. Lettecia Johnson to Lincoln, January 13, 1863, RG 204, Entry 1a (PAL 242470); Pardon File of Mary L. Easton, RG 204, Entry 1a (PAL 242469).

20. Fanny Tyler to Lincoln, February 9, 1863 (PAL 242568), Pardon File of Elizabeth Williams (PAL 242564), Robert Williams to Lincoln, February 10, 1863 (PAL 242565), and Henry C. Cooper to Lincoln, February 11, 1863 (PAL 242566), all in RG 204, Entry 1a.

21. Pardon File of Benjamin Brown (PAL 242576), Benjamin Brown to Lincoln, April 1863 (PAL 242577), C. Dodd McFarland to Lincoln, April 1863 (PAL 242578), and McFarland to Lincoln, May 26, 1863 (PAL 242579), all in RG 204, Entry 1a; pardon of Benjamin Brown, June 18, 1863, RG 59, Entry 897 (PAL 239182).

22. William J. C. Bounds, Philip Conover, and Francis M. Roe to Lincoln, September 20, 1864, RG 94, Entry 360 (PAL 294699).

23. No record of their service appears in Stryker, *Record of Officers and Men*, or Bilby, *"Freedom to All,"* 82–137.

24. *Trenton State Gazette*, January 26, 1861; January 19, 1863; January 3, 1881; and May 9 and 15, 1884; *New York Herald*, June 18, 1867.

25. *Daily National Intelligencer* (Washington, D.C.), May 6, 1864; *Evening Star* (Washington, D.C.), May 3, June 17, 20, and October 22, 1864.

26. Elizabeth Shorter to Lincoln, November 4, 1864 (PAL 243450); Pardon File of Elizabeth Shorter (243449); pardon of Elizabeth Shorter, November 5, 1864, RG 59, Entry 897 (PAL 208573b).

27. Celia Kuykendall and Giles Morris to Lincoln, December 26, 1864, including notation by Hitchcock, RG 107, Entry 18 (PAL 287421 and 287422).

28. Kuykendall, *Frontier Days*, 84.

Chapter Two

1. Moses, *Liberian Dreams*, xx–xxv.

2. Greene, "Against Wind and Tide," 7.

3. Masur, "African American Delegation," 119–23.

4. An Act for the Release of certain Persons held to Service or Labor in the District of Columbia, April 16, 1862, 12 Stat. 376–78; An Act to suppress Insurrection, to punish Treason and Rebellion, to seize and confiscate the Property of Rebels, and for other Purposes, July 17, 1862, 12 Stat. 589–92.

5. Masur, "African American Delegation," 136.

6. Lincoln to John D. Johnson and Alexander Crummell, May 5, 1862, in *African Repository* 38 (August 1862): 243.

7. Burlingame, *Abraham Lincoln*, 2:394.

8. John B. Hepburn to Lincoln, May 7, 1862, Lincoln Papers.

9. Masur, "African American Delegation," 130–31; Boyd's Washington directories for 1862 and 1864. For more on Thomas, see Taylor, *Slave in the White House*, 201–2, 206, 213–15.

10. Lincoln, "Address on Colonization to a Deputation of Negroes," August 14, 1862, in *CWL*, 5:370–75.

11. Edward M. Thomas to Lincoln, August 16, 1862, Lincoln Papers.

12. Edward M. Thomas to Lincoln, August 16, 1862, Lincoln Papers.

13. Jacob R. S. Van Vleet to Lincoln, August 17, 1862, Lincoln Papers.

14. Douglass, "The President and His Speeches," in *Frederick Douglass*, 510–13.

15. *Liberator* (Boston), September 12, 1862.

16. *An Appeal from the Colored Men of Philadelphia*, 3–8.

17. During the election of 1860, rumors circulated that Lincoln's vice presidential candidate, Hannibal Hamlin, was black. Robert Barnwell Rhett of South Carolina said in a speech, "Hamlin is what we call a mulatto. He has black blood in him, and let me tell you it is his nomination that has a remarkable peculiarity." *Cleveland Daily Leader*, July 24, 1860.

18. Thomas Paine famously wrote in 1776, "These are the times that try men's souls." The following sentence alludes to famous battles and leaders of the American Revolution and the War of 1812. At the Battle of New Orleans in 1815, African American men fought alongside whites in Andrew Jackson's army.

19. Lincoln had lived almost his entire adult life in Sangamon County, Illinois. During the election of 1860, Republicans put him forward as "the Rail-splitter," pointing to his hard work as a farm laborer as a young man.

20. The Slaveholders' Convention of Maryland of 1858 debated measures to expel free African Americans from the state. The convention adopted the following resolution: "Resolved, That this Convention consider *any measure* for the general removal of the free blacks from the State of Maryland as impolitic, inexpedient, and uncalled for by any public exigency which could justify it."

21. *Liberator* (Boston), September 5, 1862.

22. Hanchett, "George Boyer Vashon," 205–19, 333–49.

23. *Douglass' Monthly*, October 1862.

24. Masur, "African American Delegation," 138–41.

25. Hart, "Springfield's African Americans," 48; J. W. Menard to John P. Usher, April 11, 1863, in M160, reel 8.

26. *New York Times*, November 2, 1862; *Liberator* (Boston), November 7, 1862.

27. John W. Menard et al. to Lincoln, May 18, 1863, RG 48, Entry 376 (PAL 273999). Although Lavalette signed his name with an "e" in this document, his name most often appears as "Lavalette," as it is in the previous document.

28. John B. Pinney was corresponding secretary of the New York Colonization Society.

29. John D. Johnson to Lincoln, March 3, 1863, RG 48, Entry 376 (PAL 273997). A copy of this letter is in RG 46, Entry 563.

30. John W. Menard to Lincoln, September 16, 1863, RG 48, Entry 376 (PAL 274000). Menard's lengthy report, which was written as a letter to Lincoln, occupies

more than half of the fourth page of the October 24, 1863, issue of the *Anglo-African* (New York).

31. B. F. Brown to Lincoln, October 13, 1863, RG 48, Entry 376 (PAL 274001). A copy of this letter is in RG 46, Entry 563.

32. Hay, *Inside Lincoln's White House*, 217.

Chapter Three

1. Wert, "Camp William Penn," 337; Dobak, *Freedom by the Sword*, 6–7.

2. Berlin, *Wartime Genesis of Free Labor*, 97–98; Dobak, *Freedom by the Sword*, 30–33; Lincoln "Proclamation Revoking General Hunter's Order of Military Emancipation of May 9, 1862," May 19, 1862, in *CWL*, 5:222–24; Quarles, *Negro in the Civil War*, 109–12.

3. An Act to amend the Act calling forth the Militia to execute the Laws of the Union, suppress Insurrections, and repel Invasions, approved February twenty-eight, seventeen hundred and ninety-five, and the Acts amendatory thereof, and for other Purposes, July 17, 1862, 12 Stat. 597–600; An Act to suppress Insurrection, to punish Treason and Rebellion, to seize and confiscate the Property of Rebels, and for other Purposes, July 17, 1862, 12 Stat. 589–92.

4. Dobak, *Freedom by the Sword*, 33–44.

5. Lincoln, "Emancipation Proclamation," January 1, 1863, in *CWL*, 6:30.

6. Smith, *Lincoln and the U.S. Colored Troops*, 56–57; George E. Stephens to Sir, September 19, 1863, in *Black Abolitionist Papers*, 5:243 (hereafter cited as *BAP*).

7. Draft of letter to Isaac M. Schermerhorn, September 12, 1864, in *CWL*, 8:1–2; Lincoln to James C. Conkling, August 26, 1863, in *CWL*, 6:406–10.

8. Smith, *Lincoln and the U.S. Colored Troops*, 2.

9. *War of the Rebellion*, ser. 1, vol. 42, pt. 3, p. 163 (hereafter cited as *O.R.*).

10. Levin Tilmon to Lincoln, April 8, 1861, Lincoln Papers.

11. Brown, *Black Man*, 241–42.

12. Brown, *Black Man*, 242–44; *New York Times*, August 17, 1876.

13. Clipping from the London *Morning Star*, enclosed in John Sella Martin to Lincoln, July 14, 1862, Lincoln Papers.

14. John Sella Martin to Lincoln, July 14, 1862, Lincoln Papers.

15. *New York Times*, August 17, 1876.

16. Bradley, "Dr. Alexander T. Augusta," 5–8; *BAP*, 5:205–11.

17. Alexander T. Augusta to Lincoln, January 7, 1863, Compiled Military Service Record for Augusta, RG 94, Entry 519 (PAL 297233) (hereafter cited as CMSR). Augusta's letter to Stanton was written on the same day and appears in CMSR for Augusta.

18. Bradley, "Dr. Alexander T. Augusta," 5–8; *BAP*, 5:205–11.

19. *National Republican* (Washington, D.C.), March 18, 1863; Orr, "Cities at War," 470–71.

20. Seward, *William H. Seward*, 308.

21. Bogart appears to have written an "L" when he meant to start the word "Sound."

22. Willis A. Bogart to Lincoln, RG 94, Entry 409 (PAL 296682). Bogart capitalized the first word of every line but one.

23. Willis A. Bogart to William H. Seward, May 8, 1864; Harriet C. Bogart to Seward, March 6, 1866; Seward to Harriet, March 12, 1866; and Seward to Richard J. Oglesby, March 12 and 20, 1866 (copies), all in William H. Seward Papers, University of Rochester; Seward to Oglesby, March 12 and 20, 1866, in Executive Clemency Files, Illinois State Archives.

24. Drinkard, *Illinois Freedom Fighters*, 94; Miller, *Black Civil War Soldiers of Illinois*, 24, 123.

25. Washington, *They Knew Lincoln*, 105–17; Sweet, "A Representative 'of Our People,'" 21–41.

26. Robert Dale Owen (1801–77), a Scottish immigrant, was a diplomat and social reformer who served two terms in Congress as a Democrat from Indiana.

27. Phineas D. Gurley to Lincoln, April 8, 1863; Henry McNeal Turner et al. to Edwin M. Stanton, April 22, 1863; Preston King et al., to Edwin M. Stanton, April 23, 1863; William G. Raymond to Lincoln, April 25, 1863; William Slade to Lincoln, April 28, 1863; and James M. Edmunds to Lincoln, April 29, 1863, all in Lincoln Papers; Lincoln to Stanton, May 12, 1863, in *CWL*, 6:212.

28. *Anglo-African* (New York), May 23, 1863; *Canonsburg (Pa.) Weekly Notes*, March 5, 1892.

29. Deveney, *Paschal Beverly Randolph*.

30. *Trenton State Gazette*, May 18, 1861.

31. *New York Times*, July 22, 1863.

32. Randolph, *Pre-Adamite Man*; *National Republican* (Washington D.C.), July 28, 1866.

33. Paschal B. Randolph to Lincoln, October 19, 1863, RG 94, Entry 360 (PAL 299092).

34. Randolph, *P. B. Randolph, the "Learned Pundit,"* 15–19.

35. *Christian Recorder* (Philadelphia), March 7, 1895.

36. Orr, "Cities at War," 349, 443–47, 453.

37. James H. A. Johnson to Lincoln, December 28, 1863, RG 110, Entry 18 (PAL 296450).

38. *Baltimore Sun*, January 28, 1895; *Christian Recorder* (Philadelphia), March 7, 1895.

39. Lew Wallace to Charles A. Dana, August 30, 1864, in *O.R.*, ser. 1, vol. 43, pt. 1, pp. 969–70; Scharf, *History of Maryland*, 3:638–39; Stephens, *Shadow of Shiloh*, 207.

40. Samuel W. Chase, a prominent Presbyterian minister and grand master of a black branch of the Freemasons, was part of a delegation of black ministers from Baltimore who met with Lincoln at the White House on September 7, 1864, to present the president with a beautiful pulpit edition of the Bible.

41. Loyial Colard Men of Baltimore Citey to Lincoln, August 20, 1864, RG 107, Entry 18 (PAL 208909).

42. Wallace to Dana, August 30, 1864, in *O.R.*, ser. 1, vol. 43, pt. 1, pp. 969–70.

43. Wallace to Dana, August 30, 1864. On recruiting practices in Maryland, see Smith, *Lincoln and the U.S. Colored Troops*, 39–41; Orr, "Cities at War."

44. Fields, *Slavery and Freedom on the Middle Ground*, 148.

45. Possibly William Jennison, Jr., an attorney in Detroit.

46. Possibly the Detroit law firm of Maynard & Meddaugh.

47. It is unclear who this is. There were two lawyers named Wilcox in Detroit, as well as Maj. Gen. Orlando B. Willcox, who had practiced law in Detroit before the Civil War. The word I have rendered as "mjor" might be "myor," although there was no mayor of Detroit by that name.

48. Greenbury Hodge to Lincoln, August 17, 1864, RG 94, Entry 360 (PAL 296921); CMSR and pension record for Greenbury Hodge (includes obituary).

49. Douglass, *Life and Times*, 312–14; Fehrenbacher and Fehrenbacher, *Recollected Words of Abraham Lincoln*, 145.

50. Frederick Douglass to Lincoln, August 29, 1864, Lincoln Papers.

51. CMSR for Elisha S. Robison.

52. Elisha S. Robison to Lincoln, December 1864, RG 94, Entry 360 (PAL 297228); Ford, *History of Northeast Indiana*, 1:216–17.

53. Court-Martial Case Files NN-2799 and NN-2801.

54. CMSR for Francis A. Boyd; Berlin, Reidy, and Rowland, *Black Military Experience*, 350–54; Redkey, "Black Chaplains," 335–36.

55. Francis A. Boyd to Lincoln, January 12, 1865 (PAL 297326), February 25, 1865 (PAL 297327), and March 9, 1865 (PAL 297328), all in RG 94, Entry 360.

56. Berlin, Reidy, and Rowland, *Black Military Experience*, 350–54.

Chapter Four

1. An Act to amend the Act calling forth the Militia to execute the Laws of the Union, suppress Insurrections, and repel Invasions, approved February twenty-eight, seventeen hundred and ninety-five, and the Acts amendatory thereof, and for other Purposes, July 17, 1862, in 12 Stat. 597–600.

2. Belz, *Abraham Lincoln*, 119–21.

3. Higginson, *Army Life*, 238.

4. Francis H. Fletcher to Jacob C. Safford, May 28, 1864, Gilder-Lehrman Collection.

5. Shaw, *Blue-Eyed Child of Fortune*, 366; Samito, *Becoming American*, 56–62, 242.

6. Samito, "Intersection between Military Justice," 197–201.

7. John A. Andrew to Lincoln, May 13, 1864, Lincoln Papers.

8. Edward Bates to Lincoln, April 23, 1864, Lincoln Papers.

9. Belz, *Abraham Lincoln*, 122–31; Smith, *Lincoln and the U.S. Colored Troops*, 66–72; An Act making Appropriations for the Support of the Army for the Year ending the thirtieth June, eighteen hundred and sixty-five, and for other Purposes, June 15, 1864, in 13 Stat. 126–30.

10. Lincoln to Edward Bates, June 24, 1864, in *CWL*, 7:404–6; Belz, *Abraham Lincoln*, 131–32.

11. Higginson, *Army Life*, 273–74; Belz, *Abraham Lincoln*, 136–37.

12. Silber, *Daughters of the Union*, 46–47.

13. Trudeau, *Voices of the 55th*, 86; Redkey, *Grand Army of Black Men*, 237; Stephens, *Voice of Thunder*, 319–21.

14. Following the Union assault on Fort Wagner in Charleston Harbor on July 18, 1863, Confederate soldiers buried the dead black soldiers of the Fifty-Fourth Massa-

chusetts in a large unmarked grave. This attack remains famous today because of its depiction in the movie *Glory*.

15. James Henry Gooding to Lincoln, September 28, 1863, RG 94, Entry 360 (PAL 208892); Adams, *On the Altar of Freedom*. This transcription includes paragraph breaks that are not in the original letter in order to assist the reader.

16. Peter Crowl to Lincoln, October 7, 1863, enclosing Charles Burr and James Jackson to Crowl, September 27, 1863, RG 110, Entry 18 (PAL 296488); CMSRs and pension records for Charles Burr and James Jackson.

17. Matilda Burr to Lincoln, January 18, 1864, RG 94, Entry 360 (PAL 294685).

18. Ester Ann Jackson to Lincoln, January 18, 1864, RG 107, Entry 18 (PAL 287111).

19. CMSRs and pension records for Charles Burr and James Jackson.

20. John H. Harris to Lincoln, February 23, 1864, RG 99, Entry 7, NARA (PAL 255770); CMSR and pension record for John H. Harris.

21. Rosanna Henson to Lincoln, July 11, 1864, RG 99, Entry 7 (PAL 255867); CMSR for Benjamin Hinson.

22. Samito, "Intersection between Military Justice," 170–73; CMSR for Wallace Baker; *Sacramento Daily Union*, July 19, 1864.

23. This is a reference to section 5 of An Act to authorize the Employment of Volunteers in aid in enforcing the Laws and protecting Public Property, July 22, 1861, 12 Stat. 268.

24. Shorter may have begun writing "Therefore" before he realized he needed to insert "5th."

25. John F. Shorter and others to Lincoln, July 16, 1864, RG 94, Entry 360 (PAL 296952).

26. Reid, *Practicing Medicine in a Black Regiment*, 254; Trudeau, *Voices of the 55th*, 62, 105, 118, 127, 141, 213, 231, 241–42. For other writings by Shorter, see Trudeau, *Voices of the 55th*, 84–85, 150–54.

27. George Rodgers and others to Lincoln, August 1864, RG 94, Entry 360 (PAL 297221); Berlin, Reidy, and Rowland, *Black Military Experience*, 501–2; CMSRs for George Rogers, Nimrod Rowley, Samuel Sampson, and Thomas Sipple.

28. Greene, *Swamp Angels*, 125–28; Harrison, *Rev. Samuel Harrison*; CMSR for Harrison.

29. John A. Andrew to Lincoln, March 24, May 13, 1864, Lincoln Papers.

30. Lincoln to Bates, April 4, 1864, in *CWL*, 7:280; Edward Bates to Lincoln, April 23, 1864, Lincoln Papers.

31. Charles Sumner to John A. Andrew, April 30, 1864, in Palmer, *Selected Letters of Charles Sumner*, 2:237.

32. Pension record for Samuel Harrison.

33. Samuel Harrison to Lincoln, September 9, 1864, RG 99, Entry 7 (PAL 255869); Greeley, *American Conflict*, 2:521; Harrison, *Rev. Samuel Harrison*, 32.

34. In June 1864, Congress raised the pay of white enlisted men from $13 to $16 per month.

35. Berlin, Reidy, and Rowland, *Black Military Experience*, 402–3; CMSR for William Wicker.

36. Possibly "truth."

37. Mary Ann Vincent to Lincoln, September 28, 1864, RG 99, Entry 7 (PAL 255781); CMSR and pension record for Amos Vincent.

38. William Chandler to Lincoln, November 21, 1864, RG 99, Entry 7 (PAL 255811); CMSR for William Chandler.

39. Thomas Pepper to Lincoln, November 26, 1864, RG 94, Entry 360 (PAL 297212); CMSR for Thomas Pepper; pension record for George Gaunt alias Thomas Pepper.

40. Gerrit Smith (1797–1874) was a prominent radical abolitionist in New York.

41. Abbie A. Myers to Lincoln, January 16, 1865, RG 99, Entry 7 (PAL 255871).

42. Harrower and Wieckowski, *Spectacle for Men and Angels*, 218.

43. Anonymous to Lincoln, February 4, 1865, RG 94, Entry 360 (PAL 297598).

Chapter Five

1. See, for example, Clarke and Plant, "No Minor Matter," 881–927; Berlin, Reidy, and Rowland, *Freedom's Soldiers*, 19–20.

2. RG 94, Entry 416 (PAL 294898); Clarke and Plant, "No Minor Matter," 901–3.

3. CMSR for Richard M. Smith; Court-Martial Case File LL-1256.

4. Charles B. Smith to Lincoln, November 27, 1863 (PAL 294617), November 28, 1863 (PAL 294618), and December 5, 1863 (PAL 294619), all in RG 94, Entry 360.

5. CMSR for Richard M. Smith. Smith was later acquitted of assault with intent to kill. See Court-Martial Case File LL-2811.

6. Ann Benson to Lincoln, February 20, 1864, RG 94, Entry 360 (PAL 294831); CMSR for James Henry Benson.

7. CMSR for William Jackson.

8. Petition of William Jackson, April 13, 1864, RG 94, Entry 360 (PAL 296925).

9. Hay, *Inside Lincoln's White House*, 97. The governor of Maryland was also outraged by this sort of treatment of African Americans, which was widespread in the state. See Augustus W. Bradford to Montgomery Blair, May 12, 1864, Lincoln Papers.

10. Petition of Jackson.

11. Freeman Glasco to Lincoln, June 1, 1864, RG 112, Entry 12 (PAL 295888); CMSR and pension record for Freeman Glasco.

12. Frederick Douglass to Lincoln, August 29, 1864, Lincoln Papers; CMSR for Charles R. Douglass.

13. Julia Rouser to Lincoln, September 24, 1864, RG 94, Entry 360 (PAL 297229); CMSR for William Rouser.

14. As described in the James H. A. Johnson letter in chapter 3, under the federal conscription law of 1863, draftees could hire a substitute to take their place in the ranks. Historian James W. Geary explains that this system "fostered the rise of a professional class of brokers. For a fee, these agents found substitutes for individuals and often arranged to fill a local [draft] quota with men from other areas. . . . Brokers often cheated many of these prospective recruits or substitutes out of a large portion or all of their substitute fee or bounty money." See Geary, *We Need Men*, 13.

15. Henry Homer to Lincoln, October 4, 1864, RG 94, Entry 360 (PAL 296919); CMSR and pension for Henry Homer.

16. Brumbey's first letter has not been located.

17. During the Civil War, several secret societies—including the Knights of the Golden Circle, the Order of American Knights, and the Sons of Liberty—threatened to divide the North from within. Shortly before the presidential election of 1864, the ringleaders of one of these "Copperhead" organizations were arrested and tried before a military tribunal.

18. Supporters of Maj. Gen. George B. McClellan, the Democratic nominee for president.

19. In the mid-nineteenth century, political parties printed their own ballots, listing only their party's candidates for office (in other words, ballots did not list all the candidates for office from every party, as they do today). If a voter did not support all the candidates from his party, he would cross out—or "scratch"—the unwanted candidate's name from the ticket before casting it in the ballot box.

20. Richard Brumbey to Abraham and Mary Lincoln, November 10, 1864, RG 94, Entry 360 (PAL 294807); CMSR for Richard Brumbey.

21. William H. Johnson to Lincoln, November 21, 1864, RG 94, Entry 360 (PAL 296926). While the testimony is conflicting, it appears that another man who went by the names Charles R. Morris and Spencer Beverly King claimed Johnson's pension after the war. When Morris's widow attempted to continue receiving pension funds, her request was denied when it became apparent that Morris's original claim of Johnson's pension had been fraudulent.

22. Jane Welcome to Lincoln, November 21, 1864, RG 94, Entry 360 (PAL 208901); CMSR and pension record for Martin Welcome.

23. George Washington to Lincoln, December 4, 1864, RG 94, Entry 360 (PAL 208920); CMSR for George Washington.

24. Alcia Bass to Lincoln, December 7, 1864, RG 94, Entry 366 (PAL 299178); CMSR for Armor Bass; *Xenia (Ohio) Daily Gazette*, May 18, 1907.

25. Lucy Freeman to Lincoln, December 1, 1864, RG 94, Entry 366 (PAL 301653); CMSRs for three soldiers named Charles Brown.

26. Sarah Patton to Lincoln, March 7, 1865, RG 94, Entry 366 (PAL 302250); CMSR for Thomas Payton.

Chapter Six

1. Samito, "Intersection between Military Justice," 174–77, 202; Samito, *Becoming American*, chap. 4. Compare with Glatthaar, *Forged in Battle*, 116–20. Unless otherwise noted, the letters to Lincoln in this chapter are from the court-martial case files of the correspondents.

2. Reidy, and Rowland, *Black Military Experience*, 433–42; White, "Martial Law," 52–72.

3. Reidy, and Rowland, *Black Military Experience*, 442.

4. Vicksburg, Mississippi, a Confederate stronghold on the Mississippi River, fell to the Union on July 4, 1863. Port Hudson, Louisiana, fell to the Union five days later, essentially opening up the Mississippi River to Union navigation all the way down to New Orleans, which had been captured in April 1862.

5. John H. Morgan and others to Lincoln, January 16, 1864, RG 94, Entry 360 (PAL 294687).

6. Court-Martial Case File MM-2824 and MM-3274; CMSR for Barcroft.

7. Court-Martial Case File NN-3832; CMSR for William D. Mayo.

8. William D. Mayo to Lincoln, January 10, 1864, RG 94, Entry 12 (PAL 294277); CMSR for William D. Mayo.

9. The Articles of War were to be read to every regiment or company once every six months, although it was not uncommon for soldiers to claim that they had not heard them read. See Glatthaar, *Forged in Battle*, 111, 116.

10. Court-Martial Case File LL-1623; CMSR for John Johnson.

11. Court-Martial Case File NN-2392; CMSR for Adam Laws.

12. CMSR and pension record for James T. S. Taylor; *Anglo-African* (New York), January 30, April 9, June 4, 1864; Brooks, "Taylor, James T. S. (1840–1918)." Taylor's CMSR states that he was nineteen years old when he enlisted, whereas his pension states that he was born in 1840 and was twenty-three when he enlisted.

13. White, "Black Soldier from Charlottesville." The disposition of Moffat's trial is unknown.

14. James T. S. Taylor to Lincoln, November 15, 1864, RG 94, Entry 360 (PAL 297289).

15. White, "Black Soldier from Charlottesville"; Brooks, "Taylor, James T. S. (1840–1918)"; *Anglo-African* (New York), February 25, September 3, 1865.

16. Court-Martial Case File NN-1688; CMSR for James W. Castle. Castle often capitalized the first letter of each line. In his letters, Castle mistakenly dated the shooting to January 8; however, the court-martial records clearly place the incident on February 8.

17. Court-Martial Case File LL-2394; CMSR for Franklin Smith.

18. Court-Martial Case File LL-2783; CMSR for David Washington. On tying up black soldiers, see Glatthaar, *Forged in Battle*, 109, 114–17, 180, 222–23.

19. This word appears to be "cameny," but Washington's meaning is unclear.

20. David Washiton to Lincoln, November 26, 1864, RG 94, Entry 360 (PAL 208896); Berlin, Reidy, and Rowland, *Black Military Experience*, 455.

21. CMSRs for Alfred H. Chapman and Randolph Burr; Court-Martial Case File NN-3641. It is unclear what happened to Chapman after the war. The 1880 census indicates that he may have settled in South Carolina. Martha is not listed in that census.

22. CMSR for Isaiah Price; Court-Martial Case File NN-3122.

23. CMSR for John Pool.

24. John Pool to Lincoln, January 20, 1865, in Court-Martial Case File LL-2229.

25. Samuel Roosa to Lincoln, January 24, 1865, in Berlin, Reidy, and Rowland, *Black Military Experience*, 477–79; CMSRs for Jack Morris and Samuel Roosa; Court-Martial Case File LL-3106. The court-martial case files for Morris and Samuel Roosa appear to no longer exist.

26. Johnson's Island was a prison camp for Confederate officers in Lake Erie, near Sandusky, Ohio. Camp Delaware was a training site for black soldiers in Delaware, Ohio.

27. William Joseph Nelson to Lincoln, February 22, 1865, in Berlin, Reidy, and Rowland, *Black Military Experience*, 111–12; CMSR for William J. Nelson.

Chapter Seven

1. Lincoln to Sumner, May 19, 1864, in Lincoln, *Collected Works of Lincoln: First Supplement*, 243; An Act supplementary to an Act entitled "An Act to grant Pensions," approved July fourteenth, eighteen hundred and sixty-two, July 4, 1864, in 13 Stat. 387–89.

2. Lincoln, "Second Inaugural Address," in *CWL*, 8:333.

3. Lincoln, "Order of Retaliation," July 30, 1863, in *CWL*, 6:357.

4. Johnson's rendering of "n" and "u" is identical, so this word could be "agoue," meaning, "ago."

5. The words "some do" are inserted with a caret, likely indicating that Johnson intended them as a parenthetical phrase.

6. Hannah Johnson to Lincoln, July 31, 1863, RG 94, Entry 360 (PAL 208889).

7. Lincoln to Stanton, May 17, 1864, in *CWL*, 7:345–46. Lincoln had similarly balked when it came to executing hostages involving white Confederate sailors in 1861. See Weitz, *Confederacy on Trial*, 195–96.

8. Ed. D. Jennings to Lincoln, January 22, 1864, Lincoln Papers.

9. CMSR and pension record for James S. Weir; *Liberator* (Boston), June 27, 1862.

10. Weir here alludes to a story in Exodus 17 in which as long as the Israelites held up Moses's hands, they would be victorious in battle over the Amalekites.

11. It appears that a line may be missing from the scan here.

12. Nancy M. Weir to Lincoln, February 8, 1864, and January 9, 1865, RG 94, Entry 360 (PAL 297560 and 298284); CMSR for James S. Weir. Bounties were offered at the local, state, and federal levels to induce men to enlist, sometimes causing confusion among recruits and their families regarding how much money they were owed. Moreover, there was significant discrimination against black recruits, many of whom never received the money they were owed. See Smith, *Lincoln and the U.S. Colored Troops*, 66–67, 71–72; Glatthaar, *Forged in Battle*, 65–68.

13. Rankin, "Origins of Negro Leadership," 155–73.

14. During the War of 1812, African American men were part of Andrew Jackson's army that defended New Orleans.

15. In 1862, Attorney General Edward Bates issued an opinion stating that the *"free man of color . . .* if born in the United States, is a citizen of the United States." Bates, *Opinion*, 26–27.

16. Petition of Jean Baptiste Roudanez and E. Arnold Bertonneau, January 5, 1864, RG 46, Entry 565 (PAL 285189b), and RG 233, Entry 479 (PAL 285189).

17. Prior to ratification of the Fourteenth, Fifteenth, Seventeenth, Nineteenth, Twenty-Fourth, and Twenty-Sixth Amendments, the U.S. Constitution left the states with almost complete authority to determine who was eligible to vote. In this petition, however, the memorialists argued that the federal government could enfranchise African Americans by pointing out that the military had authorized white soldiers to vote in an election in Louisiana in December 1863.

18. Petition of Jean Baptiste Roudanez and Arnold Bertonneau, March 10, 1864, RG 233, Entry 479 (PAL 285187), and RG 46, Entry 565 (PAL 285187b).

19. Carpenter, *Six Months at the White House*, 267–68.

20. Lincoln to Michael Hahn, March 13, 1864, in *CWL* 7:243.

21. Cecelski, *Fire of Freedom*; Bishir, *Crafting Lives*, 167–71.

22. *Anglo-African* (New York), May 14, July 2, 1864; *North Carolina Times* (New Berne, N.C.), May 21, 1864. It is unclear why Hill did not sign the petition.

23. Annie Davis to Lincoln, August 25, 1864, RG 94, Entry 360 (PAL 208912).

24. White, "Achieving Emancipation in Maryland."

25. Zack Burden to Lincoln, February 2, 1865, RG 94, Entry 360 (PAL 208900); CMSR and pension record for Zachariah Burden. Burden appears to have written "NCC" and "CC" near his signature, although it is unclear what those notations meant.

Chapter Eight

1. Boles, *Dividing the Faith*, 167.

2. Horton and Horton, *In Hope of Liberty*, 129–30.

3. Simmons, *Men of Mark*, 662–65.

4. Leonard A. Grimes and others to Lincoln, August 21, 1863, Lincoln Papers. Grimes was also a signatory on another letter sent by a number of whites to Lincoln. See Weston Lewis and others to Lincoln, December 10, 1864, Rutherford B. Hayes Presidential Center, Fremont, Ohio (PAL 229585).

5. Lincoln to whom it may concern, August 21, 1863, in *CWL*, 6:401.

6. Edmund Kelly to Lincoln, August 21, 1863, Lincoln Papers; Simmons, *Men of Mark*, 291–95. The signatures in the Grimes letter are all in the same hand, which explains why Kelly's signature is spelled differently in this document.

7. Asher, *Incidents in the Life of the Rev. J. Asher*; Johnson, "History of Camp William Penn," 89–91; Redkey, "Black Chaplains," 337–44; *Public Ledger* (Philadelphia), December 3, 1859.

8. Jeremiah Asher to Lincoln, September 7, 1863, RG 94, Entry 360 (PAL 291234).

9. Johnson, "History of Camp William Penn," 89–90; Redkey, "Black Chaplains," 337–44.

10. Redkey, "Black Chaplains," 344.

11. Johnson, "History of Camp William Penn," 90–91; Redkey, "Black Chaplains," 337; *Report of the Twenty-Fifth Anniversary*, 13–14.

12. *Daily National Republican* (Washington, D.C.), October 6, 1863; *Christian Recorder* (Philadelphia), October 3, 1863. The *Christian Recorder* dated Lincoln's letter September 22, which had to be a typographical error, so I have used the *National Republican's* date, although the rest of these two transcriptions are from the *Christian Recorder*.

13. John A. Simms, John F. N. Wilkinson, and Thomas Cross to Lincoln, October 8, 1863, Lincoln Papers.

14. James Mitchell to Lincoln, November 5, 1863, Lincoln Papers; An Act to incorporate the "African Civilization Society," May 5, 1863, in *Laws of the State of New York*, 758–59.

15. George W. Le Vere and others to Lincoln, November 5, 1863, Lincoln Papers.

16. Draft order in the hand of James Mitchell, November 5, 1863, Lincoln Papers; *Daily National Intelligencer* (Washington, D.C.), November 16, 1863.

17. The circular is included in the Lincoln Papers. It contains the constitution of the African Civilization Society, a statement regarding the organization's desire to open schools for freedpeople in the South, and a list of officers.

18. Richard H. Cain to Lincoln, January 27, 1864, Lincoln Papers.

19. Redkey, "Black Chaplains," 349; Quinn, *Freedom Journey*, 94–95; Foner, *Freedom's Lawmakers*, 35–36; *BAP*, 1:504.

20. James D. Turner to Lincoln, April 25, 1863, Lincoln Papers.

21. Jesse W. Devine and others to Lincoln, October 14, 1863, RG 94, Entry 360 (PAL 302962); Lincoln endorsement on John S. Poler to Lincoln, August 22, 1863, RG 94, Entry 360 (PAL 294642);*Evening Star* (Washington, D.C.), June 25, 1864.

22. Chauncey Leonard to Lincoln, July 9, 1864, and John Hay to Edwin M. Stanton, July 27, 1864, both in M1064, reel 104; Joyce, "Freedmen Warriors," 42–48.

23. Hill, *Black Women Oral History Project*, 6:46–48.

24. J. R. Pierre to Lincoln, July 21, 1864, in RG 42, Entry 1; *Evening Star* (Washington, D.C.), August 3, 1864.

25. "Proclamation of a Day of Prayer," July 7, 1864, in *CWL*, 7:431–32; *Evening Star* (Washington, D.C.), August 5, 1864, April 13, 1870, July 5, 1872; *Weekly National Intelligencer* (Washington, D.C.), August 11, 1864.

26. Edward Bates, diary entry for August 6, 1864, in *Diary of Edward Bates*, 395.

27. *Daily Milwaukee News*, August 14, 1864.

28. *Star of the North* (Bloomsburg, Pa.), December 21, 1864; Burlingame, *Abraham Lincoln*, 2:829–31.

29. Randolph CMSR; *Burlington (Vt.) Free Press*, November 5, 1868; Foner, *Freedom's Lawmakers*, 175–76.

30. B. F. Randolph to Lincoln, August 23, 1864, RG 94, Entry 12 (PAL 294173).

31. *Salem (Mass.) Observer*, November 7, 1868.

Chapter Nine

1. John P. Hale (1806–73) was a Republican senator from New Hampshire.

2. Anson Burlingame (1820–70) was a Republican member of Congress from Massachusetts.

3. Aaron A. Bradley to Lincoln, April 1, 1861, and John A. Andrew to Lincoln, March 23, 1861, both in M650, reels 7 and 24.

4. Reidy, "Aaron A. Bradley"; Hahn et al., *Land and Labor, 1865*, 466–76; Hayden et al., *Land and Labor, 1866–1867*, 51, 223–24, 344–56.

5. Emery Watson to Lincoln, January 23, 1863, RG 60, Entry 9A (PAL 241326).

6. In this case Laburzan appears to have misspelled "two" and left it appearing as a "u." He left similar stray characters a few lines down.

7. Edward T. Laburzan to Lincoln, March 15, 1864, RG 94, Entry 366 (PAL 301655); CMSR for Edward T. Laburzan.

8. Berlin et al., *Wartime Genesis of Free Labor*, 87–113, 168–88, 255–59, 278–81; Hester, *Yankee Scholar*, 24, 38–39, 47, 59, 144–46, 159–60; Lincoln to David Hunter and others, February 10, 1863, and "Instructions to Tax Commissioners in South Carolina," September 16, 1863, in *CWL*, 6:98–99, 453–59.

9. Edward S. Philbrick to Albert G. Browne, March 25, 1864, Lincoln Papers.

10. Berlin et al., *Wartime Genesis of Free Labor: The Lower South*, 297–308.

11. Towne, *Letters and Diary of Laura M. Towne*; Hester, *Yankee Scholar*, 62.

12. Grimké, *Journals of Charlotte Forten Grimké*, 469–70.

13. Theodosia Burr (1783–1813) married Joseph Alston (later governor of South Carolina) in 1801. She was lost at sea in 1813 off the coast of South Carolina.

14. Possibly "Potter" or "Rutter."

15. Laura M. Towne and Don Carlos to Lincoln, May 24, 1864, Lincoln Papers.

16. Towne, *Letters and Diary of Laura M. Towne*, 294.

17. An Act to provide for the Collection of abandoned Property and for the Prevention of Frauds in insurrectionary Districts within the United States, March 3, 1863, in 12 Stat. 820–21.

18. Petition of John Habersham to Lincoln, February 23, 1865, RG 56, Entry 370 (PAL 251019).

19. Petition of Henry Fields to Lincoln, March 1, 1865, RG 56, Entry 370 (PAL 251020).

20. For an account of this meeting, see Berlin et al., *Wartime Genesis of Free Labor*, 331–38.

21. Petition of Charles Bradwell to Lincoln, March 1, 1865, RG 56, Entry 370 (PAL 251021 and 251021b); *Burlington (Iowa) Hawk-Eye*, March 4, 1865. For a full account of the meeting, see Hahn et al., *Land and Labor, 1865*, 331–38.

22. The signature is in a different hand, which explains the variant spelling of the last name.

23. Petition of Delancy Jenks to Lincoln, March 1, 1865, RG 56, Entry 370 (PAL 251016).

24. H.R. Ex. Doc. 2, 41st Cong., 3rd sess., p. xlvi (1870); H.R. Ex. Doc. 2, 44th Cong., 1st sess., p. 40 (1875); H.R. Misc. Doc. 190, 44th Cong., 1st sess., p. 5 (1876); An act for the relief of Charles L. Bradwell, September 24, 1888, in 25 Stat. 1190.

25. Berlin, Reidy, and Rowland, *Black Military Experience*, 727–28.

26. Berlin et al., *Wartime Genesis of Free Labor: The Upper South*, 231–34.

27. Berlin et al., *Wartime Genesis of Free Labor: The Upper South*, 234–36.

28. Berlin, Reidy, and Rowland, *Black Military Experience*, 727–30.

29. James Wilson to Lincoln, April 4, 1865 (PAL 297844), RG 94, Entry 360.

30. E. W. Douglass to Lincoln, April 4, 1865 (PAL 297845), RG 94, Entry 360.

31. E. W. Douglass to the Secretaries of the American Missionary Association, January 14, 1865, and E. W. Douglass to G. Whipple, March 4, 1865, American Missionary Association Collection.

Chapter Ten

1. Eben G. Trask to Lincoln, November 9, 1864, RG 107, Entry 18 (PAL 287327); Holzer, "'Tokens of Respect,'" 177–92.

2. Solomon Peck to Lincoln, January 1, 1863, Lincoln Papers.

3. John Proctor to Lincoln, April 18, 1863, Lincoln Papers; CMSR for John Proctor.

4. Silkenat and Barr, "'Serving the Lord and Abe Lincoln's Spirit,'" 86–90.

5. In his Farewell Address at Springfield, Illinois, on February 11, 1861, Lincoln said, "I now leave, not knowing when, or whether ever, I may return, with a task before me greater than that which rested upon Washington. Without the assistance of that Divine Being, who ever attended him, I cannot succeed. With that assistance I cannot fail. Trusting in Him, who can go with me, and remain with you and be every where for good, let us confidently hope that all will yet be well. To His care commending you, as I hope in your prayers you will commend me, I bid you an affectionate farewell." *CWL*, 4:190–91.

6. Benjamin Woodward to Lincoln, April 11, 1864, Lincoln Papers; pension record of Hannibal Cox.

7. White, *Midnight in America*, 39, 87, 149–51, 178–79.

8. Mrs. Luther Fowler and George Washington to Lincoln, March 19, 1865, Lincoln Papers.

9. White, *Midnight in America*, chap. 4.

Epilogue

1. Todd, *Seventy-Ninth Highlanders*, 102.

2. Swint, *Dear Ones at Home*, 61.

3. Keckley, *Behind the Scenes*, 140–41.

4. BAP, 5:276.

5. Fischer, *Liberty and Freedom*, 327; Towne, *Letters and Diary of Laura M. Towne*, 162; Julia Wilbur Diary, entry for April 16, 1865.

6. Genovese, *Roll, Jordan, Roll*, 118–19.

7. Hodes, *Mourning Lincoln*, 99, 112, 140, 244.

8. Twitty, *Before Dred Scott*; Kennington, *In the Shadow of Dred Scott*.

9. Welch, *Black Litigants*, 13–14.

10. On petitions by African Americans, see Carpenter and Moore, "When Canvassers Became Activists," 479–90; Sinha, *Slave's Cause*.

11. Quarles, *Lincoln and the Negro*, 209–10, 213.

12. Foner, *Freedom's Lawmakers*.

13. White, "Martial Law and the Expansion of Civil Liberties," 52–72; Milewski, *Litigating across the Color Line*.

14. Johnson, *Papers of Andrew Johnson*, 7:251–53; 9:296–98, 490–91; 10:41–48, 265–66, 456, 547, 549, 598, 652–53, 720, 734–35, 745; *New-York Tribune*, June 17, 1865; Jordan, *Negro Baptist History*, 63–65; *Report of the Twenty-Fifth Anniversary*, 15–16, 23–24; Oakes, *Radical and the Republican*, 247–55, 265; Simon, *Personal Memoirs of Julia Dent Grant*, 175.

15. *Knoxville Sentinel*, October 21, 1901.

Bibliography

Primary Sources

Manuscript Collections

COLLEGE PARK, MD.
National Archives at College Park, Maryland
 RG 48: Records of the Office of the Secretary of the Interior
  Entry 376: Records Relating to the Suppression of the African Slave Trade,
   1854–1872
 RG 56: General Records of the Department of the Treasury
  Entry 370: Case Files of Claims for Cotton and Captured and Abandoned
   Property, 1861–1902
 RG 59: General Records of the Department of State
  Entry 897: Appointment Records, General Pardon Records, Pardons
   and Remissions
  Entry 902: Appointment Records, General Pardon Records, Requisitions for
   Pardons, 1858–1862
 RG 60: Records of the Attorney General's Office
  Entry 9A: Letters Received, 1809–1870
 RG 112: Records of the office of the Surgeon General (Army)
  Entry 12: Central Office, Letters Received, 1818–1870
 RG 204: Records of the Office of the Pardon Attorney
  Entry 1a: Pardon Case Files, 1853–1946

FREMONT, OH.
 Rutherford B. Hayes Presidential Center
  Weston Lewis and others to Lincoln

HAVERFORD, PA.
 Quaker and Special Collections, Haverford College
  Julia Wilbur Diary (transcription by Alexandria Archaeology)

NEW ORLEANS, LA.
 Amistad Research Center, Tulane University
  American Missionary Association Collection

NEW YORK, N.Y.
 Gilder-Lehrman Collection
 National Archives at New York City

RG 21: Records of the U.S. District and Circuit Courts for the Southern District of New York

ROCHESTER, N.Y.
  University of Rochester
    William H. Seward Papers

SPRINGFIELD, ILL.
  Illinois State Archives
    Secretary of State, Executive Clemency Files, Record Series 103.096

WASHINGTON, D.C.
  Manuscript Division, Library of Congress
    Abraham Lincoln Papers
  National Archives and Records Administration (NARA)
    RG 21: Records of the United States District Court for the District of Columbia
      Entry 77: Criminal Case Files, 1863–1934
      Entry 74: Criminal Dockets, 1863–1934
      Entry 108: Miscellaneous Volumes of the District of Columbia's Justices of the Peace
    RG 42: Records of the Office of Public Buildings and Public Parks of the National Capital
      Entry 1: Letters Received, 1791–1867
    RG 45: Naval Records Collection of the Office of Naval Records and Library
      Entry 36: Miscellaneous Letters Received, 1801–1884
    RG 46: Records of the U.S. Senate
      Entry 563: Records of Legislative Proceedings, President's Messages, 1863–1865
      Entry 565: Petitions and Memorials, Resolutions of State Legislatures, and Related Documents, 1863–1865
    RG 94: Records of the Office of the Adjutant General
      Entry 12: Letters Received by (Main Series), 1861–1870
      Entry 360: Colored Troops Division, Letters Received, 1863–1868
      Entry 366: Colored Troops Division, Letters Received Relating to Recruiting, 1863–1868
      Entry 409: Enlisted Branch, Letters Received, 1862–1889
      Entry 416: Letters Received Relating to Soldiers, 1848–1862
      Entry 519: Compiled Military Service Records, Records of the Record and Pension Office, Carded Military Service Records, 1784–1903, Civil War, 1861–1865
    RG 99: Records of the Office of the Paymaster General
      Entry 7: Correspondence, Letters Received, 1799–1894
    RG 107: Records of the Office of the Secretary of War
      Entry 18: Letters Received [Main Series], 1801–1889

RG 110: Records of the Provost Marshal General's Bureau (Civil War)
  Entry 18: Records of the Central Office, Letters Received, 1863–1865
RG 153: Records of the Office of the Judge Advocate General (Army)
  Entries 11–15: General Court-Martial Case Files
RG 233: Records of the United States House of Representatives
  Entry 479: Petitions and Memorials, Resolutions of State Legislatures, and
    Related Documents Which Were Referred to Committees, 1863–1865
RG 351: Records of the Government of the District of Columbia
  Entry 125: Daily Returns of Precincts, 1861–78, and 1887

National Archives Microfilm

M160 (Records of the Office of the Secretary of the Interior Relating to the
  Suppression of the African Slave Trade and Negro Colonization, 1854–72).
M650 (Letters of Application and Recommendation during the Administrations of
  Abraham Lincoln and Andrew Johnson, 1861–1869).
M1064 (Letters Received by the Commission Branch of the Adjutant General's Office,
  1863–1870).

Electronic Databases

Accessible Archives
Ancestry.com
Fold3
NewsBank
Newspapers.com
Papers of Abraham Lincoln: Images from the National Archives and Library of
  Congress
Slavery and Anti-Slavery: A Transnational Archive (Gale)

Newspapers on Microfilm

African Repository
Anglo-African

Published Primary Sources

Adams, Virginia M., ed. *On the Altar of Freedom: A Black Soldier's Civil War Letters from the Front.* Amherst: University of Massachusetts Press, 1991.
An Appeal from the Colored Men of Philadelphia to the President of the United States. Forwarded to Washington. Philadelphia, August 1862.
Aptheker, Herbert, ed. *A Documentary History of the Negro People in the United States.* New York: Citadel Press, 1951.
Asher, Jeremiah. *Incidents in the Life of the Rev. J. Asher.* London, Charles Gilpin, 1850.

Bates, Edward. *The Diary of Edward Bates, 1859–1866*. Edited by Howard K. Beale. Washington, D.C.: Government Printing Office, 1933.

———. *Opinion of Attorney General Bates on Citizenship*. Washington, D.C.: Government Printing Office, 1862.

Berlin, Ira, Barbara J. Fields, Thavolia Glymph, Joseph P. Reidy, and Leslie S. Rowland, eds. *The Destruction of Slavery*. Ser. 1, vol. 1, of *Freedom: A Documentary History of Emancipation, 1861–1867*. New York: Cambridge University Press, 1985.

Berlin, Ira, Thavolia Glymph, Steven F. Miller, Joseph P. Reidy, Leslie S. Rowland, and Julie Saville, eds. *The Wartime Genesis of Free Labor: The Lower South*. Ser. 1, vol. 3, of *Freedom: A Documentary History of Emancipation, 1861–1867*. New York: Cambridge University Press, 1990.

Berlin, Ira, Steven F. Miller, Joseph P. Reidy, and Leslie S. Rowland, eds. *The Wartime Genesis of Free Labor: The Upper South*. Ser. 1, vol. 2, of *Freedom: A Documentary History of Emancipation, 1861–1867*. New York: Cambridge University Press, 1993.

Berlin, Ira, Joseph P. Reidy, and Leslie S. Rowland, eds. *The Black Military Experience*. Ser. 2 of *Freedom: A Documentary History of Emancipation, 1861–1867*. New York: Cambridge University Press, 1982.

———, eds. *Freedom's Soldiers: The Black Military Experience in the Civil War*. New York: Cambridge University Press, 1998.

Boyd's Washington and Georgetown Directory. Washington, D.C.: Hudson Taylor, 1864.

Brown, Katie O'Halloran, ed. "Letters of Three Ohio Soldiers in the 54th and 55th Massachusetts Colored Infantries." *Ohio Valley History* 16 (Fall 2016): 72–79.

Brown, William Wells. *The Black Man: His Antecedents, His Genius, and His Achievements*. Boston: James Redpath, 1863.

Carpenter, Francis B. *Six Months at the White House with Abraham Lincoln*. New York: Hurd and Houghton, 1866.

Chandler, Lucinda. "Reminiscences of the Sunny South." *Granite Monthly* 10 (December 1887): 377–82.

Chester, Thomas Morris. *Thomas Morris Chester, Black Civil War Correspondent: His Dispatches from the Virginia Front*. Edited by R. J. M. Blackett. Baton Rouge: Louisiana State University Press, 1989.

Douglass, Frederick. *Frederick Douglass: Selected Speeches and Writings*. Edited by Philip S. Foner and Yuval Taylor. Chicago: Lawrence Hill Books, 1999.

———. *The Life and Times of Frederick Douglass, from 1817 to 1882, Written by Himself*. London: Christian Age, 1882.

———. *The Oxford Frederick Douglass Reader*. Edited by William L. Andrews. New York: Oxford University Press, 1996.

Fehrenbacher, Don E., and Virginia Fehrenbacher, eds. *Recollected Words of Abraham Lincoln*. Stanford: Stanford University Press, 1996.

Greeley, Horace. *The American Conflict: A History of the Great Rebellion in the United States of America, 1860–'65*. 2 vols. Hartford, Conn.: O. D. Case and Co., 1864–67.

Greene, Robert Ewell. *Swamp Angels: A Biographical Study of the 54th Massachusetts Regiment*. Washington, D.C.: BoMark/Greene Publishing Group, 1990.

Grimké, Charlotte Forten. *The Journals of Charlotte Forten Grimké*. Edited by
    Brenda L. Stevenson. New York: Oxford University Press, 1988.
Hahn, Steven, Steven F. Miller, Susan E. O'Donovan, John C. Rodrigue, and
    Leslie S. Rowland, eds. *Land and Labor, 1865*. Ser. 3, vol. 1, of *Freedom: A
    Documentary History of Emancipation, 1861-1867*. Chapel Hill: University of North
    Carolina Press, 2008.
Harrison, Samuel. *Rev. Samuel Harrison: His Life Story, Told by Himself*. Pittsfield,
    Mass.: Eagle, 1899.
Harrower, David I., and Thomas J. Wieckowski, eds. *A Spectacle for Men and Angels:
    A Documentary Narrative of Camp William Penn and the Raising of Colored Regiments
    in Pennsylvania*. West Conshohocken, Pa.: Infinity, 2013.
Hay, John. *Inside Lincoln's White House: The Complete Civil War Diary of John Hay*.
    Edited by Michael Burlingame and John R. Turner Ettlinger. Carbondale:
    Southern Illinois University Press, 1997.
Hayden, René, Anthony E. Kaye, Kate Masur, Steven F. Miller, Susan E.
    O'Donovan, Leslie S. Rowland, and Stephen A. West, eds. *Land and Labor,
    1866-1867*. Ser. 3, vol. 2, of *Freedom: A Documentary History of Emancipation,
    1861-1867*. Chapel Hill: University of North Carolina Press, 2013.
Hester, James Robert, ed. *A Yankee Scholar in Coastal South Carolina: William
    Francis Allen's Civil War Journals*. Columbia: University of South Carolina Press,
    2015.
Higginson, Thomas Wentworth. *Army Life in a Black Regiment*. 1869. Reprint,
    New York: W. W. Norton, 1984.
Hill, Ruth Edmonds, ed. *The Black Women Oral History Project*. 10 vols. Westport,
    Conn.: Meckler, 1991.
Jackson, Mattie J. "The Story of Mattie J. Jackson." In *Freedom's Journey: African
    American Voices of the Civil War*, edited by Donald Yacovone, 245-74. Chicago:
    Lawrence Hill Books, 2004.
Johnson, Andrew. *The Papers of Andrew Johnson*. Edited by Leroy P. Graf, Ralph W.
    Haskins, and Paul H. Bergeron. 16 vols. Knoxville: University of Tennessee Press,
    1967-2000.
Keckley, Elizabeth. *Behind the Scenes, or Thirty Years a Slave, and Four Years in the
    White House*. New York: G. W. Carleton, 1868.
Laws of the State of New York Passed at the Eighty-Sixth Session of the Legislature. Albany:
    Weed, Parsons, 1863.
Leasher, Evelyn, ed. *Letter from Washington, 1863-1865*. Detroit: Wayne State
    University Press, 1999.
Lincoln, Abraham. *The Collected Works of Abraham Lincoln*. Edited by Roy P. Basler.
    9 vols. New Brunswick, N.J.: Rutgers University Press, 1953-1955.
————. *The Collected Works of Abraham Lincoln: Supplement, 1832-1865*. Edited by
    Roy P. Basler. Westport, Conn.: Greenwood Press, 1974.
McPherson, James M., ed. *The Negro's Civil War: How American Negroes Felt and Acted
    during the War for the Union*. New York: Pantheon, 1965.
Moses, Wilson Jeremiah, ed. *Liberian Dreams: Back-to-Africa Narratives from the
    1850s*. University Park: Penn State University Press, 1998.

Palmer, Beverly Wilson. ed. *The Selected Letters of Charles Sumner*. 2 vols. Boston: Northeastern University Press, 1990.

Quinn, Edythe Ann. *Freedom Journey: Black Civil War Soldiers and the Hills Community, Westchester County, New York*. Albany: State University of New York Press, 2015.

Randolph, Paschal B. *P. B. Randolph, the "Learned Pundit" and "Man with Two Souls": His Curious Life, Works, and Career, the Great Free-Love Trial, Randolph's Grand Defence, His Address to the Jury, and Mankind, the Verdict*. Boston: Randolph, 1872.

———. [Griffin Lee, pseud.]. *Pre-Adamite Man: The Story of the Human Race, from 35,000 to 100,000 Years Ago!* 2nd ed. New York: Sinclair Tousey, 1863.

Redkey, Edwin S., ed. *A Grand Army of Black Men: Letters from African-American Soldiers in the Union Army, 1861–1865*. New York: Cambridge University Press, 1992.

Regosin, Elizabeth A., and Donald R. Shaffer, eds. *Voices of Emancipation: Understanding Slavery, the Civil War, and Reconstruction through the U.S. Pension Bureau Files*. New York: New York University Press, 2008.

Reid, Richard M., ed. *Practicing Medicine in a Black Regiment: The Civil War Diary of Burt G. Wilder, 55th Massachusetts*. Amherst: University of Massachusetts Press, 2010.

Report of the Twenty-Fifth Anniversary of the American Baptist Missionary Convention: Held at the Meeting House of the First Colored Baptist Church, Alexandria, Va. from Friday, August 18th, to Sunday, August 27th, 1865. New Bedford, Mass.: E. Anthony and Sons, 1865.

Ripley, C. Peter, ed. *The Black Abolitionist Papers*. 5 vols. Chapel Hill: University of North Carolina Press, 1985–92.

Seward, Frederick W. *William H. Seward: An Autobiography*. New York: Derby and Miller, 1891.

Shaw, Robert Gould. *Blue-Eyed Child of Fortune: The Civil War Letters of Colonel Robert Gould Shaw*. Edited by Russell Duncan. Athens: University of Georgia Press, 1992.

Simon, John Y., ed. *The Personal Memoirs of Julia Dent Grant (Mrs. Ulysses S. Grant): 45th Anniversary Edition*. Carbondale: Southern Illinois University Press, 2020.

Smith, Eric Ledell, ed. "The Civil War Letters of Quartermaster Sergeant John C. Brock, 43rd Regiment, United States Colored Troops." In *Making and Remaking Pennsylvania's Civil War*, edited by William Blair and William Pencak, 141–63. University Park: Pennsylvania State University Press, 2001.

Stephens, George E. *A Voice of Thunder: The Civil War Letters of George E. Stephens*. Edited by Donald Yacovone. Urbana: University of Illinois Press, 1997.

Swint, Henry L., ed. *Dear Ones at Home: Letters from Contraband Camps*. Nashville: Vanderbilt University Press, 1966.

Towne, Laura Matilda. *Letters and Diary of Laura M. Towne: Written from the Sea Islands of South Carolina, 1862–1884*. Edited by Rupert Sargent Holland. Cambridge, Mass.: Riverside Press, 1912.

Trudeau, Noah Andre, ed. *Voices of the 55th: Letters from the 55th Massachusetts Volunteers, 1861–1865*. Dayton, Ohio: Morningside House, 1996.

Turner, Henry McNeal. *Freedom's Witness: The Civil War Correspondence of Henry McNeal Turner*. Edited by Jean Lee Cole. Morgantown: West Virginia University Press, 2013.

U.S. Congressional Serial Set.

War of the Rebellion: A Compilation of the Official Records of the Union and Confederate Armies. 128 vols. Washington, D.C.: Government Printing Office, 1880–1901.

Washington, Booker T. *Up from Slavery: An Autobiography*. New York: Doubleday, 1901.

White, Jonathan W., Katie Fisher, and Elizabeth Wall, eds. "The Civil War Letters of Tillman Valentine, Third U.S. Colored Troops." *Pennsylvania Magazine of History and Biography* 139 (April 2015): 165–82.

Woodson, Carter G., ed. *The Mind of the Negro as Reflected in Letters Written during the Crisis, 1800–1860*. New York: Russell and Russell, 1926.

Yacovone, Donald, ed. *Freedom's Journey: African American Voices of the Civil War*. Chicago: Lawrence Hill Books, 2004.

Secondary Sources

Articles and Chapters

Bradley, Ed. "Dr. Alexander T. Augusta." *Lincoln Editor* 14 (July–September 2014): 5–8.

Carpenter, Daniel, and Colin D. Moore. "When Canvassers Became Activists: Antislavery Petitioning and the Political Mobilization of American Voters." *American Political Science Review* 108 (August 2014): 479–98.

Clarke, Frances M., and Rebecca Jo Plant. "No Minor Matter: Underage Soldiers, Parents, and the Nationalization of Habeas Corpus in Civil War America." *Law and History Review* 35 (November 2017): 881–927.

Doig, Ivan. "Lincolniana Notes: The Genial White House Host and Raconteur." *Journal of the Illinois State Historical Society* 62 (Autumn 1969): 307–11.

Egerton, Douglas R. "The Slaves' Election: Fremont, Freedom, and the Slave Conspiracies of 1856." *Civil War History* 61 (March 2015): 35–63.

Fannin, John F. "The Jacksonville Mutiny of 1865." *Florida Historical Quarterly* 88 (Winter 2010): 368–96.

Gordon, Ann D. "Getting History's Words Right: Diaries of Emilie Davis." *Pennsylvania Magazine of History and Biography* 139 (October 2015): 197–216.

Hahn, Steven. "But What Did the Slaves Think of Lincoln?" In *Lincoln's Proclamation: Emancipation Reconsidered*, edited by William A. Blair and Karen Fisher Younger, 102–19. Chapel Hill: University of North Carolina Press, 2009.

Hanchett, Catherine M. "George Boyer Vashon, 1824–1878: Black Educator, Poet, Fighter for Equal Rights." Pts. 1 and 2. *Western Pennsylvania Historical Magazine* 68, no. 3 (July 1985): 205–19; 68, no. 4 (October 1985): 333–49.

Hart, Richard E. "Springfield's African Americans as a Part of the Lincoln Community." *Journal of the Abraham Lincoln Association* 20 (Winter 1999): 35–54.

Holzer, Harold. "'Tokens of Respect' and 'Heartfelt Thanks': How Abraham Lincoln Coped with Presidential Gifts." *Illinois Historical Journal* 77 (Autumn 1984): 177–92.

Joyce, Charles. "Freedmen Warriors, Civil Rights Fighters." *Military Images* 34 (Autumn 2016): 42–48.

Masur, Kate. "The African American Delegation to Abraham Lincoln: A Reappraisal." *Civil War History* 56 (June 2010): 117–44.

———. "Color Was a Bar to the Entrance: African American Activism and the Question of Social Equality in Lincoln's White House." *American Quarterly* 69 (March 2017): 1–22.

Palmer, William M. "Unpardoned by Lincoln: Stephen A. Douglas's House Servant." *Lincoln Forum Bulletin* 43 (Fall 2018): 4.

Rankin, David C. "The Origins of Negro Leadership in New Orleans during Reconstruction." In *Southern Black Leaders of the Reconstruction Era*, edited by Howard Rabinowitz, 155–73. Urbana: University of Illinois Press, 1982.

Redkey, Edwin S. "Black Chaplains in the Union Army." *Civil War History* 33 (December 1987): 331–50.

Reidy, Joseph P. "Aaron A. Bradley: Voice of Black Labor in the Georgia Lowcountry." In *Southern Black Leaders of the Reconstruction Era*, edited by Howard Rabinowitz, 281–309. Urbana: University of Illinois Press, 1982.

Samito, Christian G. "The Intersection between Military Justice and Equal Rights: Mutinies, Courts-Martial, and Black Civil War Soldiers." *Civil War History* 53 (June 2007): 170–202.

Silkenat, David, and John Barr. "'Serving the Lord and Abe Lincoln's Spirit': Lincoln and Memory in the WPA Narratives." *Lincoln Herald* 115 (2013): 75–97.

Slap, Andrew L. "The Tintype That Proved a Pension Claim." *Military Images* 33 (Summer 2015): 44–45.

Smith, John David. "Black Images of Lincoln in the Age of Jim Crow." *Lincoln Lore* 1681 (March 1978): 1–3.

Stowell, Daniel W. "President Lincoln Pardons John Booth." *Lincoln Editor* 8 (April–June 2008): 7.

Sweet, Natalie. "A Representative 'of Our People': The Agency of William Slade, Leader in the African American Community and Usher to Abraham Lincoln." *Journal of the Abraham Lincoln Association* 34 (Summer 2013): 21–41.

Wert, Jeffry D. "Camp William Penn and the Black Soldier." *Pennsylvania History* 46 (October 1979): 335–46.

White, Jonathan W. "Achieving Emancipation in Maryland." In *The Civil War in Maryland Reconsidered*, edited by Jean H. Baker and Charles W. Mitchell. Baton Rouge: Louisiana State University Press, forthcoming.

———. "Martial Law and the Expansion of Civil Liberties during the Civil War." In *Ex parte Milligan Reconsidered: Race and Civil Liberties from the Lincoln Administration to the War on Terror*, edited by Stewart L. Winger and Jonathan W. White, 52–72. Lawrence: University Press of Kansas, 2020.

———. *Emancipation, the Union Army, and the Reelection of Abraham Lincoln*. Baton Rouge: Louisiana State University Press, 2014.

———. "'Sweltering with Treason': The Civil War Trials of William Matthew Merrick." *Prologue* 39 (Summer 2007): 26–36.

Books

Anderson, James D. *The Education of Blacks in the South, 1860–1935.* Chapel Hill: University of North Carolina Press, 1988.

Belz, Herman. *Abraham Lincoln, Constitutionalism, and Equal Rights in the Civil War Era.* New York: Fordham University Press, 1998.

Bilby, Joseph G. *"Freedom to All": New Jersey's African-American Civil War Soldiers.* Hightstown, N.J.: Longstreet House, 2011.

Bishir, Catherine W. *Crafting Lives: African American Artisans in New Bern, North Carolina, 1770–1900.* Chapel Hill: University of North Carolina Press, 2013.

Boles, Richard J. *Dividing the Faith: The Rise of Segregated Churches in the Early American North.* New York: NYU Press, 2020.

Burlingame, Michael. *Abraham Lincoln: A Life.* 2 vols. Baltimore: Johns Hopkins University Press, 2008.

Butchart, Ronald E. *Schooling the Freed People: Teaching, Learning, and the Struggle for Black Freedom, 1861–1876.* Chapel Hill: University of North Carolina Press, 2010.

Cecelski, David S. *The Fire of Freedom: Abraham Galloway and the Slaves' Civil War.* Chapel Hill: University of North Carolina Press, 2012.

Clavin, Matthew J. *Aiming for Pensacola: Fugitive Slaves on the Atlantic and Southern Frontiers.* Cambridge, Mass.: Harvard University Press, 2015.

Conroy, James B. *Lincoln's White House: The People's House in Wartime.* Lanham, Md.: Rowman and Littlefield, 2016.

Deveney, John P. *Paschal Beverly Randolph: A Nineteenth-Century Black American Spiritualist, Rosicrucian, and Sex Magician.* Albany: State University of New York Press, 1997.

Dirck, Brian. *Lincoln the Lawyer.* Urbana: University of Illinois Press, 2007.

Dobak, William A. *Freedom by the Sword: The U.S. Colored Troops, 1862–1867.* Washington, D.C.: Center of Military History, 2011.

Donald, David Herbert. *Lincoln.* New York: Simon and Schuster, 1995.

Drinkard, Dorothy L. *Illinois Freedom Fighters: A Civil War Saga of the 29th Infantry, United States Colored Troops.* Needham Heights, Mass.: Simon and Schuster Custom Publishing, 1998.

Fields, Barbara Jeanne. *Slavery and Freedom on the Middle Ground: Maryland during the Nineteenth Century.* New Haven, Conn.: Yale University Press, 1985.

Fischer, David Hackett. *Liberty and Freedom: A Visual History of America's Founding Ideas.* New York: Oxford University Press, 2005.

Foner, Eric. *Freedom's Lawmakers: A Directory of Black Officeholders during Reconstruction.* New York: Oxford University Press, 1993.

Foote, Lorien. *The Gentlemen and the Roughs: Violence, Honor, and Manhood in the Union Army.* New York: New York University Press, 2010.

Ford, Ira, ed. *History of Northeast Indiana.* 2 vols. Chicago: Lewis, 1920.

Geary, James W. *We Need Men: The Union Draft in the Civil War*. DeKalb: Northern Illinois University Press, 1991.

Genovese, Eugene D. *Roll, Jordan, Roll: The World the Slaves Made*. New York: Random House, 1972.

Glatthaar, Joseph T. *Forged in Battle: The Civil War Alliance of Black Soldiers and White Officers*. New York: Free Press, 1990.

Hodes, Martha. *Mourning Lincoln*. New Haven, Conn.: Yale University Press, 2015.

Horton, James Oliver, and Lois E. Horton. *In Hope of Liberty: Culture, Community, and Protest among Northern Free Blacks, 1700–1860*. New York: Oxford University Press, 1997.

Jordan, Lewis G. *Negro Baptist History, U.S.A., 1750–1930*. Nashville: Sunday School Publishing Board, 1930.

Kennington, Kelly M. *In the Shadow of Dred Scott: St. Louis Freedom Suits and the Legal Culture of Slavery in Antebellum America*. Athens: University of Georgia Press, 2017.

Keyssar, Alexander. *The Right to Vote: The Contested History of Democracy in the United States*. New York: Basic Books, 2000.

Kuykendall, William L. *Frontier Days: A True Narrative of Striking Events on the Western Frontier*. N.p.: J. M. and H. L. Kuykendall, 1917.

Masur, Kate. *An Example for All the Land: Emancipation and the Struggle over Equality in Washington, D.C.* Chapel Hill: University of North Carolina Press, 2010.

Milewski, Melissa. *Litigating across the Color Line: Civil Cases between Black and White Southerners from the End of Slavery to Civil Rights*. New York: Oxford University Press, 2018.

Miller, Edward A., Jr. *The Black Civil War Soldiers of Illinois: The Story of the Twenty-Ninth U.S. Colored Infantry*. Columbia: University of South Carolina Press, 1998.

Oakes, James. *The Radical and the Republican: Frederick Douglass, Abraham Lincoln, and the Triumph of Antislavery Politics*. New York: W. W. Norton, 2007.

Quarles, Benjamin. *Lincoln and the Negro*. New York: Oxford University Press, 1962.

———. *The Negro in the Civil War*. Boston: Little, Brown, 1953.

Robinson, Armstead L. *Bitter Fruits of Bondage: The Demise of Slavery and the Collapse of the Confederacy, 1861–1865*. Charlottesville: University of Virginia Press, 2005.

Rollin, Frank A. *Life and Public Services of Martin R. Delany*. Boston: Lee and Shepard, 1883.

Samito, Christian G. *Becoming American under Fire: Irish Americans, African Americans, and the Politics of Citizenship during the Civil War Era*. Ithaca, N.Y.: Cornell University Press, 2009.

Scharf, John Thomas. *History of Maryland from the Earliest Period to the Present Day*. 3 vols. 1879. Reprint, Hatboro, Pa.: Tradition Press, 1967.

Silber, Nina. *Daughters of the Union: Northern Women Fight the Civil War*. Cambridge, Mass.: Harvard University Press, 2005.

Simmons, William J. *Men of Mark: Eminent, Progressive and Rising*. Cleveland: Geo. M. Rewell, 1887.

Sinha, Manisha. *The Slave's Cause: A History of Abolition*. New Haven, Conn.: Yale University Press, 2016.

Smith, John David. *Lincoln and the U.S. Colored Troops*. Carbondale: Southern Illinois University Press, 2013.

Stephens, Gail. *Shadow of Shiloh: Major General Lew Wallace in the Civil War*. Indianapolis: Indiana Historical Society Press, 2010.

Stryker, William S. *Record of Officers and Men of New Jersey in the Civil War, 1861–1865*. 2 vols. Trenton: J. L. Murphy, 1876.

Taylor, Elizabeth Dowling. *A Slave in the White House: Paul Jennings and the Madisons*. New York: Palgrave Macmillan, 2012.

Todd, William. *The Seventy-Ninth Highlanders: New York Volunteers in the War of the Rebellion, 1861–1865*. Albany, N.Y.: Brandow, Barton, 1886.

Twitty, Anne. *Before Dred Scott: Slavery and Legal Culture in the American Confluence, 1787–1857*. New York: Cambridge University Press, 2016.

Washington, John E. *They Knew Lincoln*. New York: E. P. Dutton, 1942.

Weitz, Mark A. *The Confederacy on Trial: The Piracy and Sequestration Cases of 1861*. Lawrence: University Press of Kansas, 2005.

Welch, Kimberly M. *Black Litigants in the Antebellum American South*. Chapel Hill: University of North Carolina Press, 2018.

White, Jonathan W. *Guide to Research in Federal Judicial History*. Washington, D.C.: Federal Judicial Center, 2010.

———. *Midnight in America: Darkness, Sleep, and Dreams during the Civil War*. Chapel Hill: University of North Carolina Press, 2017.

Dissertations

Colby, Robert. "The Continuance of an Unholy Traffic: Slave Trading in the Civil War South." PhD diss., University of North Carolina at Chapel Hill, 2019.

Greene, Ousmane Kirumu. "Against Wind and Tide: African Americans' Response to the Colonization Movement and Emigration, 1770–1865." PhD diss., University of Massachusetts Amherst, 2007.

Johnson, James Elton. "A History of Camp William Penn and Its Black Troops in the Civil War, 1863–1865." PhD diss., University of Pennsylvania, 1999.

Orr, Timothy J. "Cities at War: Union Army Mobilization in the Urban Northeast, 1861–1865." PhD diss., Pennsylvania State University, 2010.

Web-Based Sources

Berry, Stephen W. "Civil War Letters." Lecture presented at the Civil War Institute, Gettysburg College, June 16, 2019. www.c-span.org/video/?461565-9/civil-war -letters.

Brooks, Christopher, T. "Taylor, James T. S. (1840–1918)." In *Encyclopedia Virginia*. Virginia Humanities, February 12, 2021. https://encyclopediavirginia.org/entries /taylor-james-t-s-1840-1918/.

White, Jonathan W. "A Black Soldier from Charlottesville Writes to Lincoln." Blog of the John L. Nau III Center for Civil War History at the University of Virginia, September 27, 2016. https://naucenter.as.virginia.edu/blog-page/311.

Index of Correspondents

This index excludes white people who wrote letters on behalf of African Americans. Correspondents with the identical names appear under the same heading. Alternative spellings of surnames appear in parentheses.

Allen, Robert, 39–43
Ames, John, 15–18
Asher, Jeremiah, 185–88
Augusta, Alexander T., 64–66, 238
Augusta, John, 39–43

Babcock, Charles, 53
Barcroff, William J., 137–39
Bass, Alcia, 133–34
Benson, Ann, 121–22
Bertonneau, E. Arnold, 171–76, 177
Bogart, Willis A., 68–69
Bolding, John A., 66–67
Booth, Elizabeth, 11–12
Boulden, Albert, 182–84
Bounds, William J. C., 25–28
Bowers, John C., 39–43
Boyd, Francis A., 84–88
Boyle, Richard, 219–24
Bradley, Aaron A., 201–2, 237
Bradwell, Charles L., 216–18
Brown, Benjamin, 24–25
Brown, B. F., 55
Brumbey, Richard, 129–30
Burden, Zachariah, 179–80
Burr, Matilda, 95–96
Butcher, William C., 51–53
Butler (Butlar), George, 83–84

Cain, Richard H., 190–93, 237
Castle, James, 146–50
Chandler, William, 110–11
Chapman, Martha, 153–54
Conover, Philip, 25–28

Cooper, William, 39–43
Cox, Hannibal, 230–32
Cross, Thomas H., 188–89

Davis, Annie, 179
Davis, J. C., 39–43
Davis, John, 12–15
Davis, Noah, 182–84
Davis, Thomas M., 39–43
Devoe, Isaac, 66–67
Douglass, Frederick, 2, 39, 46, 50, 79–82, 116, 125–26, 199, 237–38
Dungey, John, 66–67

Evans, James, 12–15

Felton, Isaac K., 177–79
Fields, Henry, 215–16
Florville (de Fleurville), William, xv–xix
Ford, Thomas, 227–29
Foskey, M., 51–53
Freeman, Lucy, 134

Galloway, Abraham H., 177–79, 237–38
Gardner, Elias, 227–29
Gibbs, Jonathan C., 39–43
Glasco (Glascow), Freeman, 124–25
Good, John R., 177–79
Gooding, James Henry, 2, 5, 93–95
Green, Kit, 227–29
Grimes, Leonard A., 182–84

Habersham, John, 214–16, 219
Hardy (Hundy), Henry, 12–15

Harris, John H., 97–98
Harrison, June, 227–29
Harrison, Samuel, 90, 104–7
Henson, Rosanna, 98–99
Hepburn, John B., 35–36
Hermong, Charles, 66–67
Hodge, Greenbery, 77–78
Homer, Henry, 127–29

Jackson, George W., 129–30
Jackson, Hester Ann, 96
Jackson, James A., 66–67
Jackson, William, 122–24
January, 227–29
Jencks, Delancy, 218–19
Jenkins, Joseph, 227–29
Jennings, Ed. D., 168
Johnson, B., 51–53
Johnson, Hannah, 166–68
Johnson, Henry, 51–53
Johnson, Henry Andrew, 73–75
Johnson, John, 140–42
Johnson, John D., 34, 53–54
Johnson, Letticia, 20–21
Johnson, William, 66–67, 154
Johnson, William Henry, 130–31

Kelley, Joshua D., 39–43
Kelley, Uriah H., 39–43
Kelly (Kelley), Edmund, 182–85, 238,
    254n6

Laburzan, Edward T., 203–5
Lavalette, William A., 50–53
Laws, Adam, 142–44
Leonard, Chauncey, 194–95
Le Vere, George W., 189–93

Madden, Sam, 182–84
Martin, John Sella, 62–64, 237
Mayo, William D., 137–40
Menard, John Willis, 50–55, 237, 245n30
Mifflin, Daniel, 227–29
Morgan, John H., 137–38
Morris, Giles, 31–32

Muse, Daniel G., 182–84
Myers, Abbie A., 111–13

Nelson, William Joseph, 161–62

Orsey, H. W., 50–53

Pearson (Pierson), Clinton D., 177–79
Peirce (Perce), George, 12–15
Penn, William, 12–15
Pepper, Thomas, 111–12
Petersen, John, 12–15
Pierre, J. R., 195–99
Pool, John, 156–58
Porter, Peter S., 189–92
Pringle, Charles, 227–29
Proctor, John, 229–30

Randolph, Benjamin Franklin, 199–200,
    237
Randolph, Paschal Beverly, 71–73, 237
Robinson, Jacob, 227–29
Robison (Robinson), Elisha S., 82–83
Rock, George, 66–67
Rodgers, George, 101–3
Roe, Francis M., 25–28
Roosa, Samuel, 159–61
Roudanez, Jean Baptiste, 171–76
Rowley, Nimrod, 101–4
Russell, James, 12–15

Sampsons, Samuel, 101–3
Sayers, Amos B., 39–43
Shorter, Elizabeth, 28–31
Shorter, John F., 99–101
Simmons, Harry, 227–29
Simmons, Moses, 227–29
Simms, John A., 188–89
Singleton, Caesar, 227–29
Sipple, Thomas, 101–3
Slade, William, 69–71
Smallwood, John S., 205–10
Smith, A. P., 43–46
Smith, Charles B., 118–21
Smith, Franklin, 150–51

Smith, Richard, 118–21
Stafford, P., 53
Suffon, Alfred, 12–15

Talor, John, 137–38
Taylor, James T. S., 144–46, 237
Tennant (Tennat), Charles, 12–15
Thomas, Edward M., 36–39
Thomas, Jacob, 66–67
Tilmon, Levin, 61–62
Trout, David, 39–43
Tyler, Fanny, 21–24

Underdue, James, 39–43

Vail, Hiram, 116–18
Vashon, George B., 46–50
Vinson (Vincent), Mary Ann, 108–10

Walker, William E., 182–84
Walker, William J., 182–84

Washington (Washiton), David,
    151–52
Washington, George, 53, 132–33,
    232–33
Watson, Emery, 202–3
Weir, Nancy M., 168–70
Welcome, Jane, 131–32
Welles, John, 66–67
West, John, 18–20
West, John Francis, 18–20
White, Peter, 227–29
White, Sampson, 182–84
Wicker, Rachel Ann, 108
Wilkinson, John F. N., 188–89
Williams, Collen, 182–84
Williams, Jarvis M., 177–79
Williams, J. E., 50–53
Williams, Robert, 21–24
Williams, William, 182–84
Wilson, Henry M., 189–92
Wilson, James, 224–26

Subject Index

Italicized page numbers indicate illustrations.

Abbott, Anderson R., 66

Adams, Charles F., 63

Africa, 25, 33, 35, 47, 49, 55, 102, 105, 117, 189–90. *See also* colonization; Liberia

African Americans: considered citizens, 10, 27, 36, 40, 41, 59, 144–45, 168, 171, 193, 210, 217–19, 235; loyalty of, 5, 39, 41, 44–46, 59, 66, 71, 75–77, 85, 86, 140, 156, 171–76, 187, 203–5, 210, 219, 227; patriotism of, 44–48, 66, 80, 92, 95, 98, 100, 109, 138, 161, 169–70, 198. *See also* African American Union regiments; citizenship; pay

African American Union regiments: 1st South Carolina Volunteers, 59–60, 89, 91–92, 229–30; 1st USCT, 97; 2nd Engineers Corps d'Afrique, 147, 149; 2nd USCT, 144–46; 3rd U.S. Colored Cavalry, 151–52; 3rd USCT, 2, 95–96, 118–22, 124–25; 5th Massachusetts Cavalry, 125–26, 154–56; 6th USCT, 92, 187; 7th USCT, 66; 8th USCT, 110–11, 131–32, 179–80; 10th USCT, 127; 11th U.S. Colored Heavy Artillery (14th Rhode Island Artillery), 146–47, 156–58; 18th 17th Corps d'Afrique, 204; 19th USCT, 142–44, 176, *195*; 20th USCT, 101–4, 108–10, 121–22, 193; 21st USCT (3rd South Carolina Volunteers), 90; 22nd USCT, 98–99, *195*; 25th USCT, 135; 26th USCT, *113, 195*, 199–200; 27th USCT, 133–34, 153–54, 161–62, *195*; 28th USCT, 150–51, *195*; 29th USCT, 69; 30th USCT, *195*; 31st USCT, *195*; 34th USCT (2nd South Carolina Volunteers), 229–30; 39th USCT, 122–24; 41st USCT, 113; 45th USCT, 135; 54th Massachusetts Infantry, 2–3, 5, 60, 68, 78, 89–90, 93–95, 97–98, 99, 105–7, 125–26, 134, 166–67, 168–70, 182, 184, 248n14; 55th Massachusetts Infantry, 78, 89, 92, 99–101, 105, 108, 134, 154–56; 70th USCT, 159–61; 73rd USCT (1st Louisiana Native Guards), 159; 86th USCT (14th Corps d'Afrique), 137–40; 88th USCT (17th Corps d'Afrique), 203–4; 97th USCT, 205; 99th USCT (15th Corps d'Afrique), 140–42; 102nd USCT, 77–79, 82–83, 111, 130–31; 117th USCT, 128–29; 123rd USCT, 132–33

African Civilization Society, 189–93

African Methodist Episcopal (AME) Church, 34, 73, 75, 189, 190, 193

alcohol, 15–18, 118, 147–48, 154, 158, 162, 169

amendments to the U.S. Constitution. *See* Constitution, U.S.

American Colonization Society, 33, 53

American Revolution, 5, 36, 44–45, 48, 67, 245n18. *See also* Declaration of Independence; Jefferson, Thomas

Andrew, John A., 63, 90, 93, 100, 105–7, 108, 201–2

Anglo-African (New York), 92, 144, 146, 245–46n30

Antietam, 198

Baltimore, xv, 24–25, 64, 73–77, 83, 101, 122–23, 140, 142, 161–62, 183, 227, 247n40

Banks, Nathaniel P., 173–75

Baptists, 1, 62–64, 182–88, 194, 196–99, 227–29, 232–33

Bates, Edward, 21, 90–91, 106–7, 172–73, 197

Beaufort, S.C., 78–79, 107, 110, 111, 124–25, 131, 199–200, 208, 210, 227–30

Berlin, Ira, 3, 136

Bible, 5, 227, 223, 247n40; allusions to, xviii, 10, 26, 35, 40, 43–44, 50, 66, 89, 97, 117, 169, 191, 237, 253n10. *See also* Christ

black soldiers. *See* African American Union regiments

Blair, Montgomery, 54

Blumenberg, Leopold, 73–74

Boles, Richard, 181

Bowman, Samuel M., 76

Bradford, Augustus W., 75–76

Brown, John, 80, 185

Burlingame, Anson, 201, 255n2

Burnside, Ambrose, 48

Burr, Aaron, 212

Butler, Benjamin F., 61, 84–85, 88, 173, 177, 221

Cameron, Simon, 1, 59, 116–17

Camp Casey (Virginia), 69, 83, 145

Camp William Penn (Philadelphia), 92, 113–15, 118, 124, 180, 186

Canada, 33, 64, 110, 111, 130–31, 148–49, 182; correspondence from, 64–66

Casey, Silas, 145

Castle Williams (New York), 143, 153, 156

Chapin's Farm, Battle of, 131

chaplains, 4, 70, 90, 193, 219–20, 221, 222; letters from, 84–87, 104–7, 185–88, 194–95, 199–200

Chase, Salmon P., 214

Chase, Samuel W., 76, 247n40

Christ, 1, 10, 20–21, 40, 44, 67, 98, 112, 131, 132, 221, 228, 232–33, 235

Christian Recorder (Philadelphia), 34, 92, 189

citizenship, 2–3, 5, 42, 52, 98, 161, 171–79, 192, 236, 253n15. *See also* right to vote

colonization, 5, 26, 27, 33–56, 105, 189–90, 192, 194–95. *See also* Africa; Haiti; Liberia

Confederates: African American views of, 26–27, 31–32, 41–42, 45, 104, 229; dream of Lincoln, 232; invade Maryland, 75–77; lie to slaves, 160, 222, 235; massacre African Americans, 165, 166, 200, 248n14; Native American, 71; official policies toward black soldiers, 94, 165–67; seek amnesty, 31–32

Congress, African American appeals to, 3, 88, 117, 171–76, 203–5, 236, 237

Connecticut, 15, 185

conscription, 59, 70, 73–77, 83, 114, 122–24, 127, 128, 130–31, 144, 154, 179, 250n14. *See also* Enrollment Acts; substitutes

Constitution, U.S., 9, 24, 171, 173, 179, 190; amendments to, 3, 82, 253n17

contrabands (black refugees), 5, 22, 48, 66, 79–81, 94, 182, 193–95, 203–5, 211–13, 222, 227, 235; rejection of the term, 90, 98

Corinth, 68, 69

Crummell, Alexander, 34

Curtin, Andrew G., 121

Davis, Jefferson, 26, 94

Declaration of Independence, 42, 165, 172, 177

Delaware, 15, 103, 202–3; correspondence from, 83–84, 150–51

Democratic Party, 2, 14, 18, 67, 197–99, 247n26, 251n17. *See also* elections; McClellan, George B.

desertion, 116–18, 124–25, 140–43, 151–52, 154–56, 159, 161–62, 204
District of Columbia: correspondence from, 11–12, 15–24, 28–31, 38–39, 51–54, 69–71, 127, 129–30, 168, 182–84, 188–93, 195–99; emancipation in, 34, 35, 169, 196
Dix, John A., 155
Donald, David Herbert, 3
Doubleday, Abner, 84
Douglass, Charles R., 125–26, 126
Douglass, Lewis, 50
draft. See conscription
Dred Scott v. Sandford, 165, 236

Early, Jubal, 75
education: denied to slaves, 2, 40, 64, 152, 160, 229, 231; for freedpeople, 6, 73, 85, 167, 207, 222, 225, 229–31; lack of among free blacks, 42, 71, 79, 166; obtained by free blacks, 64, 73, 171; obtained by slaves, 184, 212, 229. See also schools
Egerton, Douglas R., 2
elections: presidential of 1860, 1–2, 117, 245n17, 245n19; presidential of 1864, xvi, xviii, 26, 27, 31, 73, 79, 81–82, 129–30, 161, 170, 235, 251n17
Emancipation Proclamation, 64, 71; African American commentary on, xii, xvi, xvii, 67, 167, 177, 192, 227–28, 230; Confederate response to, 166; limitations of, 179; Lincoln and, 36, 37, 59–60, 69, 79, 82
Enrollment Acts, 73, 92. See also conscription
equality: attained by African Americans, 44, 136, 198–99; black claims for, 2–3, 51–52, 100, 137–38, 146, 165–80, 200, 238; denied to African Americans, 41–42; Lincoln on, 37–38. See also Declaration of Independence; pay
ex-slaves, letters from, 21–24, 62–64, 77–82, 101–7, 125–26, 127, 140–42, 177–79, 184, 201–2, 203–26, 227–33

families, soldiers': destitution of, 82, 92, 95–96, 98–99, 127, 137–38, 148–49; mistreatment of, 76, 132–33, 170; suffering of, 93–94, 97–99, 102, 108–12, 131–33, 143, 153, 156, 160–61, 162, 165, 168, 219–24; write to Lincoln, 95–96, 98–99, 108–10, 111–13, 116–22, 125–27, 131–32, 133–35, 153–54, 166–68, 168–70. See also pay
Fifteenth Street Presbyterian Church (Washington, D.C.), 37, 69
Florida, 2, 59, 67, 118, 121, 135; correspondence from, 137–42, 144–50, 156–61. See also Olustee, battle of
Fort Barrancas (Florida), 135, 139
Fort Clinch (Florida), 118
Fort Delaware, 84, 150
Fort Donelson (Tennessee), 68
Fort Esperanza (Texas), 146–47, 148, 157
Fort Henry (Tennessee), 68
Fort Jefferson (Dry Tortugas, Florida), 139, 141, 143, 147, 148–50, 155–56, 157, 159
Fort Pickens (Florida), 135
Fort Pillow (Tennessee), 165, 167
Fort Stevens (Washington, D.C.), 75
Fort Sumter (South Carolina), 59, 61
Fort Taylor (Key West), 145
Fort Wagner (South Carolina), 60, 94, 105, 166, 248n14
Freedmen's Bureau, 46, 77, 223–24
Fremont, John C., 66–67

Gallops Island (Boston), 134, 154–55
Garnet, Henry Highland, 189
Geffrard, Fabre Nicolas, xix, 43
Georgia, 59, 62, 104, 201–2, 232; correspondence from, 213–19
Gettysburg, 90, 165
Gloucester, H. Parker, 66
Gordon, Nathaniel, 117
Grant, Ulysses S., 79, 150–51, 153
Gratiot Street Prison (St. Louis), 152

Hahn, Michael, 176
Haiti, xv, xix, 33–34, 43, 46, 47, 56, 195, 201, 202; correspondence from, 35–36
Hale, John P., 201, 255n1
Halleck, Henry Wager, 46
Hamlin, Hannibal, 44, 245n17
Hay, John, 6, 56, 124, 144, 229
Hayden, Lewis, 98
Hays, Alexander, 146
Henry, Anson G., xvi, xvii
Higginson, Thomas Wentworth, 60, 89, 91–92
Holt, Joseph, 84, 144, 148, 149–50, 156, 158
Horton, James O., and Lois, 181
Howard, Oliver Otis, 224
Hunter, David, 59–60

Illinois, 46, 50–53, 54–55, 62, 68–69, 92, 230–31, 245n19, 257n5; correspondence from, xv–xix
Indiana, 36, 115, 150, 179–80, 247n26
Iowa, 225

Jackson, Andrew, 45, 171–72
Jefferson, Thomas, 5, 35
Johnson, Andrew, 87, 149–50, 237–38

Kansas, 32, 50, 180
Keckly, Elizabeth, xvii, 235
Kentucky, xv, 78, 84, 85, 88, 199; correspondence from, 127–29, 132–33

L'Ouverture Hospital (Alexandria, Virginia), 195
land, African American struggles for, 41, 168, 202–14, 219
Liberator, The, 43, 169
Liberia, xix, 26, 27, 33–34, 36, 47, 53–54, 194
Lincoln, Abraham: assassination of, 140, 226, 235–36; considered a "friend" of African Americans, xv–xix, 6, 66, 73, 86–87, 102, 103, 120–21, 134, 225, 227, 232, 235–37; letter to African Americans, 34; endorsements on letters from African Americans, 31, 124, 126, 176, 184, 188–89, 194; pardons granted by, 9–10, 12, 18, 20, 25, 31, 144. See also elections; Emancipation Proclamation
Lincoln, Mary Todd, xvii, 129, 235
Lincoln, Willie, xvi–xvii, xviii
Louisiana, 2, 64, 73, 110, 121, 140, 159, 166, 251n4, 253n17; correspondence from, 101–4, 171–76, 203–5. See also New Orleans

Maryland, 15, 61, 97, 103, 183, 245n20, 250n9; correspondence from, 24–25, 73–77, 122–24, 161–62, 179. See also Baltimore
Massachusetts, 44, 93, 97, 100, 108, 170, 255n2; Boston, 38, 98, 99, 154–56, 182–83, 227; correspondence from, 62–64, 104–7, 134, 184, 201–2. See also African American Union regiments; Andrew, John A.; Sumner, Charles
McClellan, George B., 27, 46, 48, 130, 251n18
Michigan, 77–79, 111, 130–31, 170; correspondence from, 82–83
Militia Act of 1862, 36, 59–60, 89, 91
Milliken's Bend, 60
Mississippi, 46, 64, 227, 251n4; correspondence from, 151–52. See also Vicksburg
Missouri, 1, 152; correspondence from, 31–32
Mitchell, James, 36–37, 53–54, 189, 192
Monocacy, Battle of, 75
Morris Island, S.C., 93–98, 105, 107, 118–20, 125, 169
mutiny, 12–15, 69, 89–90, 99, 136, 139, 142–44, 150, 158

Navy, Union, 15, 36, 60, 89, 103, 137, 175, 196, 236
New Hampshire, 225, 255n1

New Jersey, 105, 183; correspondence from, 25–28, 43–46, 55, 98–99

New Orleans, xv, 62, 109, 112, 137–38, 148–49, 159, 204–5; capture by the Union, 171, 251n4; correspondence from, 102–4, 171–76; during the War of 1812, 45, 67, 173, 245n18, 253n14

New York, 38, 46, 54; black soldiers enlist at, 121, 125; correspondence from, 12–15, 55, 61–62, 66–69, 71–73, 79–82, 108–11, 111–13, 125–26, 142–44, 154–56, 166–68, 168–70; correspondents originally from (or born in), 46, 52, 93, 101–4, 138, 157, 161, 189–93; imprisonment at, 21, 24, 30–31

Nicolay, John G., 142, 156

Norfolk, Virginia, 64, 128, 235

North Carolina, 62–64, 85, 129, 133, 187, 238; correspondence from, 177–79, 219–24

Ohio, 1, 82, 105, 128, 154, 161–62, 180, 190, 232, 252n26; correspondence from, 108, 116–18, 133–34, 153–54

Oklahoma, 180

Olustee, Battle of, 61, 95, 110, 131

Owen, Robert Dale, 70, 247n26

Panama, 33–34, 50, 52. *See also* colonization

pardons, 9–32, 69, 83–84, 136–62

pay, of black laborers, 205–10, 212, 222, 223, 224–25

pay, of black soldiers, 26–27, 72, 78, 88, 129, 162; loss of as punishment, 141, 147, 150, 152, 155–56, 157; not received, 59, 108–9, 120; unequal to white soldiers, 3, 5, 60, 89–115, 136–38, 142–44, 157–58, 159–60, 166, 169

Payne, Daniel A., 75

Peninsula Campaign, 71, 194

Pennington, J. W. C., 235

Pennsylvania, 1, 10, 177, 199, 227; black volunteers from, 3, 59; correspondents originally from (or born in),

51–53, 102, 104–5, 110, 124, 179–80, 183, 210–13; correspondence from, 39–43, 95–96, 113–15, 118–22, 131–32, 135, 185–88, 193–94, 202–3. *See also* Camp William Penn; Union regiments (white)

Petersburg, Virginia, 61, 79, 98, 133, 150, 153–54, 187

Philbrick, Edward S., 206–10

Phillips, Wendell, 201

Pomeroy, Samuel, 50, 52–53

Pope, John, 68

Port Hudson, 138, 173, 204, 251n4

Presbyterians, 37, 69, 105, 189, 190, 199, 235, 247n40

presidential pardons. *See* pardons

Quarles, Benjamin, 237

Redkey, Edwin S., 4

refugees. *See* contrabands

Reidy, Joseph P., 3

Rhode Island, 44, 146–50, 156–58, 185

right to vote, xvii, 1, 5, 26, 160–61, 171–79, 180, 181, 237, 253n17. *See also* citizenship; elections

Roman Catholics, 195, 196

Roosevelt, Theodore, 238

Rowland, Leslie S., 3

Samito, Christian, 136

Saxton, Rufus, 60, 82, 209, 229

schools: established for freedpeople, 73, 85, 184, 192, 210–11, 213, 222, 225–26, 233; for free blacks, 37, 105; Sabbath, 196–99. *See also* education

Second Confiscation Act, 34, 36, 59–60, 90–91

Seward, William H., 36, 68–69

Seymour, Horatio, 67

Shaw, Robert Gould, 89–90

Shepley, George F., 173–74

Sherman, William T., 79, 81, 214, 216, 218

slavery. *See* Emancipation Proclamation; ex-slaves

slave trade: domestic, 2, 45, 116, 162, 203, 211, 221; trans-Atlantic, 117, 185, 189–90

Smith, Gerrit, 112, 250n40

Smith, James Y., 157

South Carolina, correspondence from: Beaufort, 77–79, 111, 124–25, 130–31, 199–200, 227–30; Folly Island, 99–101; Hilton Head, 232–33; Morris Island, 93–95, 97–98, 118–19; St. Helena Island, 205–13. *See also* African American Union regiments

South Carolina Sea Islands, 105, 205–13, 217, 235–36. *See also* Beaufort, South Carolina; Morris Island, South Carolina; South Carolina, correspondence from

Stanton, Edwin M., 59, 66, 89–90, 106, 107, 121, 130, 151, 152, 194, 216, 222; receives letters from African Americans, 64, 70, 149

Stephens, George E., 92

substitutes, 73–75, 95, 115, 127–29, 130–31, 132, 162, 179, 250n14. *See also* conscription

suffering. *See* families, soldiers'

suffrage. *See* right to vote

Sumner, Charles, 106, 165, 174, 201

Taney, Roger B., 236

Taylor Barracks (Kentucky), 84

teachers, letters written by, 210–13, 219–26, 227–29, 230–31, 232–33

Tennessee, 77–78, 184, 193, 227; correspondence from, 230–32. *See also* Fort Pillow

Texas, 129, 132, 144, 157, 180; correspondents from, 146–50

Towne, Laura M., 210–13, 211

Turner, James D., 70–71, 193–94

Union regiments (white): 4th Pennsylvania Cavalry, 70, 193–94; 8th Ohio Infantry, 116–18; 15th New York Independent Battery, 21; 22nd Illinois Infantry, 230–31; 51st Illinois Infantry, 68–69; 86th New York Infantry, 70. *See also* African American Union regiments

Usher, John P., 54

Vicksburg, 60, 138, 151–52, 251n4

Virginia, 1, 2, 3, 9, 21–24, 35–36, 61, 64, 66, 68, 69, 70, 79, 83, 98, 116, 127–29, 131, 144–46, 150, 153, 168, 182, 187, 190, 194, 203, 211, 231, 235; correspondence from, 84–88, 179–80, 194–95, 224–26

voting. *See* right to vote

Wagner, Louis, 113–15

Walker, William, 90–91

Wallace, Lew, 75–77

War of 1812, 5, 45, 67, 171, 173–74, 245n18. *See also* Jackson, Andrew

Washington, Booker T., 2, 238

Washington, D.C. *See* District of Columbia

Wayman, Alexander W., 73

Webster Barracks (Kentucky), 128–29

Welch, Kimberly M., 236

West Virginia, 128, 161

Whiting, William, 89

Wisconsin, 71

Yates, Richard, xvi, xvii